At Home with Thimbleberries Quilts

A Collection of
25 Country Quilts and
Decorative Accessories

Lynette Jensen

Rodale Press, Inc.
Emmaus, Pennsylvania

To Morgan...an angel among us

The author and editors who compiled this book have tried to make all of the contents as accurate and as correct as possible. Patterns, diagrams, photographs, and text have all been carefully checked and cross-checked. However, due to the variability of personal skill and so on, neither the author nor Rodale Press assumes any responsibility for any injuries suffered or for damages or other losses incurred that result from the material presented herein. All instructions and diagrams should be carefully studied and clearly understood before beginning any project.

Printed in the United States of America on acid-free ∞, recycled ♺ paper

Editor: *Jane Townswick*

Interior Book Designer and Illustrator: *Sandy Freeman*

Cover and Interior Photographer: *Mitch Mandel*

Cover Designer: *Mary Ellen Fanelli*

Interior Photo Stylists: *Mary Ellen Fanelli and Jody Olcott*

Photography Editor: *James A. Gallucci*

Assistant Designer: *Nancy Smola Biltcliff*

Copy Editor: *Jennifer R. Hornsby*

Manufacturing Coordinator: *Melinda Rizzo*

Indexer: *Nanette Bendyna*

Editorial Assistance: *Jodi Guiducci and Susan L. Nickol*

RODALE HOME AND GARDEN BOOKS

Vice President and Editorial Director: *Margaret J. Lydic*

Managing Editor, Quilt Books: *Suzanne Nelson*

Director of Design and Production: *Michael Ward*

Associate Art Director: *Carol Angstadt*

Studio Manager: *Leslie M. Keefe*

Copy Director: *Dolores Plikaitis*

Book Manufacturing Director: *Helen Clogston*

Office Manager: *Karen Earl-Braymer*

ON THE COVER: The quilts shown in the cover photos are Christmas House and Christmas Apple.

Photos not taken at Lynette Jensens's home were shot at Max and Carol Sempowski's Light Farm Bed and Breakfast, Kintnersville, PA.

Stencils from the following companies were incorporated in the design of this book: American Traditional Stencils, American Home Stencils, Inc., The Stencil Shoppe, Inc., and Liberty Design Co.

You can order any Rodale title by calling (800) 848-4735. Our customer satisfaction representatives are available 8:00 A.M. to 10:00 P.M. Monday through Friday and 8:30 A.M. to 5:00 P.M. on Saturdays. We accept MasterCard, Visa, Discover, and American Express for your convenience.

For questions or comments concerning the editorial content of this book, please write to:
Rodale Press, Inc.
Book Readers' Service
33 East Minor Street
Emmaus, PA 18098

For more information about Rodale Press and the books and magazines we publish, visit our World Wide Web site at:
http://www.rodalepress.com

Library of Congress Cataloging-in-Publication Data

Jensen, Lynette.
  At home with thimbleberries quilts : a collection of 25 country quilts and decorative accessories / Lynette Jensen.
        p.   cm.
    ISBN 0–87596–768–X hardcover
    ISBN 0–87596–984–4 paperback
    1. Patchwork—Patterns.
    2. Quilting—Patterns.
    3. Patchwork quilts.
  I. Thimbleberries, Inc. II. Title.
TT835.J45   1997
746.46'041—dc21   97–33755

Distributed in the book trade by St. Martin's Press

2 4 6 8 10 9 7 5 3   hardcover
2 4 6 8 10 9 7 5 3 1 paperback

┌─ OUR PURPOSE ─┐

"We inspire and enable people to improve their lives and the world around them."

CONTENTS

ACKNOWLEDGMENTS

The staff at Thimbleberries, Inc., has always been a constant source of energy, talent, and commitment. Their dedication is immeasurable. Deadlines are always met, workmanship is impeccable, and they all have an innate sense of what everyone expects from Thimbleberries. Their lives continue to be demanding and a bit hectic at times, yet they, too, find time to make very special quilts for themselves and others. I think they are a true reflection of today's quilters, who set aside time to enjoy quilting as a form of artistic expression. Even though we work all day with some aspect of quiltmaking, we still take projects home to make during our off hours. Often, I hear parting words like these as we leave the workplace, "I'm going to make this tonight!" My undying gratitude to Sherry Husske, Peggy Christianson, Kathy Lobeck, and Dale Ann Foster and an extra special thank you to Sue Bahr and Lisa Kirchoff for using their exceptional quiltmaking and editorial skills to turn my designs into clear, concise, and well-illustrated instructions.

Also, thank you to the very busy fingers of Leone Rusch, Esther Grischkowsky, and Julie Borg, who are responsible for the extraordinary hand and machine quilting throughout this book. Their talents enhance my designs and truly make them quilts. Julie Jergens, Tracy Schrantz, and Carla Plowman test our patterns, taking care to make sure we have included all the necessary steps to complete each project successfully. Thank you, also, to Christa and Reid for those extra hours after their busy school day. It is all greatly appreciated.

I am ever grateful for my association with Rodale Press, Suzanne Nelson, and her talented staff, who have guided me through the production of my second book. Jane Townswick has been our beacon through this project, and I thank her for her guidance and encouragement. I know that I am blessed by all of these talented people who are dedicated to the growth of Thimbleberries and all that is involved.

Thank You.

INTRODUCTION

Shortly after the photos were taken for my first book, *The Thimbleberries Book of Quilts,* my husband and I had the opportunity to purchase a beautiful old house in a neighborhood filled with homes that reflect the history of our town. Our home sits on the bank of the Crow River, which meanders gently through the middle of our town. Since our children grew up in our other home, we felt considerable nostalgia at leaving, but this was tempered by the excitement we felt at the huge new challenge ahead. I was positive I had one more house renovation in me.

Our "new" old house is a definite style change, and I have really enjoyed the different direction it demanded. Our former house was a delightful example of Prairie-style Arts and Crafts architecture, with lots of dark wood and built-in cabinets. Our new one is a charming 1930s house with arched doorways and painted woodwork, built-in bookcases and corner cupboards, and large paned windows with beautiful views of a wooded lot. Recently, I read through a journal I had kept during the months of renovation. My first entry was, "This house

needs attention, this house needs love, this house needs money!"

We decided to do everything, from top to bottom—replaster, repaint, replace light fixtures, retile, mill woodwork to match the original, and spend endless hours polishing brass knobs, rods, hinges, and door pulls. Throughout the months, my journal records comments like "They started sanding the floors today. What a huge mess, what a huge improvement!" And on another day, "Kerry came home from college today to a 'done' room complete with lots of quilts and fresh flowers. She was surprised and delighted. Her room is so sweet, so light, so fresh, so special."

Our son Matt's room is one of the most inviting hideaways in the house. Its ceiling has all sorts of angles, a dormer that allows sunlight to fill the room, and there is enough space to fill with treasures, collectibles, and quilts. All of these elements make it an inviting, welcome retreat he loves to come home to.

The quilts throughout my house echo my belief that home should always be comfortable and welcoming. When we are at home, we

have an overwhelming sense of well-being that comes from being surrounded by colors and textures, quilts, collectibles, and family pieces, and we strive to pass that same feeling on to all who enter.

Filling the house with my treasures and all the quilts for this book has been like having a blank artist's canvas on which I can apply wonderful colors, patterns, and textures. Just like other quiltmakers, I plan quilts for certain bedrooms, decorating schemes, holiday decorating, gift giving, and special family celebrations. As I wrote this book, I made sure there would be projects to fit all of those occasions.

I hope you will enjoy visiting my home through the pages of this book and that my quilt designs will make you love the wonderful heritage craft of quiltmaking as much as I do.

My Best,

Lynette Jensen

Lynette Jensen

LIVING
with
QUILTS

All quilts are meant to be enjoyed. I keep mine out where I can enjoy their color, texture, and the warm, cozy feeling they create. Here, Harvest Mix sets the fall theme for my dining room table centerpiece, which includes a cast-iron skillet filled with apples and a candle. In the next few pages, I hope you'll be inspired to find ways to fill your home with the quilts you make.

<<<< <<<< <<<<

his simply furnished guest bedroom is the perfect setting for Nine Patch Criss-Cross and Christmas House (draped on the chair in the corner). The antique doll bed holds an assortment of vintage children's books. Adding just the right homespun touch, the crocheted rug picks up the colors in the quilt. Pearl Baysinger, a member of my quilt group, taught me how to crochet rugs from leftover quilt scraps. Pearl's grandmother taught this craft to her, using a hand-carved crochet hook. I must admit that now I'm "hooked" and have filled many rooms in my house with these colorful accents.

My son Matt's room shows how you can create a masculine look with quilts. The dark, rich colors in the quilts set the tone, with Pine Tree Log Cabin casually folded and draped over Pine View (a nice way to think about displaying two bed quilts at the same time). I made the dust ruffle out of a brown and black check fabric to complete the scene. An old parade drum serves as a unique bedside table. The antique quilts on the bucket bench are some of my earliest finds and are what got me hooked on quilt-making.

Tucked in a corner, this reproduction wagon holds a mix of antique quilts and some new Thimbleberries quilts. The small quilt in the background is framed with nonglare glass. To keep it square and flat, I stitched the quilt to a mat board background, working all the way along the outside edges. This is also a good trick for displaying antique quilt blocks.

Banisters make perfect quilt racks. Here, I've folded and draped Raining Cats and Dogs and Sticks and Stones. I change the quilts with the seasons, always picking those I know I can safely launder. Peeking through the arch at the bottom of the stairs, Harvest Mix is draped over the back of the living room couch, another favorite, if unexpected, place where I like to display my quilts.

Against the neutral background of our master bedroom, the quilts and accessories add a graphic punch without becoming overwhelming. The striped dust ruffle adds a nice contrast to the checkered patterns found in the Home Place quilt on the bed, the framed Cinnamon Hearts on the wall, and the big, chunky check fabric covering the chair. The red pillow on the chair is simply a square of fabric I layered with batting and a muslin backing, then machine quilted in a meander pattern. After the quilting, I sewed the square into a ruffled pillow to add a quick and easy touch of texture to the room.

This dresser-top scene in my daughter's room shows how little finishing touches go a long way in adding colorful accents. In keeping with the light and airy mood of the room, I covered a purchased heart-shaped box with green paper. From leftover fabric scraps, I made yo-yos and glued them to the box lid. Additional yo-yos are stitched together to create a vintage-look doily under a basket of dried flowers.

I used a light touch in Kerry's sun-dappled room, choosing a soft palette of pink, purple, and green. The quilts complement the country-cottage feel of the flower-sprigged wallpaper, without appearing overly matched. In Bloom covers the bed and Wildflower nestles on a green plaid chair. Meadow Lily drapes over the door of the antique wardrobe, one of my favorite impromptu quilt racks. My basic rule for quilt display is this: After one month, I refold, reposition, or move the quilt to an entirely new room.

I love to mix and match and rotate the quilts all through my house. When I put my familiar quilts in a new place, it makes me look at and enjoy them in a fresh way. Here in our family room I tucked Daisy Days over the mantel, with Cinnamon Hearts nestled in a magazine rack in front of the fire. Brown-Eyed Susan is draped over the front door of the TV cabinet. I accordion-folded Pine Ridge and pulled it through the handles of a large basket to create a fuller, softer effect. The big chunky design on the Just Like Home pillow is an eye-catching accent on the couch.

In this corner of our living room, a vintage wicker plant stand holds rolled quilts plus some hooked rugs for texture. Christmas Apple drapes across the front of the stand. Moved from the family room, the Just Like Home pillow adds a fresh punch of color and pattern. Big pillows like this are an inexpensive way to redecorate and create a new look quickly and easily.

We use our screened porch as a relaxing haven from spring through fall. When company comes, I put out a few quilts, like the Christmas Apple and Watermelon Patch draped over the loveseat. I don't leave them out here for long, to avoid sun damage. A few of my favorite collectibles share the space as well, including vintage tin sand pails and shovels and tin lunch pails, plus some vintage watering cans, gardening tools, and seed packets.

One of my lucky finds, this antique planter was made to look like a picket fence with an arbor. I fill it with air-dried flowers from my summer garden. My low-fuss approach is to pick them at their peak, rubber band the stems together, hang them upside-down in a cool, dry, dark place and accept the fact that some will make it and some will not!

My garden also supplies the fixings for these herb bundles. I tie together sprigs of dried herbs and flowers, adding stalks of wheat and twigs for color and interest. Wrapped in squares of plaid or checked tissue paper and tied with raffia, these make delightful hostess gifts, especially when you're invited to a cookout. Placing a bundle on the coals releases a delightful aroma.

▶ ▶

Antique rolling pins and hydrangeas from my garden create an unusual juxtaposition that is sure to catch people's eye. This seemingly unrelated collection of objects, part of an ever-changing display by my back foyer, works together well because the colors and textures complement one another.

▶▶▶▶▶▶▶▶▶▶▶▶▶▶▶▶▶▶

Christmas lights twinkle an invitation through the living room archway. With the red and green Cinnamon Hearts setting the stage, I've also gathered my antique dollhouse, a well-loved rocking horse from the 1880s, and my collection of Santas. I love to put up trees in several rooms throughout the house and often leave them unadorned for a couple of days, just to enjoy the simple beauty of their greenery. Next I add the white lights and enjoy just those for a few days, before adding my collection of antique and handmade ornaments.

I love to make my own Christmas boxes for gift giving or just to have stacked around the house for decoration. I purchase papier-mâché boxes from the craft store, then apply a coat of latex paint, sand the surface, add a stencil, then wipe on a layer of stain or graining liquid. A coat of matte acrylic sealer makes them more durable and easier to dust.

Fabric chenille garland is easy to make. Cut 1-inch-wide strips of homespun fabric and sew the short ends together to make a long strip. Zigzag a length of #8 pearl cotton down the center of the strip, gathering it as you sew. Embellish with buttons or red wooden beads.

With Town Square on the wall and Christmas Candy on the coffee table, the basement family room gets dressed up for the holidays. My tip for hanging quilts on plasterboard or wood walls is to use hand-sewing needles as nails. They're so fine they don't leave big holes in the wall or quilt. The black pot is an old vegetable steamer that I stenciled with snowmen and filled with peppermints. Grouping small quilts with items that carry out their theme is an easy decorator touch.

My mother made this dollhouse for me from an apple crate when I was five. I cherish mementos from my childhood and make them part of my home. Sitting atop the Christmas House quilt, I've filled the dollhouse with greens, berries, and pinecones for a holiday scene.

▶▶▶▶▶▶▶▶▶▶▶▶▶▶▶▶▶▶▶▶▶▶▶▶▶▶▶▶▶

The Yo-Yo Table Topper anchors this Christmas arrangement. An antique doll cradle with original paint holds artificial greens, twigs and berries, papier-mâché stars, and flicker-flame lights. I also use this cradle on the floor for an accent or as the centerpiece on a buffet table. Draping the quilt at an angle adds more interest to the scene.

Terrific gift ideas, these canning jar luminaries are simple to make. Fill canning jars with bells, holiday lights, pinecones, candies... anything goes. Add a votive candle holder to the top and decorate with ribbons as desired.

THERE'S
no place like
HOME

*T*he red patches in these
Log Cabin quilt blocks
symbolize warmth and
hospitality, two qualities
that are at the heart of
any quiltmaker's home.
I bought this little wooden
dollhouse, with its chimney
and shuttered windows,
because it reminds me
of the home we now live
in. It also makes me think
of a little girl stitching
quilts for a family of dolls
with all the same love and
care we put into our
quilts today.

<<<<<<<<<<<<<<

PINE VIEW

Pine View is a strong, masculine design with an understated country flavor. I selected small- to medium-scale prints in similar color values (the same degree of lightness and darkness) and a lot of tone-on-tone prints. All of the tree trunks are the same fabric, which guides your eyes over the entire surface. Long, narrow, dark brown print strips beside the Tree blocks set off the lighter background fabrics. The fabric in the vertical stripes between the rows of trees is a larger print that does not distract from the trees. The pieced stars at the top and the bottom bring the center colors out into the dark borders.

Size

Bed Quilt: 92 × 104 inches (unquilted)

Finished Block: 5 inches square

Fabrics and Supplies

Yardage is based on 44-inch-wide fabric.

1½ yards *total* of a variety of green, red, blue, and brown fabrics for trees

1 yard beige fabric for tree background

1⅞ yards dark brown fabric for trunks and narrow border

2½ yards beige/black print fabric for side and corner triangles

1¾ yards of chestnut print fabric for lattice strips

4 yards red print fabric for border

¼ yard *each* of three gold print fabrics for stars

1 yard red print fabric for binding

8¼ yards fabric for quilt backing

Quilt batting, at least 96 × 108 inches

Rotary cutter, mat, and see-through ruler with ⅛-inch markings

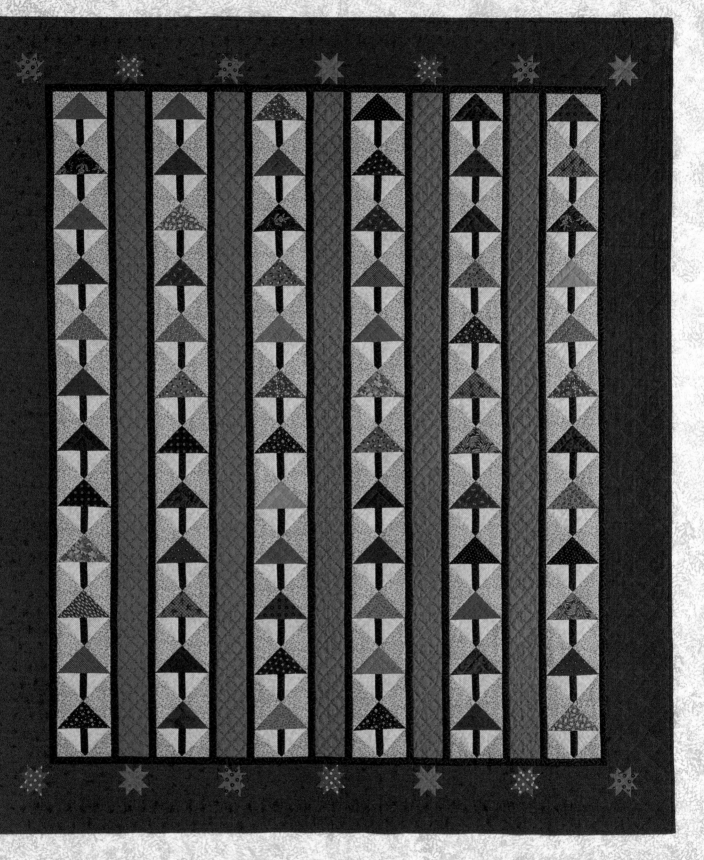

Getting Ready

- READ instructions thoroughly before you begin.

- PREWASH and press fabric.

- USE ¼-inch seam allowances throughout unless directions specify otherwise.

- SEAM ALLOWANCES are included in the cutting sizes given.

- PRESS seam allowances in the direction that will create the least bulk, and whenever possible, press toward the darker fabric.

- CUTTING DIRECTIONS for each section of the quilt are given individually. If you like to cut as you go, simply follow the directions as you get to them. If you'd rather cut all your pieces at the same time, skip ahead to find each of the cutting sections and do all the cutting before you begin to sew. 🍃

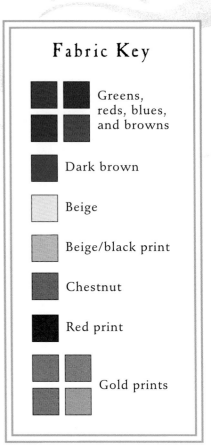

Fabric Key

Greens, reds, blues, and browns

Dark brown

Beige

Beige/black print

Chestnut

Red print

Gold prints

WHEN ORGANIZING a large group of fabrics for a scrap quilt, gather more than you'll actually need. Spread out your background fabric and start laying on top of it fabrics you know you want to use. Step back and view them from a distance to see how they look together. Then continue adding fabrics until you have found just the right mix for the look you want to achieve.

Tree Blocks
(MAKE 72)

CUTTING

From the green, red, blue, and brown tree fabrics:
- Cut six 5⅞ × 44-inch strips; from these strips, cut thirty-six 5⅞-inch squares. Cut these squares in half diagonally to make 72 triangles.

From the dark brown fabric:
- Cut eight 1½ × 44-inch strips; from these strips, cut seventy-two 1½ × 4½-inch pieces.

From the beige fabric:
- Cut five 5½ × 44-inch strips; from these strips, cut thirty-six 5½-inch squares. Cut these squares into quarters diagonally to make 144 triangles.

Piecing the Tree Blocks

1 Sew two beige background triangles to a 1½ × 4½-inch brown trunk piece, as shown in DIAGRAM 1. Trim the bottom edge of the trunk, as shown. Repeat for each trunk unit.

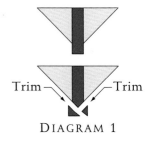

Trim —— —— Trim

DIAGRAM 1

2 Sew a tree fabric triangle onto each trunk unit, as shown in DIAGRAM 2. The individual tree square should measure 5½ inches square. If it

doesn't, check to make sure that the pieces were cut correctly and that you used accurate ¼-inch seam allowances.

DIAGRAM 2

Quilt Center

C U T T I N G

From the beige/black print fabric:
• Cut eight 9 × 44-inch strips; from these strips, cut thirty-three 9-inch squares. Cut these squares diagonally into quarters to form 132 side triangles.
• Cut two 5½ × 44-inch strips; from these strips, cut twelve 5½-inch squares. Cut these squares in half to form 24 corner triangles.

From the dark brown fabric:
• Cut thirty-one 1½ × 44-inch strips for narrow borders.

From the chestnut fabric:
• Cut eleven 4½ × 44-inch strips for lattice strips.

NOTE: The side triangles and corner triangles will be larger than necessary and will be trimmed before the narrow borders are added.

Piecing the Quilt Center

1 Referring to DIAGRAM 3, sew the side triangles to the Tree blocks. Make six vertical rows of

12 Tree blocks each. Be sure to match the seams of the Tree blocks. Add the corner triangles to the top and bottom of each row, as shown.

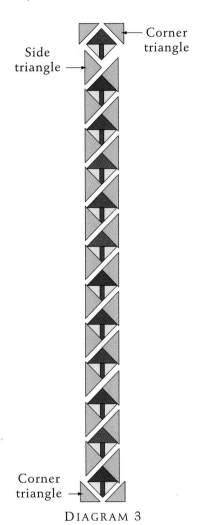

DIAGRAM 3

2 Trim off excess fabric from the side and corner triangles, taking care to allow for the ¼-inch seam allowances beyond the block corners. Before you trim, be sure to read through "Trimming Side and Corner Triangles" on page 211 to be certain you make these cuts accurately. Make sure that the corners measure accurate 90 degree angles and that all six rows measure the same.

3 Piece the short ends of the 1½ × 44-inch dark brown strips together diagonally, as shown in DIAGRAM 4. Trim the seam allowances to ¼ inch and press them open.

DIAGRAM 4

4 Measure the length of your tree block rows, and trim 12 dark brown border strips to that length. Sew a border strip to each side of the tree rows, as shown in DIAGRAM 5.

DIAGRAM 5

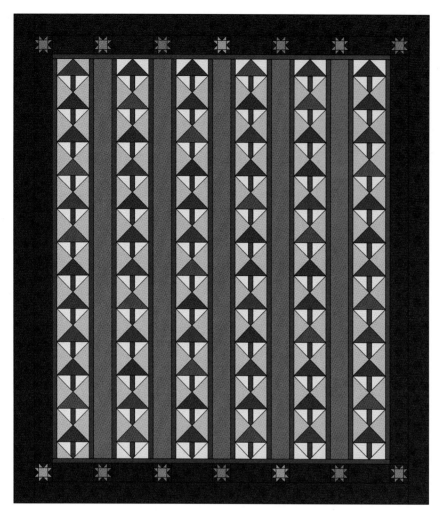

QUILT ASSEMBLY DIAGRAM

5 Piece the short ends of the 4½ × 44-inch chestnut strips together diagonally. Trim seam allowances to ¼ inch and press them open. Trim five chestnut lattice strips to the same length as your bordered tree rows. Sew a bordered tree row to each side of the lattice strips, as shown in the QUILT ASSEMBLY DIAGRAM. Press seam allowances toward the dark brown narrow borders.

6 Measure the quilt from left to right, through the center, to determine the length of the top and bottom dark brown borders. Trim two dark brown borders to the necessary length and sew them to the top and bottom of the quilt, as shown in the QUILT ASSEMBLY DIAGRAM.

7 Measure the quilt from top to bottom through the center to determine the length of the dark brown side borders. Trim two dark brown borders to the necessary length, and sew them to the sides of the quilt, as shown in the QUILT ASSEMBLY DIAGRAM.

Star Blocks
(MAKE 14)

C U T T I N G
for each Star Block

From one of the gold print fabrics:
- Cut one 2½-inch square
- Cut one 1⅞ × 9-inch strip

From the red print border fabric:
- Cut four 1½-inch squares
- Cut one 1⅞ × 9-inch strip

Piecing the Star Blocks

1 With right sides together, layer the 1⅞ × 9-inch gold print strips and the 1⅞ × 9-inch red print strips in pairs. Press each pair of strips together. Cut each of the layered strips into four 1⅞-inch squares, as shown in DIAGRAM 6. Cut the layered squares in half diagonally, and stitch a seam ¼ inch in from the diagonal edges, as shown. Press seam allowances toward the gold print fabric. Make a total of eight triangle-pieced squares for each Star block.

DIAGRAM 6

2 Sew two triangle-pieced squares together, as shown in DIAGRAM 7. Repeat to make a total of four star-point units for each Star block.

DIAGRAM 7

3 Sew a star-point unit to the top and bottom of each 2½-inch gold print square, as shown in DIAGRAM 8.

DIAGRAM 8

4 Sew a 1½-inch red print square to the sides of the remaining star-point units, as shown in DIAGRAM 9, and sew these units to the sides of the Star blocks. The Star blocks should now measure 4½ inches square.

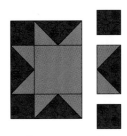

DIAGRAM 9

Borders

C U T T I N G

The yardage given allows for borders to be cut cross-grain.

From the red print border fabric:
• Cut eight 4½ × 44-inch strips for inner border
• Cut eleven 5 × 44-inch strips for outer border

Assembling the Inner Border

1 Measure the quilt from top to bottom through the center to determine the length of the side borders. Piece the short ends of five 4½-inch-wide red print strips together diagonally. Trim seam allowances and press them open. Trim two 4½-inch-wide red print borders to the necessary length, and sew them to the sides of the quilt. Press seam allowances toward the borders.

2 Measure the width of a Tree block row with two dark brown border strips attached. Cut twelve 4½-inch-wide red print rectangles to this measurement.

3 Referring to the QUILT ASSEMBLY DIAGRAM on the opposite page, sew seven stars and six 4½-inch-wide rectangles together. Press seam allowances toward the red print rectangles. Make one of these pieced border units for the top and one for the bottom inner border.

4 Sew the pieced border units to the top and bottom of the quilt. Press seam allowances toward the borders.

5 Measure the quilt from left to right through the middle to determine the length of the top and bottom outer borders. Piece together the short ends of the 5-inch-wide red print strips together with diagonal seams. Trim seam allowances to ¼ inch and press them open. Cut a top and bottom border to the length needed. Sew the borders to the top and bottom of the quilt.

Press seam allowances toward the borders.

6 Measure the quilt from top to bottom through the middle, including the borders you just added, to determine the length of the side borders. Cut the red print outer border strips to the necessary length and sew them to the quilt sides in the same manner as for the top and botttom borders. Press seam allowances toward the borders.

Putting It All Together

1 Prepare the backing by cutting the 8¼-yard length of backing fabric into thirds crosswise to make three 2¾-yard lengths. Remove the selvage edges. Sew the long edges of the three lengths together and press seam allowances open.

2 Trim the backing and batting so they are 4 inches larger than the quilt top dimensions.

3 Mark quilting designs on the quilt top.

4 Layer the backing, batting, and quilt top. Baste these layers together and quilt.

5 When quilting is complete, remove the basting stitches, and trim the excess backing and batting even with the quilt top.

Binding

NOTE: The 2¾-inch-wide binding strip will produce a ⅜-inch-wide finished binding. If you want a wider or narrower binding, adjust the width of the strips you cut. (See page 216 for pointers on how to experiment with binding width.) Refer to "Making and Attaching the Binding" on page 215 to complete your quilt.

CUTTING

From the red print binding fabric:
• Cut eleven 2¾ × 44-inch strips for cross-grain binding

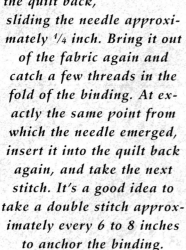

WHEN APPLYING double-fold binding to a quilt, slip stitch the binding to the back side of the quilt by hand. To do this, slip your needle into the quilt back, sliding the needle approximately ¼ inch. Bring it out of the fabric again and catch a few threads in the fold of the binding. At exactly the same point from which the needle emerged, insert it into the quilt back again, and take the next stitch. It's a good idea to take a double stitch approximately every 6 to 8 inches to anchor the binding.

Quilting DESIGNS

FOR HAND QUILTING:

❧ *Quilting in the ditch of each seam always helps to emphasize patchwork shapes in any quilt. Stitching in the ditch around the Tree blocks is a good choice for this quilt.*

❧ *You may find a purchased quilting stencil with a simple chain design will be effective in the narrow vertical strips of fabric in Pine View.*

❧ *Quilting in the ditch on each side of the narrow brown border strips will make them visually more prominent.*

❧ *Cross-hatching always produces a nice quilted texture. It is a good choice for large borders or for prints in areas where you want to camouflage your quilting stitches. In the large unpieced borders of this quilt, quilt diagonal cross-hatching lines spaced at 3-inch intervals for an easy, allover pattern that is simple to quilt.*

FOR MACHINE QUILTING:

❧ *Follow the same quilting suggestions as for hand quilting, replacing the chain design in the long, narrow vertical strips and the cross-hatching in the large unpieced borders with gentle meander quilting. Meander quilting is a continuous, free-motion type of stitching that requires no marking beforehand.*

TEA TIME

This whimsical design brightens my dining room, accompanying an antique doll cupboard filled with a blue and white toy tea set I've had since I was five years old. I chose fabrics in colors and prints that remind me of the floral prints depicted in some of the teapots in my own collection. The appliqué designs on the teapots spill into the outer borders, almost as if the flowers were floating on the edge of the quilt. This creates the effect of a large printed fabric in the border areas. Black buttonhole stitching adds a strong edge to the appliqués and a three-dimensional feel to each of the shapes.

Size

Wall Quilt: 34 inches square (unquilted)

Finished Block: 8 inches square

Fabrics and Supplies

Yardage is based on 44-inch-wide fabric.

¾ yard beige print fabric for background

⅜ yard multicolor floral fabric for corner squares

⅜ yard deep rose print fabric for flower petal appliqués and inner border

1⅓ yards blue print fabric for teapot appliqué and outer border

¼ yard medium rose print fabric for flower petal appliqués

⅛ yard gold print for flower center appliqués

¼ yard green print fabric for leaf and stem appliqués

1 yard fusible web

2 skeins black embroidery floss

½ yard blue print fabric for binding

1⅛ yards backing fabric

Quilt batting, at least 38 inches square

Rotary cutter, mat, and see-through ruler with ⅛-inch markings

TEA TIME
Getting Ready

- READ instructions thoroughly before you begin.

- PREWASH and press fabric.

- USE ¼-inch seam allowances throughout unless directions specify otherwise.

- SEAM ALLOWANCES are included in the cutting sizes given.

- PRESS seam allowances in the direction that will create the least bulk, and whenever possible, press toward the darker fabric.

- CUTTING DIRECTIONS for each section of the quilt are given individually. If you like to cut as you go, simply follow the directions as you get to them. If you'd rather cut all your pieces at the same time, skip ahead to find each of the cutting sections and do all the cutting before you begin to sew. 🍃

Fabric Key	
▨	Blue
■	Deep rose
▨	Medium rose
▨	Green
▨	Gold
▨	Beige
▨	Multicolor floral

Teapot Blocks
(MAKE 4)

CUTTING

From the beige print fabric:
- Cut four 8½-inch squares
- Cut eight 2½ × 8½-inch rectangles
- Cut one 2⅞ × 7-inch strip

From the multicolor floral fabric:
- Cut thirty-two 2½-inch squares
- Cut one 2⅞ × 7-inch strip

1 Position the fusible web (paper side facing up) over the appliqué shapes on page 29, and trace. NOTE: The shapes are reversed so that when they are fused onto fabric they will appear in the correct position. Trace onto the fusible web four

of each of the following shapes: G teapots, A petals, B petals, C petals, D leaves, E stems, and F flower centers. Cut roughly around the shapes.

2 For the G teapot shapes, draw a line approximately ⅜ inch inside the first line you traced, as shown in DIAGRAM 1. Cut away the fusible web on this drawn line, as shown. NOTE: Whenever you are fusing a large shape like the teapot, it is helpful to fuse only the outer edges of the shape. This will keep the teapots from

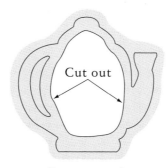

DIAGRAM 1

looking stiff and will also make it much easier to buttonhole stitch the flower shapes later.

3 With a hot dry iron, press the coated sides of the fusible web teapot shapes to the wrong side of the fabric chosen for the teapots. Let the fabric cool, and cut out the teapots along the first traced lines. Peel off the paper backing.

4 Place the fusible web flower stem and leaf shapes coated side down on the wrong sides of the fabrics chosen for the flowers. Press with a hot dry iron. Let the fabric cool, and cut out the appliqué shapes. Peel off the paper backing.

5 Referring to DIAGRAM 2 on page 26 as a placement guide, position and fuse the G teapots on the beige print background squares first, followed by the E stems, the A, B, and C petals, the F flower centers, and finally, the D leaves.

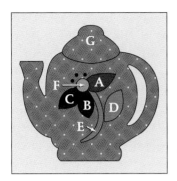

DIAGRAM 2

6 Referring to DIAGRAM 2, use three strands of black embroidery floss to appliqué a teapot and flower onto each block, using the buttonhole stitch. With three strands of floss, stitch French knots above each flower. Outline stitch the bottom of the lid, using three strands of floss. For more information on French knots, outline stitch, and buttonhole stitch, see page 210.

7 With right sides together, position a 2½-inch multi-color floral square on each corner of the Teapot blocks, as shown in DIAGRAM 3. Draw diagonal lines on the floral squares, and stitch on these lines, as shown.

Trim to ¼"

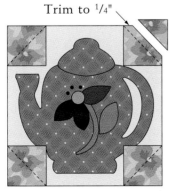

DIAGRAM 3

Trim seam allowances to ¼ inch, as shown. Press.

8 Stitch the four Teapot blocks together, matching seam intersections, as shown in DIAGRAM 4.

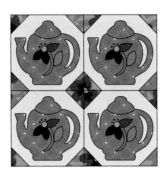

DIAGRAM 4

9 With right sides together, position a 2½-inch multi-color floral square at each end of the eight 2½ × 8½-inch beige pieces, as shown in DIAGRAM 5. Draw a diagonal line on each multicolor floral square, and stitch on these lines, as shown. Trim seam allowances to ¼ inch, as shown. Press.

Trim to ¼"

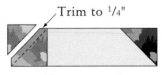

DIAGRAM 5

10 Stitch together eight of the units from Step 9 in pairs, as shown in DIAGRAM 6.

DIAGRAM 6

11 Sew one section from Step 10 to the top of the Teapot blocks and one to the bottom, as shown in DIAGRAM 7. Press.

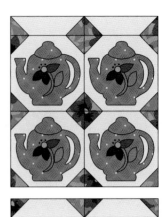

DIAGRAM 7

12 Layer the 2⅞ × 7-inch beige and multicolor floral strips, right sides together, as shown in DIAGRAM 8. Press, but do not sew. Cut the layered strips into two 2⅞-inch squares, as shown.

2⅞"

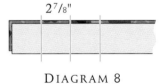

DIAGRAM 8

13 Cut the layered squares in half diagonally, as shown in DIAGRAM 9. Stitch a ¼-inch seam along the diagonal edge, as shown. Press seam allowances toward the multicolor floral fabric.

DIAGRAM 9

14 Stitch the triangle-pieced squares to the ends of the remaining two sections from Step 10, as shown in DIAGRAM 10.

DIAGRAM 10

15 Sew the two rows to the sides of the Teapot blocks, as shown in DIAGRAM 11. Press.

DIAGRAM 11

QUILT ASSEMBLY DIAGRAM

Borders

C U T T I N G

for Inner Border

NOTE: The yardage given allows for border pieces to be cut cross-grain.

From the deep rose fabric:
• Cut four 1½ × 44-inch strips

Attaching the Inner Border

1 Measure the quilt from left to right through the middle to determine the length of the top and bottom border strips. Cut the deep rose inner border strips to the necessary length. Sew the inner border strips to the top and bottom of the center section of the quilt, as shown in the QUILT ASSEMBLY DIAGRAM. Press seam allowances toward the border strips.

2 Measure the quilt from top to bottom through the middle, including the border strips you just added, to determine the length of the side border strips. Cut the deep rose inner border strips to the necessary length, and sew them to the sides of the quilt, as shown. Press seam allowances toward the border strips.

C U T T I N G

for Outer Border

From the blue print fabric:
• Cut four 6½ × 44-inch strips

Attaching the Outer Border

1 Measure the quilt from left to right through the middle to determine the length of the top and bottom outer border strips. Cut two blue print border strips to the necessary length, and sew them to the top and bottom, as shown in the QUILT ASSEMBLY DIAGRAM. Press seam allowances toward the outer borders.

2 Measure the quilt from top to bottom through the middle, including the border strips you just added, to determine the length of the side outer border strips. Cut two blue

TO HANG *wall quilts, try attaching a casing that is made of the same fabric as the quilt back at the top of the quilt. Often, it is helpful to attach a second casing at the bottom of the quilt. That way, you can insert a dowel to help weight the quilt and make it hang free of ripples.*

TIPS AND TRICKS

border strips to the necessary length and sew them to the sides of the quilt. Press seam allowances toward the outer border.

3 Stay stitch ⅛ inch from the raw edges of the outer border strips to stabilize them for the appliqué process.

Appliquéing the Outer Border

1 Prepare the border appliqués in the same manner as for the Teapots. Trace 16 of each of the following shapes: A petals, B petals, C petals, F flower centers, D leaves, and E stems. Fuse each shape to the wrong side of the fabric chosen for the flower appliqués.

2 Referring to the QUILT AS-SEMBLY DIAGRAM on page 27 as a placement guide, position and fuse the flower shapes in place on each of the outer border strips.

3 Using three strands of black embroidery floss, buttonhole stitch around each appliqué piece in the same manner as for the Teapots. Using three strands of floss, stitch French knots above the flowers.

Putting It All Together

1 Trim the backing and batting so they are 4 inches larger than the quilt top dimensions.

2 Mark quilting designs on the quilt top.

3 Layer the backing, batting, and quilt top. Baste the layers together and quilt.

4 When quilting is complete, remove basting and trim the excess backing and batting even with the quilt top.

Binding

NOTE: The 2¾-inch binding strips will produce a ⅜-inch-wide binding. If you want a wider or narrower binding,

adjust the width of the strips you cut. (See page 216 for pointers on how to experiment with binding width.) See "Making and Attaching the Binding" on page 215 to complete your quilt.

CUTTING

From the blue print fabric:
• Cut four 2¾ × 44-inch strips for cross-grain binding

Quilting DESIGNS

FOR HAND QUILTING:

Keep the quilting in this quilt very simple to serve as background to the appliqué shapes. Quilt lines of cross-hatching spaced at 1¾-inch intervals in the center background areas and in the outer borders.

Quilt around the outlines of each teapot, flower appliqué, square, and narrow border to make them stand out from the cross-hatched areas.

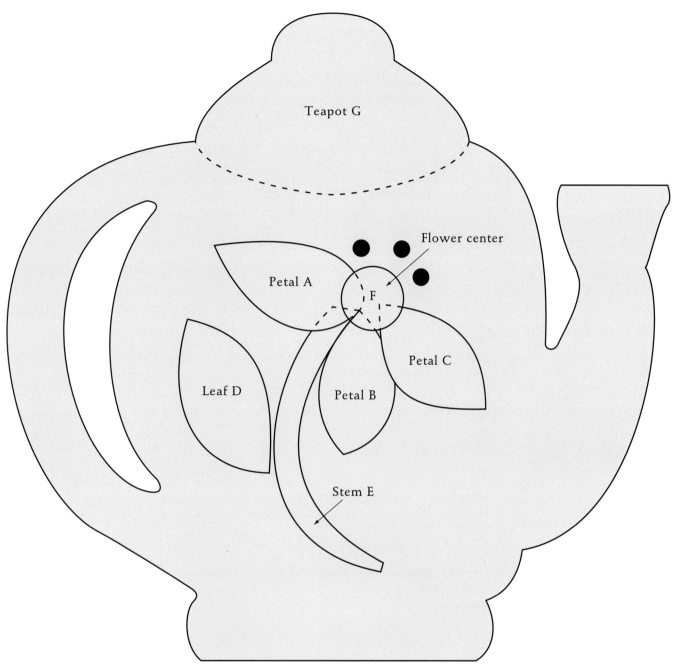

Teapot G

Flower center

Petal A

F

Petal C

Leaf D

Petal B

Stem E

TEAPOT APPLIQUÉ PATTERNS

NINE PATCH CRISS-CROSS

Because the reds, blues, and golds in this quilt are similar in value, they create strong diagonal lines that make the quilt design appear more complicated than it is. A narrow, dark inner border surrounds the pieced center, functioning like an accent mat around a framed picture. The bold red print in the outer border contains a bit of gold that repeats the color in the center of the quilt. The large cream and black bias binding is an important design element because it echoes the cream tone in the light squares and adds a final flourish to the edges of the quilt.

Size

Bed Quilt: 78 × 96 inches (unquilted)

Finished Block: 6 inches square

Fabrics and Supplies

Yardage is based on 44-inch-wide fabric.

1⅝ yards red print fabric for Nine Patch blocks

1⅓ yards gold print fabric for Nine Patch blocks

1⅓ yards cream print fabric for alternate blocks

1⅝ yards blue print fabric for alternate blocks

⅝ yard dark brown print fabric for inner border

2¼ yards red check fabric for outer border

1¼ yards black and cream plaid fabric for bias binding

6 yards fabric for quilt backing

Quilt batting, at least 82 × 100 inches

Rotary cutter, mat, and see-through ruler with ⅛-inch markings

G e t t i n g   R e a d y

- READ instructions thoroughly before you begin.

- PREWASH and press fabric.

- USE ¼-inch seam allowances throughout unless directions specify otherwise.

- SEAM ALLOWANCES are included in the cutting sizes given.

- PRESS seam allowances in the direction that will create the least bulk, and whenever possible, press toward the darker fabric.

- CUTTING DIRECTIONS for each section of the quilt are given individually. If you like to cut as you go, simply follow the directions as you get to them. If you'd rather cut all your pieces at the same time, skip ahead to find each of the cutting sections and do all the cutting before you begin to sew. 🍃

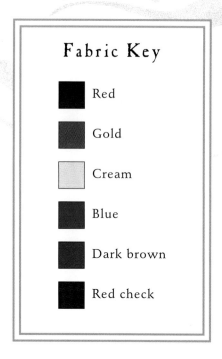

Fabric Key

■ Red

■ Gold

□ Cream

■ Blue

■ Dark brown

■ Red check

Nine Patch Blocks

(MAKE 65)

CUTTING

From the red print fabric:
- Cut sixteen 2½ × 44-inch strips for Strip Set I
- Cut four 2½ × 44-inch strips for Strip Set II

From the gold print fabric:
- Cut eight 2½ × 44-inch strips for Strip Set I
- Cut eight 2½ × 44-inch strips for Strip Set II

Piecing
the Nine Patch Blocks

1 To make Strip Set I, sew a 2½ × 44-inch red strip to either side of a 2½ × 44-inch gold strip, as shown in DIAGRAM 1.

Press seam allowances toward the darker fabric. Make eight of Strip Set I. Cut each Strip Set I into one hundred thirty 2½-inch segments, as shown.

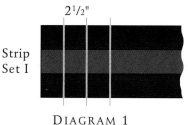

2½"

Strip Set I

DIAGRAM 1

2 To make Strip Set II, sew a 2½ × 44-inch gold strip to either side of a 2½ × 44-inch red strip, as shown in DIAGRAM 2. Press seam allowances toward

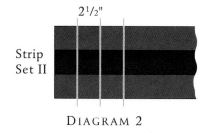

2½"

Strip Set II

DIAGRAM 2

the darker fabric. Make four of Strip Set II. Cut each Strip Set II into sixty-five 2½-inch segments, as shown.

TO ROTARY CUT segments from a strip set, start by squaring up the end of the strip set so that it is perpendicular to a seam line. Trim away any selvage edges with this first cut. Use the markings on your rotary ruler and cutting mat to continuously line up the strip set. If it begins to look uneven, trim the cut edge again to make sure it stays perpendicular to the seam line. Check often for accuracy as you cut.

TIPS AND TRICKS

3 Sew a Strip Set I segment to opposite sides of a Strip Set II, as shown in DIAGRAM 3. Make 65 of these Nine Patch blocks.

DIAGRAM 3

Alternate Blocks
(MAKE 65)

CUTTING

From the cream print fabric:
• Cut eight 4³⁄₄ × 44-inch strips; from these strips cut sixty-five 4³⁄₄-inch squares.

From the blue print fabric:
• Cut thirteen 3⁷⁄₈ × 44-inch strips; from these strips, cut one hundred thirty 3⁷⁄₈-inch squares. Cut the squares in half diagonally to make two hundred sixty triangles.

Piecing the Alternate Blocks

1 Sew blue triangles to opposite sides of each 4³⁄₄-inch cream square, as shown in DIAGRAM 4. Press seam allowances toward the triangles.

DIAGRAM 4

2 Sew blue triangles to the remaining sides of the cream squares, as shown in DIAGRAM 5. Make 65 alternate blocks.

DIAGRAM 5

Joining the Blocks

1 Sew five Nine Patch blocks and five alternate blocks together in a row, alternating the blocks, referring to the QUILT ASSEMBLY DIAGRAM on page 34. Make 13 horizontal rows.

2 Referring to the QUILT ASSEMBLY DIAGRAM for block placement, sew the rows together, matching seam intersections.

Borders

CUTTING

NOTE: The yardage given allows for the border pieces to be cut cross-grain.

From the dark brown print fabric:
• Cut seven 2¹⁄₂ × 44-inch strips for the inner border

From the red check fabric:
• Cut nine 7¹⁄₂ × 44-inch strips for the outer border

Attaching the Borders

1 Measure the quilt from left to right through the middle to determine the length of the top and bottom border strips. Diagonally piece and cut the dark brown inner border strips to the necessary length, and sew them to the top and bottom of the quilt, referring to the QUILT ASSEMBLY DIAGRAM on page 34.

2 Measure the quilt from top to bottom through the middle, including the border strips you just added, to determine the length of the side border strips. Diagonally piece and cut the dark brown inner border strips to the necessary lengths, and sew them to the sides of the quilt, referring to the QUILT ASSEMBLY DIAGRAM on page 34.

3 For the top and bottom outer border strips, measure as you did for the inner border in Step 1. Diagonally piece the red check outer border strips, trim them to the necessary lengths, and sew them to the top and bottom of the quilt.

4 For the side outer border strips, measure as for the inner border. Diagonally piece the red check outer strips, trim them to the necessary lengths, and sew them to the sides of the quilt.

Putting It All Together

1 Cut the 6-yard length of backing in half crosswise. Remove selvages and sew the two lengths together. Press the seam open. Trim backing and batting to 4 inches larger than quilt top.

2 Mark quilting designs on the quilt top.

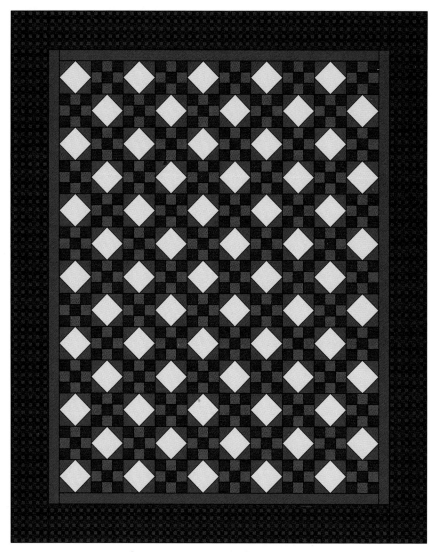

QUILT ASSEMBLY DIAGRAM

3 Layer the backing, batting, and quilt top. Baste these layers together, and quilt.

4 Remove the basting and trim the excess backing and batting even with the quilt top.

Binding

NOTE: The 2¾-inch bias strips will produce a ⅜-inch-wide binding. If you want a wider or narrower binding, adjust the width of the cut strips. (See page 216 for pointers on binding width.) See "Making and Attaching the Binding" on page 215 to complete your quilt.

From the black and cream plaid:
• Cut enough 2¾-inch bias strips to make a 370-inch strip for bias binding

Quilting DESIGNS

FOR HAND QUILTING:

❧ Because of the colors and prints in this quilt, quilting designs will not be highly visible, except in the light blocks. Simple stitch-in-the-ditch quilting will work well to highlight the shapes in the pieced areas.

❧ Choose a purchased quilting stencil with a floral motif to complement the light alternating squares on-point.

❧ You can treat the two borders as one by using a purchased quilting stencil with a large feathered chain design, or choose another large design you like. I find it helpful to keep a variety of large border stencils on hand. That way, I'm prepared with a choice of quilting designs for any border or combination of borders.

FOR MACHINE QUILTING:

❧ An overall pattern of meander quilting will work well for machine quilting the pieced areas of this quilt.

❧ You can machine quilt the light on-point squares and the borders with the very same types of designs listed under hand quilting.

JUST LIKE HOME

I have always loved to give rooms in my home an exciting, fresh look by making some new pillows. I think this is a clever way to introduce a touch of color, brighten up a corner, or just add a bit of handwork to soften the look of a chair or any other piece of furniture. Simply lining up three or four pillows can add a colorful accent that will dramatically change the appearance of a couch or loveseat. The House block in this Just Like Home pillow is big, bold, and graphic. With its narrow ruffle, this pillow makes a fun pictorial accessory for any room.

Size

Pillow without ruffle: 18 inches square (unquilted)

Fabrics and Supplies

Yardage is based on 44-inch-wide fabric.

3/8 yard beige print fabric for backgrounds and sawtooth border

1/8 yard red print #1 fabric for house

1/8 yard dark gold print fabric for inner roof and windows

3/4 yard black print fabric for outer roof, door, and ruffle

1/8 yard gold print fabric for stars

1/4 yard blue print fabric for sawtooth

1/4 yard red print #2 fabric for outer border

5/8 yard muslin for backing for pillow top

5/8 yard dark red print fabric for pillow back

18-inch square pillow form

Rotary cutter, mat, and see-through ruler with 1/8-inch markings

JUST LIKE HOME
Getting Ready

- READ instructions thoroughly before you begin.

- PREWASH and press fabric.

- USE ¼-inch seam allowances throughout unless directions specify otherwise.

- SEAM ALLOWANCES are included in the cutting sizes given.

- PRESS seam allowances in the direction that will create the least bulk, and whenever possible, press toward the darker fabric.

- CUTTING DIRECTIONS for each section of the quilt are given individually. If you like to cut as you go, simply follow the directions as you get to them. If you'd rather cut all your pieces at the same time, skip ahead to find each of the cutting sections and do all the cutting before you begin to sew. ✎

Fabric Key

- ▢ Beige
- ■ Red #1
- ▦ Dark gold
- ▦ Black
- ▦ Gold
- ■ Blue
- ■ Red #2
- ▦ Dark red backing

House Block
(MAKE 1)

CUTTING

From the beige print fabric:
- Cut one 5⅜-inch square

From the red print #1 fabric:
- Cut one 1½ × 3½-inch rectangle
- Cut four 1½ × 5-inch rectangles
- Cut two 1½-inch squares
- Cut two 1½ × 2-inch rectangles

From the dark gold print fabric:
- Cut two 1½ × 2½-inch rectangles
- Cut two 2½-inch squares

From the black print fabric:
- Cut one 5⅜-inch square
- Cut one 3½ × 4-inch rectangle

Piecing the House Block

1 Layer the 5⅜-inch beige square and the black square right sides together, as shown in DIAGRAM 1. Cut the layered squares in half diagonally and stitch a ¼-inch seam along each diagonal edge. Press seam allowances toward the black fabric.

DIAGRAM 1

2 Position a 2½-inch dark gold print square on the black corner of the triangle-pieced square, right sides together, as shown in DIAGRAM 2. Draw a diagonal line on the dark gold square, as shown, and stitch on this line. Trim the seam allow-

ances to ¼ inch, and press. Make two of these units.

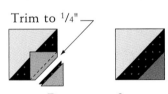

Trim to ¼"

DIAGRAM 2

3 Sew the two pieced units together as shown in DIAGRAM 3, completing the roof unit.

DIAGRAM 3

4 Sew a 1½ × 3½-inch red #1 rectangle to the 3½ × 4-inch black rectangle to make the door unit, as shown in DIAGRAM 4. Press seam allowances toward the black fabric.

DIAGRAM 4

5 To make a window unit, sew a 1½-inch red square to the top and a 1½ × 2-inch red rectangle to the bottom of a 1½ × 2½-inch dark gold rectangle, as shown in DIAGRAM 5. Press seam allowances toward the red fabric. Repeat to make a second window unit.

DIAGRAM 5

6 Sew a 1½ × 5-inch red rectangle to both sides of the window units, as shown in DIAGRAM 6. Press seam allowances toward the red fabric. Sew the window units to both sides of the door unit, as shown. Press seam allowances toward the black fabric.

DIAGRAM 6

7 Sew the roof and lower house units together to complete the House block, as shown in DIAGRAM 7. At this point, the House block should measure 9½ inches square.

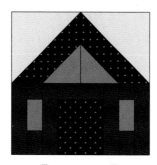

DIAGRAM 7

Star Blocks
(MAKE 4)

CUTTING

From the gold print fabric:
• Cut four 1½ × 3½-inch rectangles
• Cut eight 1½-inch squares

From the beige print fabric:
• Cut eight 1½ × 2½-inch rectangles
• Cut sixteen 1½-inch squares

Piecing the Star Blocks

1 Position a 1½-inch gold print square on the corner of a 1½ × 2½-inch beige print rectangle, as shown in DIAGRAM 8. Draw a diagonal line on the gold print square, and stitch on this line, as shown. Trim seam allowances to ¼ inch. Press seam allowances toward the gold fabric. Sew a 1½-inch beige square to the gold triangle, as shown below. Make a total of eight of these units, as shown.

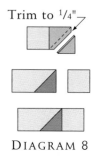

Trim to ¼"

DIAGRAM 8

2 Position a 1½-inch beige square on the corner of a 1½ × 3½-inch gold rectangle, as shown in DIAGRAM 9. Draw a diagonal line on the beige square, as shown, and stitch on this line. Trim seam allowances to ¼ inch. Press seam allowances toward the gold fabric. Repeat at the opposite corner of the gold print rectangle, as shown below. Make a total of four of these units.

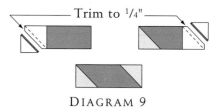

Trim to ¼"

DIAGRAM 9

3 Sew two units from Step 1 to each of the units from Step 2, completing the Star blocks, as shown in DIAGRAM 10. At this point, the Star blocks should measure 3½ inches square.

DIAGRAM 10

Sawtooth Border

CUTTING

From the beige print fabric:
• Cut one 3⅞ × 44-inch strip

From the blue print fabric:
• Cut one 3⅞ × 44-inch strip

Piecing the Sawtooth Border

1 Layer the 3⅞ × 44-inch beige print and blue print strips right sides together. Press the strips together, but do not sew. Cut the layered strips into six 3⅞-inch squares, as shown in DIAGRAM 11.

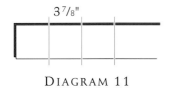

3⅞"

DIAGRAM 11

2 Cut the layered squares in half diagonally, and stitch a ¼-inch seam along each diagonal edge, as shown in DIAGRAM 12. Press seam allowances toward the darker fabric.

DIAGRAM 12

3 Sew three triangle-pieced squares together, completing a sawtooth border, as shown in DIAGRAM 13. Make four of these sawtooth borders. Press.

DIAGRAM 13

4 Sew a sawtooth border to the top and bottom of the House blocks, as shown in DIAGRAM 14. Press.

DIAGRAM 14

5 Sew a Star block to both ends of the remaining two sawtooth borders, as shown in DIAGRAM 15. Sew these borders to the sides of the House block, as shown.

DIAGRAM 15

Outer Border

CUTTING

From the red print #2 fabric:
• Cut two 2 × 15½-inch strips
• Cut two 2 × 18½-inch strips

Attaching the Outer Border

1 Sew the 2 × 15½-inch red #2 strips to the top and bottom of the pillow, as shown in the PILLOW ASSEMBLY DIAGRAM. Press seam allowances toward the borders.

PILLOW ASSEMBLY DIAGRAM

2 Sew the 2 × 18½-inch red #2 strips to the sides of the pillow, as shown. Press seams allowances toward the borders.

Putting It All Together

1 Trim the muslin backing and batting so they are 4 inches larger than the pillow top dimensions.

2 Layer the muslin backing, batting, and pillow top. Baste the layers together and quilt.

3 When quilting is complete, remove basting and trim the excess backing and batting even with the pillow top.

TO PREPARE the pillow top before attaching the ruffle, I suggest hand basting the edges of all three layers of the pillow top together. This will prevent the edge of the pillow top from rippling when you attach the ruffle.

TIPS AND TRICKS

Pillow Ruffle

CUTTING

From the black print fabric:
• Cut five 2½ × 44-inch strips

GATHERING RUFFLES

🖉 HERE'S ANOTHER quick and easy way to gather a ruffle. Do a wide, long zigzag stitch over two strands of regular-weight sewing thread or a heavier thread positioned ¼ inch in from the raw edges of the ruffle. NOTE: You will need a length of thread at least 2 times the circumference of your pillow. Secure one end of the heavy thread by stitching across it. Then zigzag over the heavy thread all the way around the ruffle, taking care not to sew through it. Pull on the heavy thread to gather up the ruffle to fit the edges of your pillow top.

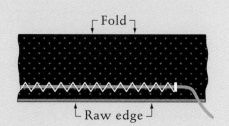

Attaching the Ruffle

1 Sew the 2½ × 44-inch black strips together with diagonal seams to make a continuous ruffle strip. For more information on diagonal seams, see page 211. Trim seam allowances to ¼ inch. Press seam allowances open.

2 With wrong sides together, fold the continuous ruffle strip in half lengthwise, and run gathering stitches all the way around the strip, ¼ inch from the raw edges, as shown in DIAGRAM 16.

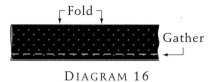

DIAGRAM 16

3 Pull up the gathering stitches until the ruffle fits the pillow top, taking care to allow fullness in the rufffle at each corner, as shown in DIAGRAM 17. Sew the ruffle to the pillow top, using a scant ¼-inch seam allowance.

DIAGRAM 17

Pillow Back

From the dark red print backing fabric:
• Cut two 18½ × 21-inch pieces

Assembling the Pillow Back

1 Fold the two dark red backing pieces in half, wrong sides together, to form two 10½ × 18½-inch double-thick back pieces. Overlap the two folded edges by 2 inches, as shown in DIAGRAM 18. Baste across the overlapped areas ¼ inch in from each edge to secure them in place, as shown. The doubled layers of fabric will make the pillow back more stable and add a nice finishing touch.

2 Place the pillow back and the pillow top right sides together, as shown in DIAGRAM 19, making sure that the folded edge of the ruffle faces the center of the pillow top. Pin the edges of the pillow front and back together, and stitch around the outside edge, using a ⅜-inch seam allowance.

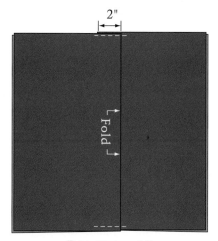

DIAGRAM 18

DIAGRAM 19

3 Trim the pillow back and corner seam allowances, if needed to reduce bulk, turn the pillow right side out, and fluff up the ruffle. Insert the pillow form through the back opening. If desired, slipstitch the back opening closed.

Quilting DESIGNS

FOR HAND OR MACHINE QUILTING:

✿ *Quilt in the ditch around the outside of the house, around each of the windows, and around the stars and the triangles. Quilt two vertical lines inside the door, spacing them an inch in from the sides of the door.*

✿ *Quilt in the ditch of each of the border seams.*

HARVEST MIX

For this quilt, I gathered fabrics in colors that signal the end of summer, when the trees around my home turn to glorious shades of rust, ochre, brown, and gold. I chose a different main color for each of the blocks in the center of the quilt. They all share the same background print, creating a feeling of unity. The mellow, medium-value fabric in the side triangles frames the blocks gently, and two coordinated plaids in the borders add strong visual interest. The tan and red prints in the corner blocks draw the eye outward to the edges of the quilt.

Size

Lap Quilt: 56 × 66 inches
Finished Block: 8 inches square

Fabrics and Supplies

Yardage is based on 44-inch-wide fabric.

⅛ yard *each* of two check fabrics for Triangle-Pieced Square blocks

¼ yard *each* of three rust print fabrics for Nine Patch blocks

1¼ yards beige print fabric for all pieced blocks

⅛ yard *each* of four dark fabrics for Ohio Star points

One 4½-inch square *each* of four plaids for Ohio Star centers

⅛ yard *each* of nine coordinating print fabrics for Sixteen Patch blocks

⅝ yard tan print for side and corner triangles

¼ yard gold print for corner blocks

¼ yard red print for corner blocks

1½ yards chestnut/black check for inner border

2 yards black/rust plaid for outer border

¾ yard brown plaid for binding

3⅓ yards fabric for Option I quilt backing

1½ yards black/tan check fabric for Option II pieced quilt backing

2¼ yards small chestnut/black check fabric for Option II pieced quilt backing

Quilt batting, at least 60 × 70 inches

Rotary cutter, mat, and see-through ruler with ⅛-inch markings

Getting Ready

- READ instructions thoroughly before you begin.

- PREWASH and press fabric.

- USE ¼-inch seam allowances throughout unless directions specify otherwise.

- SEAM ALLOWANCES are included in the cutting sizes given.

- PRESS seam allowances in the direction that will create the least bulk, and whenever possible, press toward the darker fabric.

- CUTTING DIRECTIONS for each section of the quilt are given individually. If you like to cut as you go, simply follow the directions as you get to them. If you'd rather cut all your pieces at the same time, skip ahead to find each of the cutting sections and do all the cutting before you begin to sew. 🌿

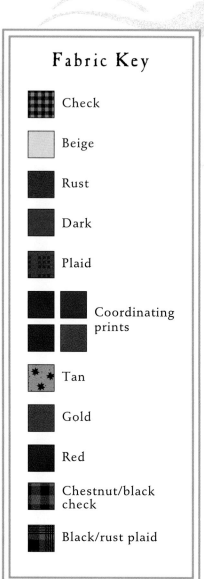

Fabric Key

- Check
- Beige
- Rust
- Dark
- Plaid
- Coordinating prints
- Tan
- Gold
- Red
- Chestnut/black check
- Black/rust plaid

Triangle-Pieced Blocks
(MAKE 2)

C U T T I N G

for Each Triangle-Pieced Square Block

TRIANGLE-PIECED SQUARE
BLOCK DIAGRAM

From the check fabric:
- Cut one 2⅞ × 26-inch strip

From the beige print fabric:
- Cut one 2⅞ × 26-inch strip

Piecing the Triangle-Pieced Square Blocks

1 With right sides together, layer a check 2⅞ × 26-inch strip and a beige 2⅞ × 26-inch strip. Press together but do not sew. Cut the layered strips into eight 2⅞-inch squares. Repeat.

2 Cut the layered squares in half diagonally, as shown in DIAGRAM 1. Stitch ¼ inch from the diagonal edges. Press seam allowances toward the check fabric. Make a total of 16 triangle-pieced squares for each block.

DIAGRAM 1

3 To piece the blocks, sew four of the triangle-pieced squares together in a row. Repeat to make four rows and sew them together; see DIAGRAM 2. Make two Triangle-Pieced Square blocks, each measuring 8½ inches square.

DIAGRAM 2

Nine Patch Blocks
(MAKE 3)

C U T T I N G

for Each Nine Patch Block

NINE PATCH
BLOCK DIAGRAM

From one of the rust print fabrics:
- Cut four 2½-inch squares
- Cut one 4½-inch square

From the beige print fabric:
- Cut four 2½ × 4½-inch pieces

Piecing
the Nine Patch Blocks

1 Sew a 2½ × 4½-inch beige piece to the top and bottom of each of the 4½-inch rust squares, as shown in DIAGRAM 3.

DIAGRAM 3

2 Sew a 2½-inch rust square to each end of the remaining 2½ × 4½-inch beige pieces, as shown in DIAGRAM 4.

DIAGRAM 4

3 Sew the units from Step 2 to the sides of each Step 1 unit, as shown in DIAGRAM 5. At this point, the Nine Patch blocks should measure 8½ inches square.

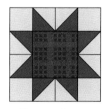

DIAGRAM 5

Ohio Star Blocks
(MAKE 4)

C U T T I N G

for Each Ohio Star Block

OHIO STAR
BLOCK DIAGRAM

From one of the dark fabrics:
- Cut one 2⅞ × 14-inch strip

From the beige print fabric:
- Cut four 2½-inch squares
- Cut one 2⅞ × 14-inch strip

From one of the plaid fabrics:
- Cut one 4½-inch square

Piecing
the Ohio Star Blocks

1 Layer the 2⅞ × 14-inch dark and beige strips right sides together. Press, but do not sew. Cut the layered strips into four 2⅞-inch squares; see DIAGRAM 6. Cut the squares in half diagonally and stitch a ¼-inch seam along each diagonal edge, for a total of eight triangle-pieced squares. Repeat for each of the remaining blocks.

DIAGRAM 6

2 Sew the triangle-pieced squares together in pairs to make four star-point units for each Ohio Star block. Sew a star-point unit to the top and bottom of each 4½-inch plaid square, as shown in DIAGRAM 7.

DIAGRAM 7

3 Sew a 2½-inch beige square to the remaining star-point units, as shown in DIAGRAM 8. Sew these units to the sides of each Ohio Star block, as shown. At this point, the Ohio Star blocks should measure 8½ inches square.

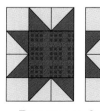

DIAGRAM 8

Sixteen Patch Blocks
(MAKE 9)

CUTTING

for Each Sixteen Patch Block

SIXTEEN PATCH
BLOCK DIAGRAM

From one of the coordinating print fabrics:
• Cut one $2\frac{1}{2} \times 22$-inch strip

From the beige print fabric:
• Cut one $2\frac{1}{2} \times 22$-inch strip

Piecing the Sixteen Patch Blocks

1 With right sides together, sew a $2\frac{1}{2} \times 22$-inch coordinating print fabric strip to a $2\frac{1}{2} \times 22$-inch beige strip. Press seam allowances toward the coordinating print fabric. Crosscut the strip set into eight $2\frac{1}{2}$-inch segments, as shown in DIAGRAM 9. Repeat for each of the remaining Sixteen Patch blocks.

$2\frac{1}{2}$"

DIAGRAM 9

2 Sew four units together in a row, alternating colors, referring to DIAGRAM 10. Make two of these rows and sew them together for each of the nine Sixteen Patch blocks. At this point, the Sixteen Patch blocks should measure $8\frac{1}{2}$ inches square.

DIAGRAM 10

Quilt Center

CUTTING

From the tan print fabric:
• Cut three 13-inch squares; cut these into quarters diagonally to make 12 side triangles
NOTE: You will use only 10 of the triangles in the quilt.
• Cut two 8-inch squares; cut these in half diagonally to make four corner triangles
NOTE: The side and corner triangles will be larger than necessary and will be trimmed after they have been added to the pieced blocks.

Assembling the Quilt Center

NOTE: When sewing the blocks into rows, press the seam allowances between blocks in the opposite direction from the previous row. This allows for easy

matching and sewing at block intersections.

1 Sew the pieced blocks together in diagonal rows, as shown in DIAGRAM 11 on the opposite page, beginning and ending each row with side triangles as needed. Do not attach the corner triangles yet.

2 Sew the diagonal rows together, pinning the block intersections for accuracy. Press all seam allowances between rows in the same direction.

3 Sew the triangles to the corners of the quilt top, referring to DIAGRAM 11.

4 Trim excess fabric from the side and corner triangles, making sure to allow a $\frac{1}{4}$-inch seam allowance beyond the block corners. Before you trim, be sure to see "Trimming Side and Corner Triangles" on page 211 to be certain you make these cuts accurately.

Borders and Corner Blocks

CUTTING

NOTE: The yardage given allows for border strips to be cut lengthwise.

From the gold and red print fabrics:
• Cut two $7\frac{1}{4}$-inch squares of each fabric for the corner blocks; cut the squares diagonally into quarters, forming eight triangles

DIAGRAM 11

From the chestnut/black check fabric:
• Cut two 6½ × 38-inch strips for the top and bottom inner borders
• Cut two 6½ × 48-inch strips for the side inner borders

From the black/rust plaid fabric:
• Cut two 5 × 49-inch strips for the top and bottom outer borders
• Cut two 5 × 69-inch strips for the side outer borders

Piecing the Corner Blocks

1 Layer a gold triangle and a red triangle. Sew a ¼-inch seam along one of the bias edges, as shown in DIAGRAM 12, being careful not to stretch the triangles. Also, make sure to sew on the same bias edge for each pair of triangles so that the pieced triangles will all have the red fabric on the same side. Press seam allowances toward the red fabric. Make eight of these units, as shown.

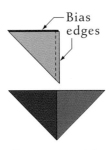

DIAGRAM 12

2 Sew two of these units together to make a corner block measuring 6½ inches square, as shown in DIAGRAM 13. Make a total of four corner blocks.

DIAGRAM 13

Inner Border

1 Measure the quilt through the center from left to right to determine the length for the top and bottom border strips. Trim the two 6½ × 38-inch chestnut/black check strips to this measurement. Sew these borders to the top and bottom of the quilt, referring to the QUILT ASSEMBLY DIAGRAM on page 48. Press seam allowances toward the border.

2 Measure the quilt through the center from top to bottom, including seam allowances but *not* the top and bottom border strips. Cut the 6½ × 48-inch chestnut/black check strips to the length needed. Sew a corner square to each end of these border strips, referring to the QUILT ASSEMBLY DIAGRAM. Sew the side border strips to the quilt, and press seam allowances toward the border.

Outer Border

1 Measure the quilt as in Step 1 of "Inner Border," and include the inner border in this measurement. Cut the 5 × 49-inch black/rust plaid outer border

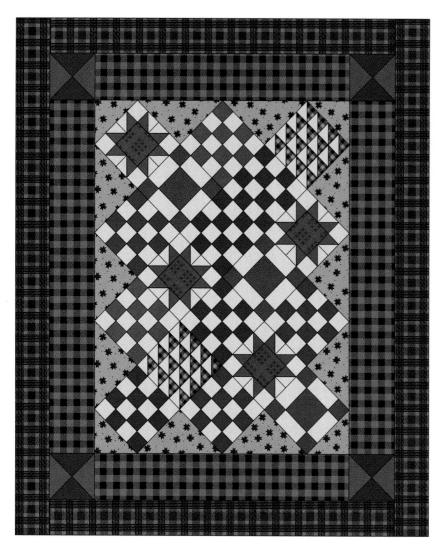

QUILT ASSEMBLY DIAGRAM

TRY PIECING quilt backs using a variety of large pieces of coordinating fabrics. They will add interest to a quilt as well as offer an opportunity to make use of leftover fabrics. These pieces can be placed vertically or horizontally.

backing and batting to about 4 inches larger than the quilt top.

2 Mark quilting designs on the quilt top.

3 Layer the backing, batting, and quilt top. Baste the layers together, and quilt by hand or machine.

4 When quilting is complete, remove the basting stitches and trim the excess backing and batting even with the quilt top.

strips to this measurement and sew them to the top and bottom of the quilt, referring to the QUILT ASSEMBLY DIAGRAM. Press.

2 Measure the quilt from top to bottom through the middle, including the border strips you just added, to determine the length of the side border strips. Cut the 5 × 69-inch black/rust plaid strips to this measurement and sew them to the sides of the quilt. Press.

Putting It All Together

NOTE: Choose the backing option you like best for your quilt.

Option I Backing

1 Cut the 3⅓-yard length of backing fabric in half crosswise. Remove the selvages and sew the two lengths together. Press this seam open. Trim the

Option II Backing

CUTTING

From the black/tan check fabric:
• Cut one 43 × 53-inch piece

From the small chestnut/black check fabric:
• Cut two 11 × 43-inch strips
• Cut two 11 × 74-inch strips

Assembling the Pieced Back

1 With right sides together, sew the 11 × 43-inch chestnut/black strips to the top and bottom of the 43 × 53-inch black/tan check piece, referring to DIAGRAM 14. Press seam allowances toward the borders.

2 Sew the 11 × 74-inch chestnut/black strips to the sides, referring to DIAGRAM 14. Press seam allowances toward the borders.

Option II backing

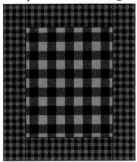

DIAGRAM 14

3 Trim the backing and batting so they are about 4 inches larger than the quilt top.

4 Mark quilting designs on the quilt top.

5 Layer the pieced backing and batting. Center the quilt top over the backing and the batting. Baste the three layers together, and then quilt.

Binding

NOTE: The 2¾-inch-wide plaid bias strips will produce a ⅜-inch-wide binding. If you want a wider or narrower binding, adjust the width of the strips you cut. (See page 216 for pointers on how to experiment with binding width.) Refer to "Making and Attaching the Binding" on page 215 to complete your quilt.

CUTTING

From the brown plaid fabric:
• Cut enough 2¾-inch bias strips to make a 260-inch binding strip

Quilting
DESIGNS

FOR HAND QUILTING:

❧ *Try quilting in the ditch around all of the pieces in each block to make the shapes stand out visually from the background as well as from each other. In the side triangles, try quilting angled lines spaced at 1¼-inch intervals, as shown in* QUILTING DIAGRAM 1. *This will echo the shapes of the triangles.*

❧ *For an easy way to add texture to the inner borders, try filling them with lines of* diagonal cross-hatching *spaced at 2¾-inch intervals.*

❧ *I used a purchased quilting stencil with a simple chain design for the outer border, as shown in* QUILTING DIAGRAM 2, *which makes a nice contrast to the straight lines in the inner border.*

FOR MACHINE QUILTING:

❧ *Quilting similar designs by machine will work nicely. A medium-size pattern of meander quilting stitches can be very effective in the middle border and is easier to machine quilt than long straight lines of cross-hatching.*

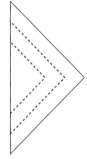

QUILTING DIAGRAM 1

QUILTING DIAGRAM 2

PINE TREE LOG CABIN

Log Cabin quilts, traditional favorites, typically feature lots of colors. They almost call out to us to curl up and get cozy in them. In Pine Tree Log Cabin, I coordinated a variety of reds, greens, chestnusts, and creams to create richness and depth in the pieced "logs." The large Pine Tree blocks in the border corners have beige prints in the background and a green print in the pine trees, which relates them visually to the Log Cabin blocks. As a final touch, I repeated some of the same colors in the border to create a strong frame around the center of the quilt.

Size

Bed Quilt: 64¾ × 90 inches (unquilted)

Finished Block: 8¾ inches square

Fabrics and Supplies

Yardage is based on 44-inch-wide fabric.

2½ yards *total* of a variety of six light fabrics (or, 14 × 44 inches each) for Log Cabin blocks

2½ yards *total* of a variety of six dark fabrics (or, 14 × 44 inches each) for Log Cabin blocks

¼ yard gold print #1 fabric for Log Cabin block center squares

½ yard green print fabric for Tree blocks

⅝ yard beige print fabric for Tree background

1 yard gold print #2 fabric for inner border

½ yard dark green print fabric for middle border

1½ yards dark red print fabric for outer border

1 yard gold print #1 fabric for binding

5½ yards fabric for quilt backing

Quilt batting, at least 69 × 95 inches

Rotary cutter, mat, and see-through ruler with ⅛-inch markings

Getting Ready

- READ instructions thoroughly before you begin.

- PREWASH and press fabric.

- USE ¼-inch seam allowances throughout unless directions specify otherwise.

- SEAM ALLOWANCES are included in the cutting sizes given.

- PRESS seam allowances in the direction that will create the least bulk, and whenever possible, press toward the darker fabric.

- CUTTING DIRECTIONS for each section of the quilt are given individually. If you'd like to cut as you go, simply follow the directions as you get to them. If you'd rather cut all your pieces at the same time, skip ahead to find each of the cutting sections and do all the cutting before you begin to sew. 🍃

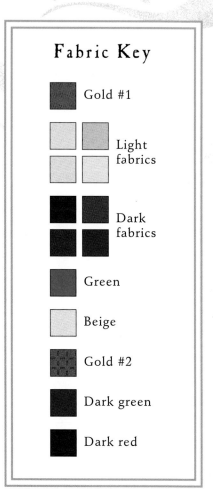

Fabric Key

- Gold #1
- Light fabrics
- Dark fabrics
- Green
- Beige
- Gold #2
- Dark green
- Dark red

Log Cabin Blocks
(MAKE 40)

CUTTING

From the variety of light fabrics:
- Cut at least thirty-seven 1¾ × 44-inch strips

From the variety of dark fabrics:
- Cut at least thirty-nine 1¾ × 44-inch strips

From the gold print #1 fabric:
- Cut two 1¾ × 44-inch strips; from these strips, cut forty 1¾-inch center squares

Piecing the Log Cabin Blocks

NOTE: You may vary the position of the light fabrics from block to block, or place them in the same position in each block. The same is true for the dark fabrics. Follow Steps 1 through 3 to piece each of the 40 Log Cabin blocks.

1 With right sides together, stitch a 1¾ × 44-inch light strip to a 1¾-inch gold print square. Press the seam allowance toward the gold strip. Trim the strip even with the edge of the center square, creating a two-piece unit, as shown in DIAGRAM 1.

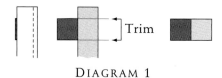

DIAGRAM 1

2 Turn the two-piece unit to the right a quarter turn. Stitch a different 1¾-inch-wide light strip to the two-piece unit. Press and trim the edges of this strip even with the edges of the two-piece unit, as shown in DIAGRAM 2.

DIAGRAM 2

3 Working counter-clockwise around the center square, continue adding alternating light and dark strips to complete the Log Cabin block, referring to DIAGRAM 3 for placement. Press each seam allowance toward the strip just added, and trim each strip before adding the next. Each Log Cabin block should measure 9¼ inches square when completed. Adjust seam allowances if needed.

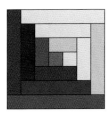

DIAGRAM 3

4 Sew the five blocks together in eight horizontal rows, referring to the QUILT ASSEMBLY DIAGRAM. Sew the horizontal rows together, matching the intersections of the blocks.

Tree Blocks
(MAKE 4)

C U T T I N G

From the green print fabric:
• Cut two 2⅞ × 44-inch strips
• Cut one 1¾ × 44-inch strip; from this strip, cut four 1¾ × 9-inch-long pieces
• Cut four 4½-inch squares for trees

• Cut four 2½-inch squares for tree bases

From the beige print fabric:
• Cut two 2⅞ × 44-inch strips
• Cut eight 2½-inch squares
• Cut four 6½-inch squares

Piecing the Tree Blocks

1 Layer two 2⅞ × 44-inch green and beige strips. Press, but do not sew. Layer the remaining 2⅞-inch-wide strips in the same manner. Cut the layered strips into twenty-eight 2⅞-inch squares. Cut the layered squares in half diagonally, and stitch a ¼-inch seam along the diagonal edges, as shown in DIAGRAM 4. Press. Make 56 triangle-pieced squares.

DIAGRAM 4

2 Draw a diagonal line on each of the 6½-inch beige squares, as shown in DIAGRAM 5. *Do not* cut.

DIAGRAM 5

3 Fold the 1¾ × 9-inch green strips in half lengthwise, wrong sides together. Press.

4 Position a green strip on each beige square so that the raw edges are even with the diagonal line. Stitch together with a ¼-inch seam, as shown

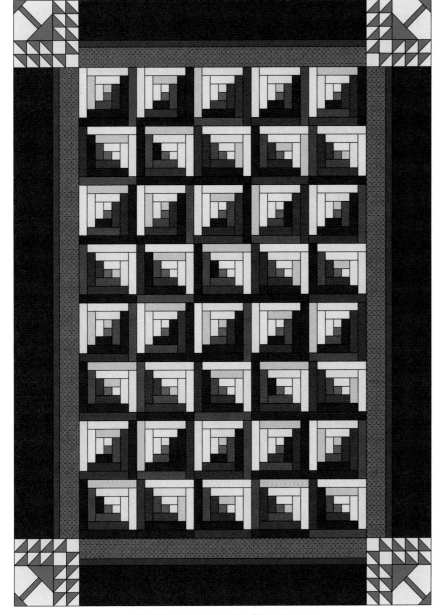

QUILT ASSEMBLY DIAGRAM

in DIAGRAM 6. Fold the green strip over the raw edges and hand stitch in place, as shown.

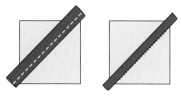

DIAGRAM 6

5 Position a 4½-inch green square on one end of each beige square, as shown in DIAGRAM 7. Position a 2½-inch green square on the opposite end of each beige square. Draw a diagonal line across each of the green squares, and stitch on these lines, as shown. Make four of these tree base units.

DIAGRAM 7

6 Trim away the excess fabric ¼ inch from each seam allowance, creating the tree base units, as shown in DIAGRAM 8. Press.

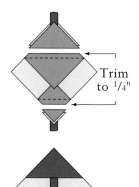

Trim to ¼"

DIAGRAM 8

7 Sew together eight sections of three triangle-pieced squares each, as shown in DIAGRAM 9. Sew two of these sections to each of the four tree base units, as shown.

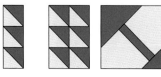

DIAGRAM 9

8 Sew together four triangle-pieced units with a beige square at the end, referring to DIAGRAM 10 for placement. Press. Make four of these sections.

DIAGRAM 10

9 Sew together three triangle-pieced units, a beige square, and another triangle-pieced unit at the end, referring to DIAGRAM 11 for placement. Press. Make four of these sections.

DIAGRAM 11

10 Sew the sections made in Step 8 and 9 to each tree base unit, as shown in DIAGRAM 12, creating the Tree blocks. Press. At this point, the Tree blocks should measure 10½ inches square. Adjust seam allowances if needed.

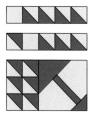

DIAGRAM 12

Borders

C U T T I N G

NOTE: The three border strips are sewn to the quilt as one unit. The yardage given allows for the border pieces to be cut cross-grain.

From the gold print #2:
• Cut seven 3½ × 44-inch inner border strips

From the dark green print fabric:
• Cut seven 1½ × 44-inch middle border strips

From the dark red print fabric:
• Cut seven 6½ × 44-inch outer border strips

Attaching the Borders

1 Measure the quilt from left to right through the center to determine the length of the top and bottom border strips. Diagonally piece the strips in each color to get the length needed. Cut two 3½-inch-wide gold strips, two 1½-inch-wide dark green strips, and two 6½-inch-wide dark red strips to this measurement. Sew the three border strips together in the order shown in DIAGRAM 13. Add these top and bottom border strips to the quilt, referring to the QUILT ASSEMBLY DIAGRAM on page 53.

DIAGRAM 13

2 For the side border strips, measure the quilt from top to bottom, including the seam allowances but not the top and bottom borders. As in Step 1, diagonally piece strips in each color to get the length needed, and cut them to this measurement. Sew the three border strips together for the side borders, referring to DIAGRAM 13. Sew a Tree corner block to each end of the side borders, referring to the QUILT ASSEMBLY DIAGRAM for placement. Sew the side borders to the quilt.

Putting It All Together

1 Cut the 5½-yard length of backing in half crosswise. Remove the selvages and sew the long edges of the two lengths together. Press this seam open.

TRY PEARL COTTON #12 for hand quilting. It gives quilting stitches a heavier, stronger appearance, which is often a nice addition to a casual, rustic design. Experiment a bit to find a nice small needle that has an eye large enough to hold this slightly larger thread.

TIPS AND TRICKS

Quilting DESIGNS

FOR HAND OR MACHINE QUILTING:

🍃 *The long, straight lines in the Log Cabin blocks make it seem natural to quilt along the seam lines of each "log." Whether you like to quilt by hand or machine, it will be easy to quilt this way, because no marking there is required.*

🍃 *Quilt the Pine Tree corner blocks in the same manner as the other blocks.*

🍃 *Treat borders as a single unit. Quilt lines at 1¼-inch intervals, from the Log Cabin blocks out to the outer edges of the quilt. This will repeat the lines formed by the "logs" in the Log Cabin blocks.*

Trim the backing and batting so they are about 4 inches larger than the quilt top.

2 Mark quilting designs on the quilt top.

3 Layer the backing, batting, and quilt top. Baste these layers together and quilt.

4 When quilting is complete, remove basting and trim the excess backing and batting even with the quilt top.

Binding

NOTE: This quilt has a narrower binding and requires attaching it with a ¼-inch seam allowance, so that the tips of the pine trees

in the border corner blocks will not be cut off. See "Making and Attaching the Binding" on page 215 to complete your quilt.

From the gold #1 fabric:
• Cut nine 2½ × 44-inch strips for cross-grain binding

GLORIES
from my
GARDEN

*B*eautiful flowers
are like an invitation, with
brilliant colors and gentle
fragrances that capture your
senses, drawing you closer.
From early spring through
late fall, I plant delphiniums,
mums, asters, hollyhocks,
and blue veronicas so lovely
they almost pull you from
the courtyard right up to the
front door of my house. In
my quilts, I try to capture all
the colors and gentle beauty
I see in my garden.

‹‹‹‹‹ ‹‹‹‹‹ ‹‹‹‹‹

CHECKERBOARD CHERRIES

The deep reds and greens of the small tone-on-tone prints in this quilt make it fit right into my country home, and I like the pleasant picture created by round plump cherries floating on a cream background. Because the checkerboard in itself is such a strong design image, I selected calm fabrics with just enough print to create visual interest and texture. Then I repeated those fabrics in the cherry appliqués to create harmony throughout the quilt. The primitive stitching around the appliqué designs adds surface texture as well as a decorative outline.

Size

Wall Quilt: 15 inches square (unquilted)

Finished Block: 4 inches square

Fabrics and Supplies

Yardage is based on 44-inch-wide fabric.

¼ yard beige print fabric for background

⅜ yard green print fabric for leaves, checkered lattice, border, and binding

¼ yard red print fabric for cherries, checkered lattice, and border

⅛ yard brown print fabric for stems

⅝ yard fabric for quilt backing

Lightweight quilt batting, at least 19 inches square

¼ yard fusible web, 16 inches wide

1 skein black embroidery floss

Rotary cutter, mat, and see-through ruler with ⅛-inch markings

Getting Ready

- READ instructions thoroughly before you begin.

- PREWASH and press fabric.

- USE ¼-inch seam allowances throughout unless directions specify otherwise.

- SEAM ALLOWANCES are included in the cutting sizes given.

- PRESS seam allowances in the direction that will create the least bulk, and whenever possible, press toward the darker fabric.

- CUTTING DIRECTIONS for each section of the quilt are given individually. If you like to cut as you go, simply follow the directions as you get to them. If you'd rather cut all your pieces at the same time, skip ahead to find each of the cutting sections and do all the cutting before you begin to sew.

- INSTRUCTIONS are given for quick cutting and piecing the blocks. Note that for some of the pieces, the quick-cutting method will result in leftover fabric. 🍃

Fabric Key

- Beige
- Green
- Red
- Brown

Cherry Blocks
(MAKE 4)

CUTTING

From the beige print fabric:
- Cut four 4½-inch squares

1 Position the fusible web (paper side facing up) over the appliqué shapes on page 62. Trace 12 cherries, 12 leaves, and four stems onto the fusible web. Roughly cut around the shapes.

2 Place fusible web shapes, coated side down, on the wrong side of the fabrics chosen for the appliqué shapes. Press with a hot dry iron, following the manufacturer's directions for your brand of fusible web. Let

the fabric cool, cut out on the traced lines, and remove the paper backing.

3 Center the appliqué pieces on each 4½-inch beige square, as shown in the PLACE-MENT DIAGRAM. Press in place with a hot dry iron.

4 Appliqué the shapes in place. Shapes may be ironed on and left as they are, machine or hand appliquéd, or stitched with a primitive stitch, using two

strands of black embroidery floss. For more information on the primitive stitch, see page 210.

This is how appliqué shapes should appear when ironed on the background squares
PLACEMENT DIAGRAM

WHEN YOU want to separate six-strand embroidery floss into groups of two or three strands each, pull out one thread at a time. Then put the individual strands together in groups of two or three. This will make the floss fluff up and appear fuller when it is stitched.

TIPS AND TRICKS

Checkered Lattice and Border

From the green print fabric:
• Cut three 1½ × 44-inch strips
• Cut two 1½ inch squares

From the red print fabric:
• Cut three 1½ × 44-inch strips

Piecing the Checkerboard Lattice and Borders

NOTE: To make the checkerboard lattice and borders, you will need to construct a Strip Set I and a Strip Set II.

1 For Strip Set I, sew a red strip to both sides of a green strip, as shown in DIAGRAM 1. Cut into twenty-seven 1½-inch segments, as shown.

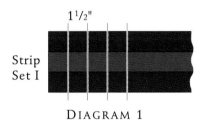

DIAGRAM 1

2 For Strip Set II, sew a green strip to both sides of a red strip, as shown in DIAGRAM 2. Cut into twenty-six 1½-inch segments, as shown.

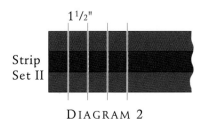

DIAGRAM 2

3 To make the lattice, sew a 1½-inch green square to one Strip Set I segment, as shown in DIAGRAM 3. Repeat to make another unit like this.

DIAGRAM 3

4 Sew a Cherry block to each side of these units, as shown in DIAGRAM 4.

DIAGRAM 4

5 To make the horizontal lattice, sew a Strip Set II segment to both sides of a Strip Set I segment, as shown in DIAGRAM 5.

DIAGRAM 5

6 Join the Cherry blocks to this horizontal lattice strip, as shown in DIAGRAM 6.

DIAGRAM 6

7 To make the top and bottom checkered border strips, sew five Strip Set I segments and four Strip Set II segments together, alternating colors, beginning and ending with a Strip Set I segment, as shown in DIAGRAM 7. Make two of these border strips. Sew the top and bottom border strips to the quilt.

DIAGRAM 7

8 To make the side border strips, sew seven Strip Set I segments and eight Strip Set II segments together, alternating colors, beginning and ending with a Strip Set II segment, as shown in DIAGRAM 8. Make two of these borders strips. Then sew the side border strips to the sides of the quilt, completing the quilt top, as shown in the QUILT ASSEMBLY DIAGRAM on page 62.

DIAGRAM 8

QUILT ASSEMBLY DIAGRAM

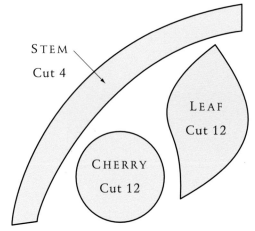

STEM
Cut 4

LEAF
Cut 12

CHERRY
Cut 12

Note: Leaf will appear in the
correct position when traced
onto fusible web

Putting It All Together

1 Trim the backing and batting so they are 4 inches larger than the quilt top dimensions.

2 Layer the backing, batting, and quilt top. Baste the layers together, and quilt by hand or machine.

3 When quilting is complete, remove basting and trim the excess backing and batting even with the quilt top.

Binding

NOTE: The 2¼-inch strip will make a ¼-inch-wide finished binding. If you want a wider or narrower binding, adjust the width of the strips you cut. (See page 216 for pointers on how to experiment with binding width.) See "Making and Attaching the Binding" on page 215 to complete your quilt.

CUTTING

From the green fabric:
• Cut two 2¼ × 44-inch strips for cross-grain binding

Quilting
DESIGNS

☙ *Because of the pieced checkerboard squares in this quilt, the only spaces to quilt are in the ditch of each of the checkerboard squares and around the cherry branches, the cherries, and the leaves. The texture created by this subtle quilting is just enough to enhance the pieced design and give the appliqué added visual depth.*

TULIP STAND

To define the tulips in this quilt and make them stand out visually, choose a strong floral print for the petals and three coordinating green prints for the stems and leaves. Repeating these tulip and stem fabrics in the quilt center and echoing the border fabric in the checkerboard center squares will help create a feeling of unity throughout your quilt. A mellow maple color in the inner border will separate the center of the quilt from the tulip border, and using that same fabric in your binding will act as a gentle reminder of that same soft shade.

Size

Bed Quilt: 72 × 88 inches (unquilted)

Finished Blocks: 4 and 8 inches square

Fabrics and Supplies

Yardage is based on 44-inch-wide fabric.

2 yards dark red print fabric for Four Patch blocks, tulips, and corner blocks

⅞ yard green check fabric for Four Patch blocks, corner blocks, and stems

2¾ yards medium red print fabric for plain blocks, corner blocks, and outer border

2¾ yards beige print fabric for background

¾ yard maple print fabric for inner border

⅜ yard dark green print fabric for leaves

½ yard light green print fabric for leaves

⅞ yard chestnut print fabric for binding

5½ yards fabric for quilt backing

Quilt batting, at least 76 × 92 inches

Rotary cutter, mat, and see-through ruler with ⅛-inch markings

TULIP STAND
Getting Ready

- READ instructions thoroughly before you begin.

- PREWASH and press fabric.

- USE ¼-inch seam allowances throughout unless directions specify otherwise.

- SEAM ALLOWANCES are included in the cutting sizes given.

- PRESS seam allowances in the direction that will create the least bulk, and whenever possible, press toward the darker fabric.

- CUTTING DIRECTIONS for each section of the quilt are given individually. If you like to cut as you go, simply follow the directions as you get to them. If you'd rather cut all your pieces at the same time, skip ahead to find each of the cutting sections and do all the cutting before you begin to sew. ✎

Fabric Key

 Dark red

 Green check

 Medium red

 Beige

 Maple

 Dark green

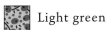 Light green

Four Patch Blocks
(MAKE 24 FULL AND 20 PARTIAL BLOCKS)

CUTTING

From the dark red print fabric:
- Cut five 2½ × 44-inch strips

From the green check fabric:
- Cut five 2½ × 44-inch strips

Piecing
the Four Patch Blocks

1 Sew the five 2½ × 44-inch-wide dark red and green check strips together in pairs. Press the seam allowances toward the darker fabric. Crosscut this strip set into sixty-eight 2½-inch segments, as shown in DIAGRAM 1.

2½"

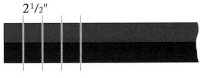

DIAGRAM 1

2 Sew 48 of the segments together in pairs to make 24 full blocks, as shown in DIAGRAM 2. The remaining units will be the 20 partial blocks, as shown.

Full block   Partial block
DIAGRAM 2

Quilt Center and Corner Squares

CUTTING

From the medium red print fabric:
- Cut five 4½ × 44-inch strips; from these strips, cut thirty-nine 4½-inch squares

From the beige print fabric:
- Cut eight 4½ × 44-inch strips; from these strips, cut fifty-eight 4½-inch squares, twenty-four 2½ × 4½-inch rectangles, and one 4½ × 22-inch strip
- Cut eight 2½ × 4½-inch rectangles

From the dark red print fabric:
- Cut one 2½ × 22-inch strip
- Cut two 2½-inch squares

From the green check fabric:
• Cut one 2½ × 22-inch strip
• Cut two 2½-inch squares

Assembling the Quilt Center and Corner Blocks

NOTE: To assemble the quilt center, use 24 full and 20 partial Four Patch blocks, thirty-five 4½-inch medium red squares, fifty-eight 4½-inch beige squares, twenty-four 2½ × 4½-inch beige rectangles, two 2½-inch dark red squares, and two 2½-inch green check squares.

1 Assemble the quilt center in 11 vertical rows, as shown in DIAGRAM 3. Sew the 11 vertical rows together, as shown. Press.

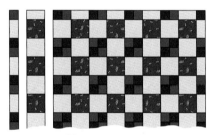

DIAGRAM 3

2 Make the corner blocks; set aside. Sew the 2½ × 22-inch dark red and green check strips to both sides of the 4½ × 22-inch beige strip. Press seams toward the darker fabric. Crosscut the strip set into eight 2½-inch segments, as shown in DIAGRAM 4.

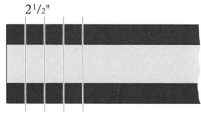

2½"

DIAGRAM 4

3 Sew a 2½ × 4½-inch-wide beige rectangle to the top and bottom of the 4½-inch medium red squares, as shown in DIAGRAM 5. Press seam allowances toward the darker fabric.

DIAGRAM 5

4 Sew a unit from Step 2 to the sides of each square, as shown in DIAGRAM 6. Press seam allowances away from each square. The four corner blocks should measure 8½ inches at this point.

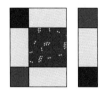

DIAGRAM 6

Borders

CUTTING

NOTE: The yardage given allows for the borders to be cut cross-grain.

From the maple print fabric:
• Cut five 2½ × 44-inch strips for the inner border
• Cut eight 2½ × 8½-inch rectangles for the tulip border

From the dark red print fabric:
• Cut twelve 4⅞-inch squares; cut these squares in half

diagonally to form twenty-four triangles for the tulips
• Cut six 5¼-inch squares; cut these squares diagonally into quarters to form twenty-four triangles for the tulips

From the green check fabric:
• Cut three 2 × 44-inch strips for stems

From the dark green print fabric:
• Cut three 2½ × 44-inch strips; from these strips, cut twenty-four 2½ × 4½-inch rectangles for leaves

From the light green print fabric;
• Cut four 2½ × 44-inch strips; from these strips, cut twenty-four 2½ × 6½-inch rectangles for leaves

From the beige print fabric:
• Cut six 5¼-inch squares; cut these squares diagonally into quarters to form twenty-four triangles for the tulip backgrounds
• Cut six 1¾ × 44-inch strips for stem backgrounds
• Cut four 2½ × 44-inch strips; from these strips, cut twenty-four 2½ × 6½-inch rectangles for leaf backgrounds
• Cut three 2½ × 44-inch strips; from these strips, cut twenty-four 2½ × 4½-inch rectangles for leaf backgrounds

From the medium red fabric:
• Cut ten 6½ × 44-inch strips for the outer border

Inner Border

1 Piece the 2½-inch-wide maple print border strips together with diagonal seams, as shown in DIAGRAM 7. Trim seam allowances to ¼ inch and press them open.

Trim to ¼"

DIAGRAM 7

2 Measure the quilt from left to right through the middle to determine the length of the top and bottom borders. Cut two inner border strips to this length

and sew the maple print inner borders to the top and bottom of the quilt, referring to the QUILT ASSEMBLY DIAGRAM.

3 Measure the quilt from top to bottom through the middle, including the borders you just added, to determine the length of the side borders. Cut two inner border strips to the necessary lengths and sew the maple print inner borders to the sides of the quilt, as shown in the QUILT ASSEMBLY DIAGRAM.

Tulip Border

1 With right sides together, sew a 1¾ × 44-inch beige strip to both sides of a 2 × 44-inch green check strip. Make three strip sets. Press seam allowances toward the darker fabric. Crosscut the strip sets into twenty-four 4½-inch stem units, as shown in DIAGRAM 8.

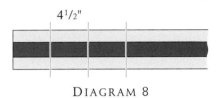

4½"

DIAGRAM 8

2 With right sides together, position a 2½ × 6½-inch beige rectangle on a 2½ × 4½-inch dark green rectangle, as shown in DIAGRAM 9. Draw a diagonal line on the beige rectangle, as shown, and stitch on the line. Trim seam allowance to ¼ inch. Press. Repeat to make 24 left leaf units, as shown.

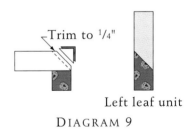

Trim to ¼"

Left leaf unit

DIAGRAM 9

QUILT ASSEMBLY DIAGRAM

3 With right sides together, position a 2½ × 6½-inch light green rectangle on a 2½ × 4½-inch beige piece, as shown in DIAGRAM 10 on page 68. Draw a diagonal line on the light green rectangle, as shown, and stitch on the line. Trim seam allowances to ¼ inch. Press. Repeat to make 24 right leaf units, as shown.

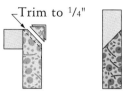

Trim to ¹/₄"

Right leaf unit

DIAGRAM 10

4 To piece the tulip units, sew the smaller dark red triangles to the beige triangles, right sides together, as shown in the left portion of DIAGRAM 11, and sew the larger dark red triangle to these units, as shown.

DIAGRAM 11

5 To assemble a Tulip block, sew a stem unit to the bottom of the tulip unit, as shown in the left portion of DIAGRAM 12. Sew the right and left leaf units to the sides of the tulip unit, as shown in the right part of DIAGRAM 12. At this point, the Tulip block should measure 8½ inches square.

Tulip unit

DIAGRAM 12

6 Sew five Tulip blocks together for the top and bottom borders. Add a 2½ × 8½-inch maple rectangle to each end,

as shown in DIAGRAM 13. Sew these borders to the top and bottom of the quilt, referring to the QUILT ASSEMBLY DIAGRAM on page 67.

7 Sew seven Tulip blocks together for each side border. Add a 2½ × 8½-inch maple rectangle and a corner block to each end, as shown in DIAGRAM 14. Sew these borders to the sides of the quilt, referring to the QUILT ASSEMBLY DIAGRAM on page 67.

Outer Border

1 Piece the 6½-inch-wide medium red border strips together with diagonal seams in the same manner as for the maple inner border. Trim seams to ¼-inch and press open.

2 Measure the quilt from left to right through the middle to determine the length of the top and bottom borders. Cut two outer border strips to this length, and sew the medium red print outer borders to the top and bottom of the quilt, referring to the QUILT ASSEMBLY DIAGRAM on page 67.

3 Measure the quilt from top to bottom through the middle, including the borders you just added, to determine the lengths of the side borders. Cut two outer border strips to this length, and sew the medium red print outer borders to the sides of the quilt, referring to the QUILT ASSEMBLY DIAGRAM on page 67.

Putting It All Together

1 Prepare the backing for the quilt by cutting the 5½-yard length of backing fabric in half crosswise to make two 2¾-yard lengths. Remove the selvages and sew the long edges of the two lengths together. Press seam open. Trim the backing and batting so they are about 4 inches larger than the quilt top.

DIAGRAM 13

DIAGRAM 14

2 Mark quilting designs on the quilt top.

3 Layer the backing, batting, and quilt top. Baste the layers together and quilt.

4 When the quilting is complete, remove the basting stitches and trim the excess backing and batting even with the quilt top.

Binding

NOTE: The 2¾-inch strips will produce a ⅜-inch-wide binding. If you want a wider or narrower binding, adjust the width of the strips you cut. (See page 216 for pointers on how to experiment with binding width.) See "Making and Attaching the Binding" on page 215 to complete your quilt.

C U T T I N G

From the chestnut print fabric:
• Cut nine 2¾ × 44-inch strips for cross-grain binding

Quilting DESIGNS

FOR MACHINE QUILTING:

🌀 *The 4-inch blocks in the center of the quilt feature the continuous-line floral quilting design shown in* QUILTING DIAGRAM 1.

🌀 *Choose medium-scale meander quilting for all background areas, as well as behind tulips, leaves, and the feathered chain designs in the outer borders. This meander quilting pattern, as shown in* QUILTING DIAGRAM 2, *enhances the feathered chain in the outer borders and makes them more visually prominent.*

🌀 *The stems of the tulips are quilted with two vertical lines that divide each stem into three ½-inch sections.*

🌀 *In the 2-inch maple borders, the 1¼-inch chain quilting design shown in* QUILTING DIAGRAM 3 *effectively separates these borders from the other quilted areas.*

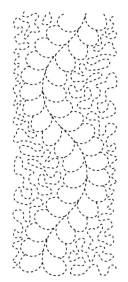

QUILTING DIAGRAM 2

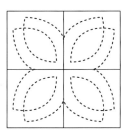

QUILTING DIAGRAM 1

QUILTING DIAGRAM 3

BROWN-EYED SUSAN

Wall Quilt and Bed Quilt

An old-fashioned flower-seed cat-alog inspired the design for Brown-Eyed Susan. The plaid flower centers create a sense of texture, and the colorful prints surrounding them are bright and beckoning. For the border, I used a dark red print with hints of the same gold tones as the lattice posts and other prints in the quilt center. A mellow background fabric unifies the blocks throughout the quilt, and the bias-cut plaid binding is a subtle hint of color that coordinates the border and corner blocks with the flower centers.

Wall Quilt

Size

Wall Quilt: 60 inches square (unquilted)

Finished Block: 12 inches square

Fabrics and Supplies

Yardage is based on 44-inch-wide fabric.

3/8 yard *each* of nine coordinating print fabrics for Flower blocks

4½-inch squares of nine coordinating plaid fabrics for flower centers

1¼ yards beige plaid fabric for background

¾ yard blue print fabric for lattice

⅛ yard gold print fabric for lattice posts

1½ yards red print fabric for borders

⅓ yard brown print fabric for corner squares

¾ yard red plaid fabric for bias binding

4 yards fabric for quilt backing

Quilt batting, at least 64 inches square

Rotary cutter, mat, and see-through ruler with ⅛-inch markings

G e t t i n g   R e a d y

- READ instructions thoroughly before you begin.

- PREWASH and press fabric.

- USE ¼-inch seam allowances throughout unless directions specify otherwise.

- SEAM ALLOWANCES are included in the cutting sizes given.

- PRESS seam allowances in the direction that will create the least bulk, and whenever possible, press toward the darker fabric.

- CUTTING DIRECTIONS for each section of the quilt are given individually. If you like to cut as you go, simply follow the directions as you get to them. If you'd rather cut all your pieces at the same time, skip ahead to find each of the cutting sections and do all the cutting before you begin to sew. 🍃

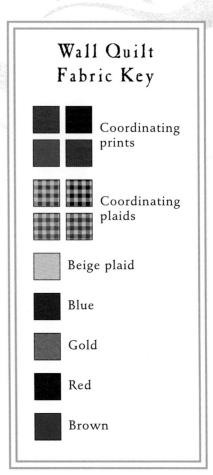

Wall Quilt Fabric Key

Coordinating prints

Coordinating plaids

Beige plaid

Blue

Gold

Red

Brown

Flower Blocks
(MAKE 9)

CUTTING

From each of the nine coordinating print fabrics:
- Cut two 2½ × 4½-inch pieces and two 2½ × 8½-inch pieces
- Cut one 2⅞ × 44-inch strip

From each of the nine coordinating plaid fabrics:
- Cut one 4½-inch square

From the beige plaid fabric:
- Cut thirty-six 2½-inch squares
- Cut nine 2⅞ × 44-inch strips

Piecing the Flower Blocks

1 Using one of the nine coordinating print fabrics, sew two 2½ × 4½-inch pieces to the top and bottom of a coordinating plaid 4½-inch square. Sew the 2½ × 8½-inch pieces to the sides, as shown in DIAGRAM 1. Do the same for each of the remaining Flower blocks.

DIAGRAM 1

2 To make the sawtooth sections, layer one 2⅞ × 44-inch beige plaid strip and one of the print fabric strips right sides together. Press these fabrics together, but do not sew. Cut the layered strips into eight 2⅞-inch squares. Cut the layered squares in half diagonally, and sew a ¼-inch seam allowance along the diagonal edge, as shown in DIAGRAM 2. Make a total of 16

triangle-pieced squares in each of the nine coordinating flower fabrics.

DIAGRAM 2

3 Sew four triangle-pieced squares together, as shown in DIAGRAM 3. Make four of these units in each of the nine flower fabrics.

DIAGRAM 3

4 Sew two of these triangle-pieced units to the top and bottom of each Flower block, as shown in DIAGRAM 4.

DIAGRAM 4

5 Sew a beige plaid 2½-inch square to each of the remaining triangle-pieced units, as shown in DIAGRAM 5.

DIAGRAM 5

6 Sew these units to the sides of each Flower block, as shown in DIAGRAM 6, making sure that the triangle squares match each other in each Flower block. At this point, the Flower blocks should measure 12½ inches square.

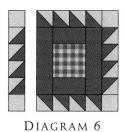

DIAGRAM 6

Quilt Center

From the blue print fabric:
• Cut twenty-four 2½ × 12½-inch lattice strips

From the gold print fabric:
• Cut sixteen 2½-inch squares

Assembling the Quilt Center

1 Sew four blue 2½ × 12½-inch strips and three Flower blocks together in a row, as shown in DIAGRAM 7. Make three of these rows.

2 Sew three blue 2½ × 12½-inch strips and four gold 2½-inch squares together, as shown in DIAGRAM 8. Make four of these strips.

3 Stitch the rows together to make the quilt center, as shown in DIAGRAM 9.

Border

From the red print fabric:
• Cut four 8½ × 46-inch strips on the lengthwise grain

From the brown fabric:
• Cut four 8½-inch squares

Attaching the Border

1 Measure the quilt from left to right through the center.

DIAGRAM 7

DIAGRAM 8

DIAGRAM 9

From the 8½ × 46-inch red strips, cut four borders to the actual length needed for your quilt. Sew two of them to the top and bottom of the quilt.

2 Measure the quilt from top to bottom, not including the border strips you just added, and add ½ inch for seam allowances. Cut two border strips to this length and sew an 8½-inch brown square to each end of the two border strips.

3 Sew the side border strips to the sides of the quilt, as shown in the WALL QUILT ASSEMBLY DIAGRAM. Press seam allowances toward the borders.

KEEP an old-fashioned mechanical lead pencil handy for marking lines. The lead is always sharp; therefore, the lines you mark will always be thin and crisp.

TIPS AND TRICKS

Putting It All Together

1 Prepare the backing for the quilt by cutting the 4-yard length of backing fabric in half crosswise to make two 2-yard lengths. Remove the selvages and sew the long edges of the two lengths together with one center seam. Press this seam open.

2 Trim the backing and batting so they are 4 inches larger than the quilt top dimensions.

WALL QUILT ASSEMBLY DIAGRAM

3 Mark quilting designs on the quilt top.

4 Layer the backing, batting, and quilt top. Baste the layers together, and quilt.

5 When quilting is complete, remove basting and trim the excess backing and batting even with the quilt top.

Binding

NOTE: The 2¾-inch-wide plaid bias strips will produce a ⅜- to ½-inch-wide finished binding. If you want a wider or narrower binding, adjust the width of the strips you cut. (See page 216 for pointers on how to experiment

with binding width.) Refer to "Making and Attaching the Binding" on page 215 to complete your quilt.

CUTTING

From the red plaid fabric:
• Cut enough 2¾-inch-wide bias strips to make a 255-inch strip

BROWN-EYED SUSAN

Bed Quilt

Size

Bed Quilt: 74 × 88 inches
(unquilted)

Finished Block: 12 inches
square

Fabrics and Supplies

*Yardage is based on
44-inch-wide fabric.*

4 yards red print fabric for
Flower blocks and lattices

³⁄₈ yard plaid fabric for
flower centers

1½ yards beige print fabric
for background

¼ yard tan print fabric for
lattice posts

2 yards large red plaid fabric
for borders

⅓ yard brown print fabric for
corner squares

1 yard plaid fabric for bias
binding

5¼ yards fabric for quilt
backing

Quilt batting, at least
78 × 92 inches

Rotary cutter, mat, and
see-through ruler with
⅛-inch markings

Flower Blocks

(MAKE 20)

CUTTING

From the red print fabric:
• Cut forty 2½ × 4½-inch pieces
and forty 2½ × 8½-inch pieces
• Cut twelve 2⅞ × 44-inch strips

From the plaid fabric:
• Cut twenty 4½-inch squares

From the beige print fabric:
• Cut eighty 2½-inch squares
• Cut twelve 2⅞ × 44-inch strips

Piecing
the Flower Blocks

Follow Steps 1 through 5 under
"Piecing the Flower Blocks" on
page 72. Make 320 triangle-
pieced squares for the 20 Flower
blocks in the bed quilt.

Quilt Center

CUTTING

From the red print fabric:
• Cut forty-nine 2½ × 12½-inch
strips

From the tan print fabric:
• Cut thirty 2½-inch squares

Assembling
the Quilt Center

NOTE: Refer to Steps 1 and 2
under "Assembling the Quilt Center" on page 73.

Bed Quilt
Fabric Key

■ Red

▨ Beige

□ Tan

▨ Large red plaid

■ Brown

1 Sew five red 2½ × 12½-inch
strips and four Flower blocks
together in a row. Make five
rows.

2 Sew four red 2½ × 12½-inch
strips and five tan 2½-inch
squares together. Make six lattice
strips.

3 Stitch the rows together to
complete the quilt center, as
shown in the BED QUILT AS-
SEMBLY DIAGRAM on page 76.

Border

CUTTING

NOTE: The yardage given allows
for the border pieces to be cut
cross-grain.

From the large red plaid:
• Cut eight 8½ × 44-inch strips

From the brown print fabric:
• Cut four 8½-inch squares

BED QUILT ASSEMBLY DIAGRAM

Attaching the Border

1 Piece the 8½ × 44-inch red plaid strips together. Trim seam allowances to ¼ inch, and press them open.

2 Measure the quilt from left to right through the center. From the 8½-inch-wide plaid strip, cut two border strips to the length needed and sew the border strips to the top and bottom edges of the quilt, referring to the BED QUILT ASSEMBLY DIAGRAM.

3 Measure the quilt from top to bottom through the center, not including the border strips you just added. Add ½ inch for seam allowances. From the 8½-inch-wide plaid strip, cut two border strips to this length.

4 Sew the 8½-inch brown corner squares to each end of the side border strips. Sew the border strips to the quilt sides.

Putting It All Together

1 For the backing, cut the 5¼-yard length of backing fabric in half crosswise to make two 2⅝-yard lengths. Remove the selvages and sew the long edges of the two lengths together. Press this seam open.

2 Trim the backing and batting so they are 4 inches larger than the quilt top dimensions.

3 Layer the backing, batting, and quilt top. Mark quilting designs on the quilt top. Baste the layers together, and quilt.

4 When quilting is complete, remove the basting stitches, and trim the excess backing and batting even with the quilt top.

Binding

NOTE: The 2¾-inch-wide plaid bias strips will produce a ⅜- to ½-inch-wide binding. If you want a wider or narrower binding, adjust the width of the strips you cut. (See page 216 for pointers on binding width.) Refer to "Making and Attaching the Binding" on page 215 to complete your quilt.

From the plaid fabric:
• Cut enough 2¾-inch bias strips to make a 340-inch strip

FOR HAND QUILTING:

❧ Quilt ½-inch diagonal cross-hatched lines in the flower centers.

❧ Quilt in the ditch around the flower pieces.

❧ Stitch in the ditch of the seams on each side of the lattice strips and lattice posts.

❧ Use a quilting stencil that has a soft, simple curved design for the border.

❧ Quilt the corner blocks with 2-, 3-, and 4-inch concentric circles.

WATERMELON PATCH

For realistic images like the watermelon wedges in this little quilt, I coordinated a group of colors and prints as luscious and tempting as the first thick slices of this fruit in summer. I chose four different green prints, ranging from rich, dark greens to medium shades. For the flesh of the melons, I chose a juicy red print with just enough black to represent the look of the seeds. For the rinds, I used a green check fabric cut on the bias, which creates a pleasing effect in these curved spaces. The wide variety of prints adds visual texture throughout the entire quilt.

Size

Wall Quilt: 44 inches square (unquilted)

Finished Blocks: 9 inches square

Fabrics and Supplies

Yardage is based on 44-inch-wide fabric.

⅜ yard beige print fabric for background

1 yard red print fabric for watermelon, lattice posts, corner squares, and borders

¾ yard green check fabric for rind, pieced block borders, and lattice strips

¼ yard green print fabric #1 for pieced block borders

1⅛ yards dark green print fabric #2 for pieced block borders and outer borders

⅜ yard green print fabric #3 for pieced block borders, lattice, and corner blocks

⅜ yard black print fabric for block border

2⅔ yards fabric for quilt backing

¾ yard green check fabric #1 for bias binding

Quilt batting, at least 48 inches square

1 yard fusible web

1 skein black embroidery floss

Rotary cutter, mat, and see-through ruler with ⅛-inch markings

WATERMELON PATCH
Getting Ready

- READ instructions thoroughly before you begin.

- PREWASH and press fabric.

- USE ¼-inch seam allowances throughout unless directions specify otherwise.

- SEAM ALLOWANCES are included in the cutting sizes given.

- PRESS seam allowances in the direction that will create the least bulk, and whenever possible, press toward the darker fabric.

- CUTTING DIRECTIONS for each section of the quilt are given individually. If you like to cut as you go, simply follow the directions as you get to them. If you'd rather cut all your pieces at the same time, skip ahead to find each of the cutting sections and do all the cutting before you begin to sew. ✐

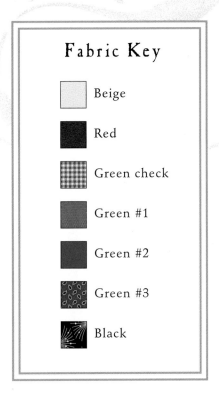

Fabric Key

☐	Beige
■	Red
▦	Green check
■	Green #1
■	Green #2
▦	Green #3
■	Black

Watermelon Units
(MAKE 16)

CUTTING

From the beige print fabric:
- Cut sixteen 4½-inch squares

1 Position the fusible web (paper side facing up) over the watermelon shapes on page 83. Trace 16 watermelons and 16 rinds onto the fusible web. Roughly cut around the shapes.

2 Place the fusible web shapes, coated side down, on the wrong side of the red fabric for watermelons and the green check fabric for the rinds. Press with a hot dry iron, following the manufacturer's directions for your brand of fusible web. Let the shapes cool, cut out watermelons and rinds on the tracing lines, and remove the paper backing.

Appliquéing the Watermelon Units

1 Center the appliqué pieces on the 4½-inch beige squares, as shown in DIAGRAM 1, layering the rinds over the watermelons. Press in place with a hot dry iron.

DIAGRAM 1

2 Primitive stitch the shapes in place with two strands of black embroidery floss, as shown in DIAGRAM 2. For more information on the primitive stitch, see page 210. To make the three watermelon seeds on each watermelon, do straight stitches using four strands of black embroidery floss. For more information on the straight stitch, see page 210.

DIAGRAM 2

WHEN DOING machine buttonhole stitching or feather stitching around appliqué shapes, thread two strands of regular sewing thread through one needle. This will produce a heavier decorative stitch.

TIPS AND TRICKS

Watermelon Blocks
(MAKE FOUR)

CUTTING

From the red print fabric:
• Cut thirty-six 1½-inch squares for the center squares and pieced borders
• Cut four 1½ × 44-inch strips; from these strips, cut sixteen 1½ × 11½-inch borders

From the green check fabric:
• Cut two 1½ × 44-inch strips for the pieced border

From the green print #1 fabric:
• Cut two 1½ × 44-inch strips for the pieced border

From the dark green print #2 fabric:
• Cut two 1½ × 44-inch strips for the pieced border

From the green print #3 fabric:
• Cut two 1½ × 44-inch strips for the pieced border
• Cut sixteen 1½ × 4½-inch lattice strips
• Cut sixteen 2½-inch corner squares

From the black print fabric:
• Cut four 1½ × 44-inch strips; from these strips, cut sixteen 1½ × 11½-inch borders

Assembling the Watermelon Blocks

1 Sew a watermelon unit to each side of a 1½ × 4½-inch green #3 strip, as shown in DIAGRAM 3. Repeat for the remaining watermelon units. Press seam allowances toward the green fabric.

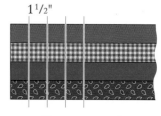

DIAGRAM 3

2 Sew a 1½ × 4½-inch green #3 strip to both sides of four 1½-inch red squares, as shown in DIAGRAM 4. Make four of these lattice strips. Press seam allowances toward the green fabric.

DIAGRAM 4

3 Sew a watermelon unit to both sides of a lattice strip, as shown in DIAGRAM 5. Repeat for the remaining lattice strips to make a total of four watermelon blocks. Press seam allowances toward the green fabric.

DIAGRAM 5

4 To make the pieced borders for each watermelon block, sew one of each of the 1½ × 44-inch green strips together along the lengthwise edges to form a strip set, as shown in DIAGRAM 6. Make two of these strip sets. Press seam allowances in one direction. Crosscut the strip sets into thirty-two 1½-inch segments, as shown.

1½"

DIAGRAM 6

5 Sew pieced border segments to both sides of sixteen of the 1½-inch red squares, as shown in DIAGRAM 7. Press seam allowances away from the red fabric.

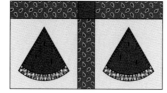

DIAGRAM 7

6 Sew a pieced border segment to the top and bottom of each watermelon block, as shown in DIAGRAM 8. Press seam allowances toward the pieced borders.

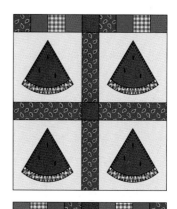

DIAGRAM 8

7 Sew a 1½-inch red square to both ends of the remaining eight pieced border segments, as shown in DIAGRAM 9. Press seam allowances away from the red fabric.

DIAGRAM 9

8 Attach the side pieced borders to the sides of each watermelon block, as shown in DIAGRAM 10. Press seam allowances toward the pieced borders.

DIAGRAM 10

9 Sew a 1½ × 11½-inch black print border strip to each of the sixteen 1½ × 11½-inch red border strips, as shown in DIAGRAM 11. Press seam allowances toward the black fabric.

DIAGRAM 11

10 Sew a pieced border to the top and bottom of each watermelon block, as shown in DIAGRAM 12, making sure the red strip is on the outside.

DIAGRAM 12

11 Add a 2½-inch green #3 corner square to both ends of the remaining eight pieced border units, as shown in DIAGRAM 13. Press seam allowances away from the green fabric.

DIAGRAM 13

12 Attach the pieced side borders to the sides of each watermelon block, as shown in DIAGRAM 14. Press.

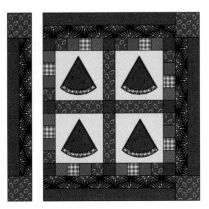

DIAGRAM 14

Lattice Strips, Posts, and Borders

C U T T I N G

NOTE: The yardage given allows for the border pieces to be cut cross-grain.

From the green check fabric:
• Cut twelve 2½ × 15½-inch lattice strips

From the red fabric:
• Cut nine 2½-inch squares for lattice posts
• Cut four 4½-inch corner squares

From the dark green print #2 fabric:
• Cut four 4½ × 44-inch outer border strips

Attaching the Lattice Strips and Borders

1 Sew a 2½ × 15½-inch green check lattice strip between two watermelon blocks, as shown in DIAGRAM 15 on page 82. Add a green check 2½ × 15½-inch lattice strip to both sides of the row, as shown. Press seam allowances toward the green check fabric. Make two of these rows.

2 Stitch two green check lattice strips and three 2½-inch red lattice posts together in a row, as shown in DIAGRAM 16 on page 82. Press seam allowances toward the green check lattice strips. Make three of these rows.

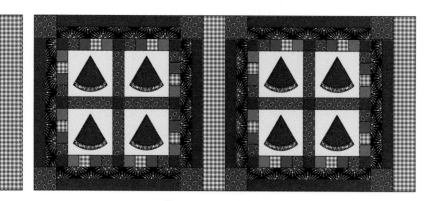

DIAGRAM 15

DIAGRAM 16

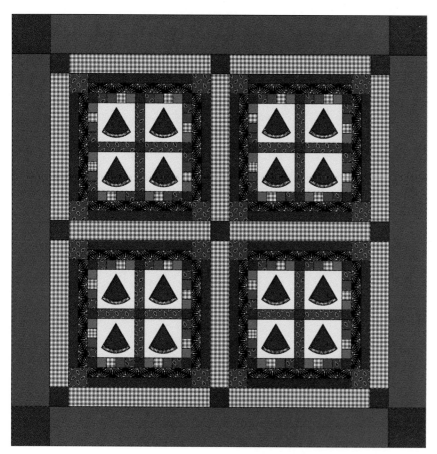

QUILT ASSEMBLY DIAGRAM

3 Sew the rows of the quilt together, as shown in the QUILT ASSEMBLY DIAGRAM. Press seam allowances toward the green check fabric.

4 Measure the quilt from left to right, through the center, to determine the length of the top and bottom border strips. Cut two green #2 strips to the length needed. Attach the top and bottom border strips to the quilt, referring to the QUILT ASSEMBLY DIAGRAM. Press seam allowances toward the green check fabric.

5 For the side border strips, measure the quilt from top to bottom. Do *not* include the top and bottom border strips in your measurement. Add ¼ inch on each end for seam allowances, and cut two green #2 strips to this length. Sew a 4½-inch red corner square to each end of the border strips. Attach the side border strips to the quilt, as shown. Press seam allowances toward the green check fabric.

Putting It All Together

1 Prepare the backing for the quilt by cutting the 2⅔-yard length of backing fabric in half crosswise to make two 1⅓-yard lengths. Remove the selvages.

2 Sew the two long edges together. Press seam allowances open. Trim backing and batting so they are 4 inches larger than the quilt top.

3 Mark quilting designs on the quilt top.

4 Layer the backing, batting, and quilt top. Baste the layers together, and quilt.

5 When quilting is complete, remove the basting stitches, and trim the excess backing and batting even with the quilt top.

Binding

NOTE: The 2¾-inch bias strips will produce a ⅜-inch-wide binding. If you want a wider or narrower binding, adjust the width of the strips you cut. (See page 216 for pointers on how to experiment with binding width.) See "Making and Attaching the Binding" on page 215 to complete your quilt.

C U T T I N G

From the green check fabric:
• Cut enough 2¾-inch bias strips to make a 200-inch strip

Quilting DESIGNS

FOR MACHINE QUILTING:

✿ *Use a variety of meander quilting patterns in different sizes. A small pattern of meander quilting in the background of the watermelon blocks will make the melon wedges stand out visually.*

✿ *A single feathered chain design from a purchased quilting stencil is quilted in the outer border, along with a small pattern of meander quilting around the chain.*

✿ *Quilt a medium-size pattern of meander quilting for the rest of the quilt, matching your thread as closely as possible to your fabrics.*

FOR HAND QUILTING:

✿ *Quilt in the ditch around each watermelon slice to enhance the wedge shapes.*

✿ *Select a purchased stencil with a simple quilting motif and a coordinating corner design for the outer borders.*

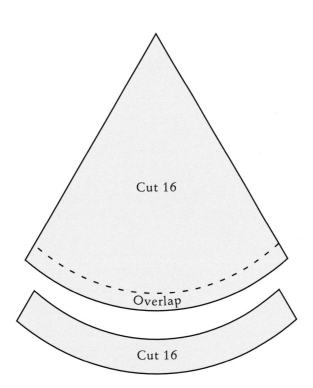

Cut 16

Overlap

Cut 16

APPLIQUÉ PATTERN PIECES

WILDFLOWER

This quilt combines a large variety of print fabrics with a lovely large-scale floral print at the center of each of the pieced Wildflower blocks. If you love to collect fabric, this is a quilt you're sure to enjoy making. Choose a light tone-on-tone print for the alternating blocks to make the pieced blocks more prominent. A variety of greens will give the shaded effect of real leaves. An interesting mix of colorful squares around the edge of the pieced center will add to the appearance of a bed of wildflowers, one that will not fade when winter months arrive.

Size

Bed Quilt: 82 × 95 inches (unquilted)

Block Size: 9 inches square

Fabrics and Supplies

Yardage is based on 44-inch-wide fabric.

½ yard large floral print for block centers

1¾ yards *total* of a variety of medium prints for Wildflower blocks and border squares

2 yards light tan print for Wildflower blocks

⅜ yard *total* of a variety of blue prints for Wildflower blocks

¼ yard *each* of five green prints for Wildflower blocks

3¼ yards beige dot fabric for alternate blocks, side triangles, corner triangles, and the pieced border

2 yards green tone-on-tone print for pieced border and outer border

1 yard green tone-on-tone print for binding

7½ yards fabric for quilt backing

Quilt batting, at least 86 × 99 inches

Rotary cutter, mat, and see-through ruler with ⅛-inch markings

Getting Ready

• READ instructions thoroughly before you begin.

• PREWASH and press fabric.

• USE ¼-inch seam allowances throughout unless directions specify otherwise.

• SEAM ALLOWANCES are included in the cutting sizes given.

• PRESS seam allowances in the direction that will create the least bulk, and whenever possible, press toward the darker fabric.

• CUTTING DIRECTIONS for each section of the quilt are given individually. If you like to cut as you go, simply follow the directions as you get to them. If you'd rather cut all your pieces at rhe same time, skip ahead to find each of the cutting sections and do all the cutting before you begin to sew. ✐

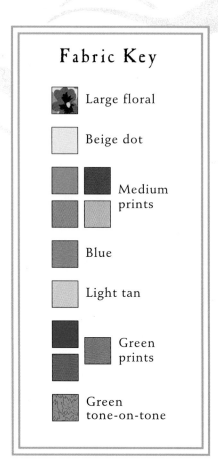

Fabric Key

■ Large floral

□ Beige dot

■ ■ Medium
■ ■ prints

■ Blue

□ Light tan

■ ■ Green
■ prints

▨ Green
tone-on-tone

Wildflower Blocks
(MAKE 30)

C U T T I N G

From the large floral fabric:
• Cut three 3½ × 44-inch strips; from these strips, cut thirty 3½-inch squares for block centers

From the medium print fabrics:
• Cut a total of twenty 1½ × 44-inch strips

From the light tan print fabric:
• Cut forty-two 1½ × 44-inch strips

From the blue print fabrics:
• Cut five 1½ × 44-inch strips

From the five green print fabrics:
• Cut a total of eleven 1½ × 44-inch strips

Piecing
the Wildflower Blocks

1 To make Strip Set I, sew a 1½ × 44-inch light tan strip to both sides of a 1½ × 44-inch green print strip, as shown in DIAGRAM 1. Press seam allowances toward the green fabric. Make 11 of these strip sets, and crosscut them into one hundred twenty 3½-inch segments, as shown.

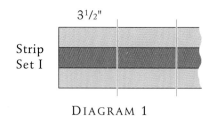

3½"

Strip
Set I

DIAGRAM 1

2 To make Strip Set II, sew a 1½ × 44-inch medium print strip to both sides of a 1½ × 44-inch light tan strip, as shown in DIAGRAM 2. Press seam allowances toward the medium fabric. Make ten of these strip sets, and crosscut into two hundred forty 1½-inch segments, as shown.

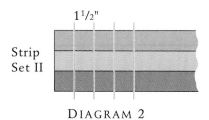

1½"

Strip
Set II

DIAGRAM 2

3 To make Strip Set III, sew a 1½ × 44-inch light tan strip to both sides of a 1½ × 44-inch blue print strip, as shown in DIAGRAM 3. Press seam allowances toward the blue fabric. Make five of these strip sets, and crosscut them into one hundred twenty 1½-inch segments, as shown.

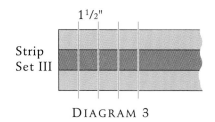

1½"

Strip
Set III

DIAGRAM 3

4 Sew a Strip Set II segment to both sides of the Strip Set III segments to make the nine-patch units, as shown in DIAGRAM 4. Press. Make 120 nine-patch units.

DIAGRAM 4

5 To complete each Wildflower block, sew the units from Steps 1 and 4 and a 3½-inch large floral square together in three horizontal rows, as shown in DIAGRAM 5. Press. Sew these horizontal rows together. Press. At this point, the Wildflower blocks should measure 9½ inches square.

DIAGRAM 5

Quilt Center

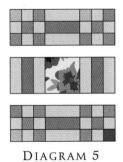

CUTTING

From the beige dot fabric:
• Cut twenty 9½-inch squares for the alternate blocks.
• Cut five 14-inch squares. Cut the squares diagonally in both directions to form 20 triangles. You will need only 18 of these for the side triangles. NOTE: Both the side triangles and corner triangles are larger than necessary and will be trimmed after they have been added to the pieced blocks.

• Cut two 10-inch squares. Cut the squares in half diagonally to form four corner triangles.

Assembling the Quilt Center

1 Sew the Wildflower blocks and the 9½-inch alternate blocks together in diagonal rows, as shown in DIAGRAM 6. Begin and end with the side triangles. NOTE: Do not attach the corner triangles at this time. Press seam allowances between blocks in the opposite direction of the previous row for easy matching.

2 Sew all the diagonal rows together, pinning block

intersections for accuracy. Press all seam allowances between rows in the same direction.

3 Sew the corner triangles to the quilt, referring to DIAGRAM 6. Trim the excess fabric from the side and corner triangles, taking care to allow a ¼-inch seam allowance beyond the corners of each block. Before you begin, see "Trimming Side and Corner Triangles" on page 211 to be certain you make these cuts accurately. Use a ruler, cutting mat, and rotary cutter to measure and cut accurate seam allowances beyond the block corners. At this point, the quilt should measure 64¼ × 77 inches. If it doesn't, adjust seam allowances so that the borders will fit.

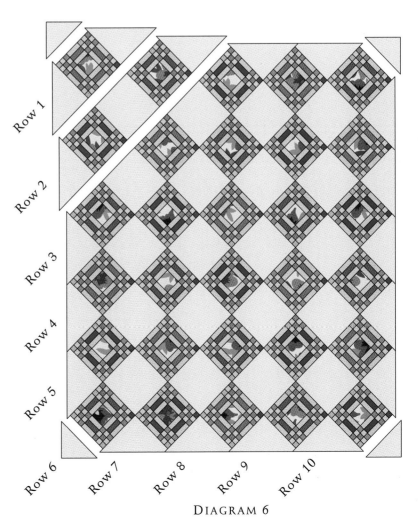

Row 1
Row 2
Row 3
Row 4
Row 5
Row 6
Row 7
Row 8
Row 9
Row 10

DIAGRAM 6

Borders

CUTTING

for Pieced Border

NOTE: The yardage given allows for border pieces to be cut cross-grain.

From the beige dot fabric:
• Cut three 5½ × 44-inch strips. From these strips, cut seventeen 5½-inch squares. Cut these squares in half diagonally in both directions to form 66 side triangles for the pieced border.
• Cut two 3-inch squares. Cut squares in half diagonally to form four corner triangles for the pieced border.

From the green tone-on-tone print fabric:
• Cut three 5½ × 44-inch strips. From these strips, cut seventeen 5½-inch squares. Cut these squares diagonally in both directions to form 66 side triangles for the pieced border.
• Cut six 3-inch squares. Cut the squares in half diagonally to form 12 corner triangles for the pieced border.

From the medium print fabrics:
• Cut seven 3½ × 44-inch strips. From these strips, cut seventy 3½-inch squares for the pieced border.

Assembling the Pieced Border

1 To make the top pieced border strip, sew together 15 medium print squares, 14 green side triangles, 14 beige side triangles, 2 beige corner triangles, and 2 green corner triangles in diagonal rows,

as shown in DIAGRAM 7. Note that there will be one beige and one green corner triangle at each end of the border strip. Repeat for the bottom pieced border strip.

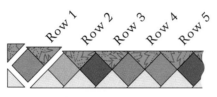

DIAGRAM 7

2 Sew the top and bottom pieced border strips to the quilt, referring to the QUILT ASSEMBLY DIAGRAM. Press.

3 Referring to DIAGRAM 8 and the QUILT ASSEMBLY

DIAGRAM, sew the pieced side border strips together in the same manner. Use 20 medium print squares, 19 green side triangles, 19 beige side triangles, and 4 green corner triangles for each border strip. NOTE: All of the corner triangles on the side pieced border strips are green.

DIAGRAM 8

4 Sew the side pieced borders to the sides of the quilt, and press.

QUILT ASSEMBLY DIAGRAM

C U T T I N G

for Outer Border

From the green tone-on-tone print fabric:

• Cut nine 5½ × 44-inch strips

Attaching the Outer Border

1 Sew the 5½-inch green border strips together with diagonal seams. Trim seam allowances to ¼ inch, and press seams open. For more information on diagonal seams, see page 211.

2 Measure the quilt from left to right through the middle to determine the length of the top and bottom border strips. Cut the top and bottom outer border strips to the necessary length, sew them to the top and bottom of the quilt, and press.

3 Measure the quilt from top to bottom through the middle, including the border strips you just added, to determine the lengths of the side border strips. Cut the side outer border strips to the necessary length, sew them to the sides of the quilt, and press.

Putting It All Together

1 Prepare the backing for the quilt by cutting the 7½-yard length of backing fabric in thirds crosswise to make three 2½-yard lengths. Remove the selvages,

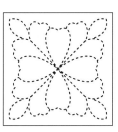

MARK UNPIECED *blocks before assembling the quilt center. It's easier to handle individual blocks than a large quilt top.*

TIPS AND TRICKS

and sew the long edges of the three lengths together so that the seams run horizontally. Press seams open.

2 Trim the backing and batting so they are 4 inches larger than the quilt top dimensions.

3 Mark quilting designs on the quilt top.

4 Layer the backing, batting, and quilt top. Baste the layers together, and quilt.

5 When quilting is complete, remove the basting stitches, and trim excess backing and batting even with the quilt top.

Binding

NOTE: The 2¾-inch strips will produce a ⅜-inch-wide binding. If you want a wider or narrower binding, adjust the width of the strips you cut. (See page 216 for pointers on how to experiment with binding width.) See "Making and Attaching the Binding" on page 215 to complete your quilt.

C U T T I N G

From the green tone-on-tone fabric:

• Cut ten 2¾ × 44-inch strips for cross-grain binding

Quilting DESIGNS

FOR HAND QUILTING:

🌿 Choose a purchased quilting stencil, as shown in QUILTING DIAGRAM 1, for quilting the alternating block.

🌿 Half of that same purchased stencil, turned as shown in QUILTING DIAGRAM 2, will work beautifully when quilted in the half-square triangles at the outer edges of the quilt.

🌿 The pieced blocks are quilted in the ditch of each seam. Cross-hatching adds texture to the outer border and frames the quilt center.

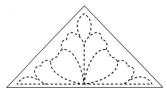

QUILTING DIAGRAM 1   QUILTING DIAGRAM 2

HOME

for the HOLIDAYS

Christmas is a cozy season. In the midst of the cold and snow of a Minnesota winter, I make my home a warm and soothing haven. I love to fill every corner with a mix of holiday collectibles, antique toys, ornaments, and quilts. My holiday memories wouldn't be complete without the deep, rich colors and soft textures of my favorite quilts.

TOWN SQUARE

Tree Skirt and Tablecloth

Town Square makes an outstanding table topper, couch throw, wall quilt, or tree skirt. I chose a very dark green print to give the trees a stately appearance and to help balance them with the chunky red houses. The subtle print in the houses makes the appliqué motifs almost glow in the windows. Strong dark green and dark brown prints create an effective frame around the fence border without distracting from it. And the gold fabric in the center star is echoed by the gold prints in the corner squares of each border.

Size

Tablecloth: 60 inches square (unquilted)

Tree Skirt: 52 inches square

Fabrics and Supplies

Yardage is based on 44-inch-wide fabric.

FOR TABLECLOTH AND TREE SKIRT

²⁄₃ yard small black/brown check fabric for roofs, tree trunks, and windows

²⁄₃ yard red print for houses

⅞ yard beige print for background

⅝ yard green print for trees

Five assorted 4 × 16-inch gold/brown fabric scraps for window appliqués

¾ yard gold print for center star, house corner squares, and center binding

⅞ yard cream print for fence border

¾ yard red print for fence border background

1 skein red embroidery floss

½ yard fusible web, 16 inches wide

Rotary cutter, mat, and see-through ruler with ⅛-inch markings

FOR TABLECLOTH ONLY

¼ yard large black/brown check fabric for fence border corner squares

1½ yards green print for checkerboard border and binding

¾ yard dark brown print for checkerboard border

¼ yard dark gold print for checkerboard border corner squares

Quilt batting, at least 64 inches square

3¾ yards backing fabric

FOR TREE SKIRT ONLY

¼ yard red/brown plaid fabric for fence border corner squares

¾ yard green print binding fabric

3½ yards backing fabric

Quilt batting, at least 56 inches square

Getting Ready

- READ instructions thoroughly before you begin.
- PREWASH and press fabric.
- USE ¼-inch seam allowances throughout unless directions specify otherwise.
- SEAM ALLOWANCES are included in the cutting sizes given.
- PRESS seam allowances in the direction that will create the least bulk, and whenever possible, press toward the darker fabric.
- CUTTING DIRECTIONS for each section of the quilt are given individually. If you like to cut as you go, simply follow the directions as you get to them. If you'd rather cut all your pieces at the same time, skip ahead to look for each of the cutting sections and do all the cutting before you begin to sew.
- INSTRUCTIONS are given for quick cutting and piecing the blocks. Note that for some of the pieces, the quick-cutting method will result in leftover fabric. ✐

Fabric Key

▉	Red
▉	Small black/brown check
▉	Green
▉	Gold
▉	Dark gold
▢	Beige
▤	Cream
▦	Large black/brown check
▨	Dark brown

House Blocks
(MAKE 4)

CUTTING

From the small black/brown check fabric:
- Cut two 8⅞-inch squares; cut the squares in half diagonally
- Cut two 3½ × 44-inch strips

From the red print fabric:
- Cut eight 2 × 12-inch pieces
- Cut four 3 × 12-inch pieces
- Cut eight 3 × 3½-inch pieces
- Cut two 2 × 44-inch strips

From the beige print fabric:
- Cut four 8⅞-inch squares; cut the squares in half diagonally
- Cut four 4⅞-inch squares; cut the squares in half diagonally

From the gold print fabric:
- Cut four 4½-inch squares

Piecing the House Blocks

1 With right sides together, stitch the 2 × 44-inch red print strip to the 3½ × 44-inch small black/brown check strip. Make two of these strip sets. Cut into sixteen 3½-inch segments. See DIAGRAM 1.

3½"

DIAGRAM 1

2 Sew one of these segments to each side of a 3 × 3½-inch red piece. Make eight of these units, as shown in DIAGRAM 2.

DIAGRAM 2

3 Sew the Step 2 units to both sides of a 3 × 12-inch red strip, as shown in DIAGRAM 3. Make four of these units. Sew a 2 × 12-inch red strip to both sides of this unit, as shown. Make four house units.

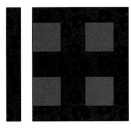

DIAGRAM 3

4 Sew a small beige print triangle to both sides of a 4½-inch gold print square; see DIAGRAM 4. Make four of these units.

DIAGRAM 4

5 Sew the Step 4 units to the bottom edges of the house units, as shown in DIAGRAM 5. Sew the black/brown roof triangles to the house tops, matching center points. Sew the large beige triangles to both sides of the house units, matching center points. At this point the House block should measure 16½ inches square.

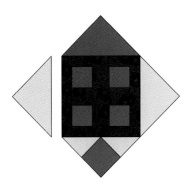

DIAGRAM 5

Window Appliqués
(MAKE 16)

1 Position the fusible web (paper side up) over the appliqué pieces on page 101, and trace. Roughly cut out the shapes.

2 Place the coated side of the fusible web on the wrong side of the fabrics chosen for the window appliqués. NOTE: Use a different fabric for the candle flame than for the candle itself. Press with a hot dry iron, following the manufacturer's directions for your brand of fusible web. Let the fabric and fusible web cool, cut out the pieces on the drawn lines, and remove the paper backing.

3 Center the appliqué pieces in each window. Press in place with a hot dry iron. With three strands of embroidery floss, stitch around the shapes using the primitive stitch or the buttonhole stitch. For more information on the primitive and buttonhole stitches, see page 210.

Tree Blocks
(MAKE 4)

CUTTING

From the green print fabric:
• Cut four 4½ × 8½-inch pieces
• Cut five 2½ × 44-inch strips; from these strips, cut twenty 2½ × 8½-inch pieces

From the beige print fabric:
• Cut three 2½ × 44-inch strips; from these strips, cut forty 2½-inch squares

• Cut two 3½ × 12-inch strips

From the gold print fabric:
• Cut eight 4½-inch squares
• Cut one 8½-inch square for star center

From the black/brown check fabric:
• Cut one 2½ × 12-inch strip

Piecing the Tree Blocks

1 With right sides together, position a 4½-inch gold print square over a 4½ × 8½-inch green piece, as shown in DIAGRAM 6. Draw a diagonal line from corner to corner on the gold square and stitch on the diagonal line, as shown. Trim the seam allowance to ¼ inch and press toward the green fabric.

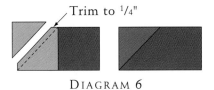

Trim to ¼"

DIAGRAM 6

2 Repeat this procedure for the opposite corner of the green piece, as shown in DIAGRAM 7. Make four of these tree top units.

DIAGRAM 7

3 With right sides together, position a 2½-inch beige square on both corners of a 2½ × 8½-inch green piece, as shown in DIAGRAM 8 on page 96. Draw diagonal lines from corner to corner, stitch on these lines, and

trim seams as in Step 1. Repeat this process to make 20 of these branch units.

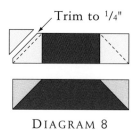

DIAGRAM 8

4 Sew a 3½ × 12-inch beige strip to both sides of the 2½ × 12-inch small black/brown check strip. Cut into four 2½-inch trunk units, as shown in DIAGRAM 9.

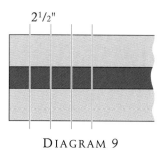

DIAGRAM 9

5 For each tree, sew together five of the units from Step 3. Sew a tree top unit to the top edge and a trunk unit to the bottom edge of each tree, as shown in DIAGRAM 10. At this point, the Tree block should measure 8½ × 16½ inches.

DIAGRAM 10

Quilt Center

1 Stitch a Tree block to opposite sides of the 8½-inch gold print square to make a tree/center star unit, as shown in DIAGRAM 11.

2 Stitch a House block to both sides of the remaining Tree blocks, as shown in DIAGRAM 12.

3 Stitch the house/tree sections to both sides of the tree/center star section, as shown in DIAGRAM 13.

DIAGRAM 11

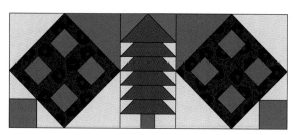

DIAGRAM 12

DIAGRAM 13

Fence Border

CUTTING

From the cream print fabric:
• Cut three 2½ × 44-inch strips
• Cut seven 2½ × 44-inch strips; cut these strips into forty 2½ × 6½-inch pieces

From the red print fabric:
• Cut six 2½ × 44-inch strips
• Cut three 2½ × 44-inch strips;

cut these strips into forty
2½-inch squares

From the black/brown plaid
fabric:
• Cut four 6½-inch squares

Piecing
the Fence Border

1 With right sides together, sew
a 2½ × 44-inch red print strip
to both sides of a 2½ × 44-inch
cream print strip. Make three of
these strip sets. Cut into forty
2½-inch segments, as shown in
DIAGRAM 14.

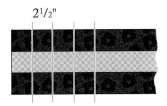

2½"

DIAGRAM 14

2 With right sides together, position a 2½-inch red square
on one end of a 2½ × 6½-inch
cream piece. Draw a diagonal line
on the red square from corner to
corner and stitch just a hair to the
outside of the diagonal line. Trim
the seam allowance to ¼ inch
and press toward the cream
fabric, as shown in DIAGRAM 15.
Make 20 of these fence units
with the points on the right,
and reverse the direction of the

Trim to ¼"

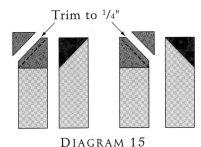

DIAGRAM 15

diagonal line on the remaining 20
to create points on the left side,
as shown.

3 To construct each of the four
fence borders, sew ten Step 1
fence sections and ten Step 2
fence sections together, as shown
in DIAGRAM 16. Sew a 6½-inch
large black/brown check square

to each end of two of the fence
border strips, as shown.

4 Stitch two fence sections to
the top and bottom of the
quilt center. Stitch the remaining
fence/corner square sections to
the sides of the quilt, as shown
in the TABLECLOTH ASSEMBLY
DIAGRAM.

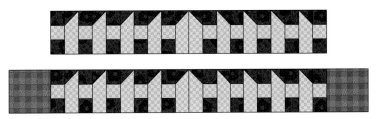

DIAGRAM 16

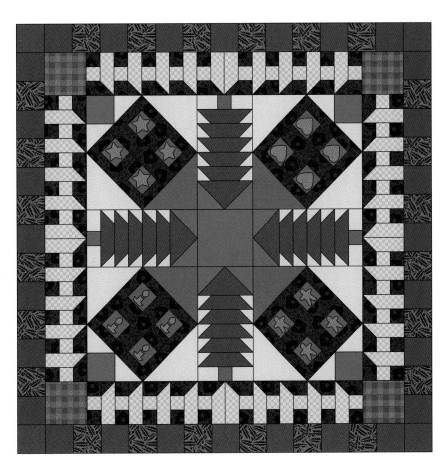

TABLECLOTH ASSEMBLY DIAGRAM

5 If you are making a tree skirt, skip ahead to Step 5 under "Putting It All Together." If you are making the tablecloth, make the checkerboard border next.

DIAGRAM 18

Checkerboard Border

From the green print fabric:
• Cut three 4½ × 44-inch strips
• Cut four 4½-inch squares

From the dark brown print fabric:
• Cut three 4½ × 44-inch strips

From the dark gold print fabric:
• Cut four 4½-inch squares

Piecing the Checkerboard Border

1 Sew a 4½ × 44-inch green print strip to a 4½ × 44-inch dark brown print strip, as shown in DIAGRAM 17. Make three strip sets in this manner. Cut into twenty-four 4½-inch segments, as shown.

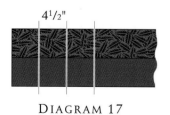

4½"

DIAGRAM 17

2 To construct each border section, sew six checkerboard segments together, as shown in DIAGRAM 18. Add a 4½-inch green square to each brown ending square, as shown. Sew a 4½-inch dark gold print square to both ends of two of the four checkerboard border sections, as shown.

3 Stitch two checkerboard sections to the top and bottom of the quilt center, referring to the TABLECLOTH ASSEMBLY DIAGRAM on page 97. Stitch the remaining checkerboard/corner square sections to the sides of the tablecloth.

> FOR A QUILT that has a pieced outer border, I like to sew a 2-inch-wide strip of scrap fabric to the outside edges of the border. That way, when I attach the quilt to a quilt frame or insert it into a hoop, the tension will not cause the seams to pull apart.
>
> TIPS AND TRICKS

Putting It All Together

1 For the tablecloth, prepare the backing by cutting the 3¾-yard length of backing fabric in half crosswise to make two 1⅞-yard lengths. Remove the selvages and sew the long edges of the two lengths together. Press this seam open.

2 Trim the backing and batting so they are 4 inches larger than the quilt top dimensions. Mark quilting designs on the quilt top.

3 Layer the backing, batting, and quilt top. Baste the layers together and quilt.

4 When quilting is complete, remove the basting and trim the excess backing and batting even with the quilt top.

5 For the tree skirt, prepare the backing by cutting the 3½-yard length of backing fabric in half crosswise to make two 1¾-yard lengths. Remove the selvages and sew the long edges of the two lengths of fabric together with one center seam. Press this seam open. Repeat Steps 2 through 4 for the tree skirt.

6 For the tree skirt, use the Center Circle Template on page 101 to draw a 4¾-inch diameter circle at the center of the tree skirt, as shown in DIAGRAM 19. Draw a straight line from the circle to the midpoint of one edge of the tree skirt, as shown. NOTE: This line must go through the center of a tree. Machine stitch ¼ inch outside the circle and ¼ inch away from the

straight line on each side. Cut on the straight line and on the circle.

Tree skirt
DIAGRAM 19

Binding

NOTE: The 2¾-inch-wide bias strips will make a ⅜- to ½-inch-wide binding. If you want a wider or narrower binding, adjust the width of the strips you cut. (See page 216 for pointers on how to experiment with binding width.) See "Making and Attaching the Binding" on page 215 to complete your quilt.

CUTTING

From the green print fabric, for binding the outer edges:
• For the tablecloth, cut six 2¾ × 44-inch cross-grain strips

• For the tree skirt, cut seven 2¾ × 44-inch cross-grain strips

From the gold print fabric, for the tree skirt center:
• Cut enough 2½-inch-wide bias strips to make a 56-inch strip

Attaching the Binding

1 Piece the binding strips together diagonally, trim the seams, and press the seam allowances open.

2 Fold the binding in half lengthwise, wrong sides together, and press.

3 With raw edges even, and using a ⅜-inch-wide seam allowance, stitch the binding to the tablecloth or the tree skirt, mitering corners where necessary. For the tree skirt, begin and end at the opening by the center circle, as shown in DIAGRAM 20. For information on mitering corners, see "Border Basics" on page 211.

4 Turn the binding to the back side of the tablecloth or tree skirt and hand stitch the folded edges in place.

5 Bind the center opening of the tree skirt in the same way, allowing 20 inches of gold bias binding to extend beyond each opening edge to serve as ties, as shown in DIAGRAM 21.

Sew the folded edges of the binding together along the tie extensions, turning in the raw ends.

Tree skirt
DIAGRAM 20

Tree skirt
DIAGRAM 21

Quilting
DESIGNS

FOR HAND QUILTING:

❧ Stitch in the ditch, outlining the houses, the window appliqué shapes, the pine trees, the fence posts, and the checkerboard squares.

❧ Inside the pieced pine trees, quilt the triangular shape of each branch, as shown in QUILTING DIAGRAM 1.

❧ Inside the house roofs, quilt lines that will echo the triangular shapes, as shown in QUILTING DIAGRAM 2.

❧ In the center star, quilt diagonal lines from each point to the opposite point, as shown in QUILTING DIAGRAM 3.

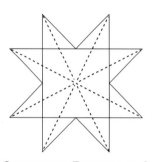

QUILTING DIAGRAM 2

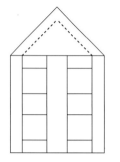

QUILTING DIAGRAM 3

FOR MACHINE QUILTING:

❧ Quilt curved, swooping lines to represent boughs in the trees and bark in the trunks, as shown in QUILTING DIAGRAM 4.

❧ Outline quilt around the houses, the appliqué shapes, the pine trees, the fence posts, and the checkerboard squares. Quilt the fence posts in a "roller coaster" design to emphasize their vertical lines, as shown in QUILTING DIAGRAM 5.

❧ Free-motion meander quilting works well for large background areas, such as around the houses and behind the fence posts. Vary the size of your meander quilting in different portions of the quilt to add interesting surface textures.

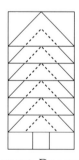

QUILTING DIAGRAM 1

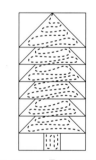

QUILTING DIAGRAM 4

QUILTING DIAGRAM 5

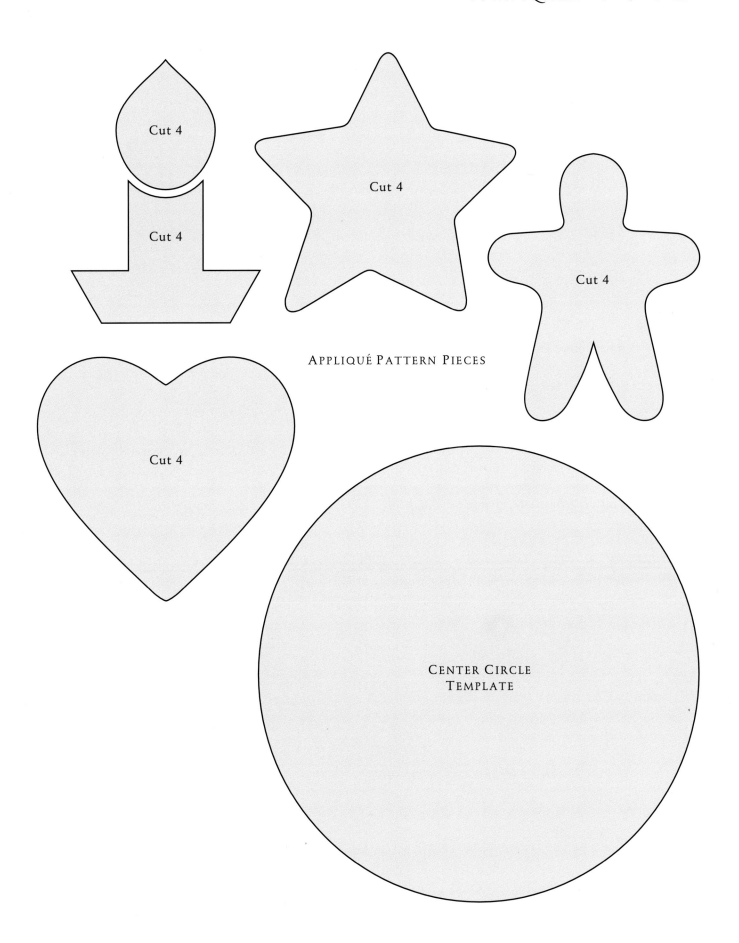

Cut 4

Cut 4

Cut 4

Cut 4

Cut 4

APPLIQUÉ PATTERN PIECES

CENTER CIRCLE
TEMPLATE

Yo-Yo Table Topper

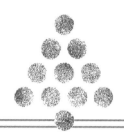

An updated version of an old-fashioned favorite, this yo-yo table topper makes a wonderful complement to the wood tones of a country pine table or adds a touch of warmth to any holiday table setting. Cotton homespun plaids in deep reds, greens, and creams in the tree motifs and borders create an overall look that is both country and casual. I like to cut out all my yo-yos at one time and keep them handy, to work on whenever I have a little time to spare—on car trips, whenever I'm waiting for someone or something, or during moments spent relaxing on my porch.

Size

Table Topper: 24 inches square (unquilted)

Fabrics and Supplies

Yardage is based on 44 inch-wide fabric.

⅛ yard black plaid homespun for trunk

1⅔ yards green plaid homespun for tree and outer border

1½ yards beige plaid homespun for tree background

1½ yards red plaid homespun for inner border

Quilting thread to match

Getting Ready

- READ instructions thoroughly before you begin.
- PREWASH and press fabric.
- TRACE the yo-yo circle onto template material and cut it out. 🖉

Fabric Key

■ Black plaid

■ Green plaid

□ Beige plaid

■ Red plaid

C U T T I N G

NOTE: Trace around the template on the wrong side of the fabric.

From the black plaid homespun:
- Cut 6 circles

From the green plaid homespun:
- Cut 133 circles

From the beige plaid homespun:
- Cut 122 circles

From the red plaid homespun:
- Cut 120 circles

Assembling the Table Topper

1 Turn the edges of each circle under ⅛ inch, gauging this distance by eye. Take care to keep the seam allowances of each circle the same size. Use a single strand of quilting thread to make running stitches close to the fold, taking care to make

these stitches approximately ¼ inch long and ¼ inch apart. Consistency in the length and spacing of your gathering stitches will produce finished yo-yos that are the same size.

2 To form each yo-yo, pull up the gathering thread so that the circle is gathered on the right side, as shown in DIAGRAM 1. The other side of each yo-yo will be flat. Take two stitches through the gathered folds at the center, knot, and clip the thread close to the fabric.

DIAGRAM 1

3 Lay the yo-yos on a flat surface, working on a quarter-section of the design at a time, as shown in DIAGRAM 2.

4 Stitch the yo-yos together with very fine whipstitches at the outer edges, as shown in DIAGRAM 3 on the opposite page. To do so, place yo-yos right sides together and whipstitch about a ⅛-inch section. Make a secure knot and clip the thread. Continue adding yo-yos in this fashion.

THREAD YOUR needle with the end of the thread that comes off the spool first. It is less likely to fray or tangle.

TIPS AND TRICKS

5 Stitch yo-yos together in rows, butting edges, completing a quarter of the table topper at a time. Sew the four quarters together and add the corner yo-yos, as shown in the TABLE TOPPER ASSEMBLY DIAGRAM.

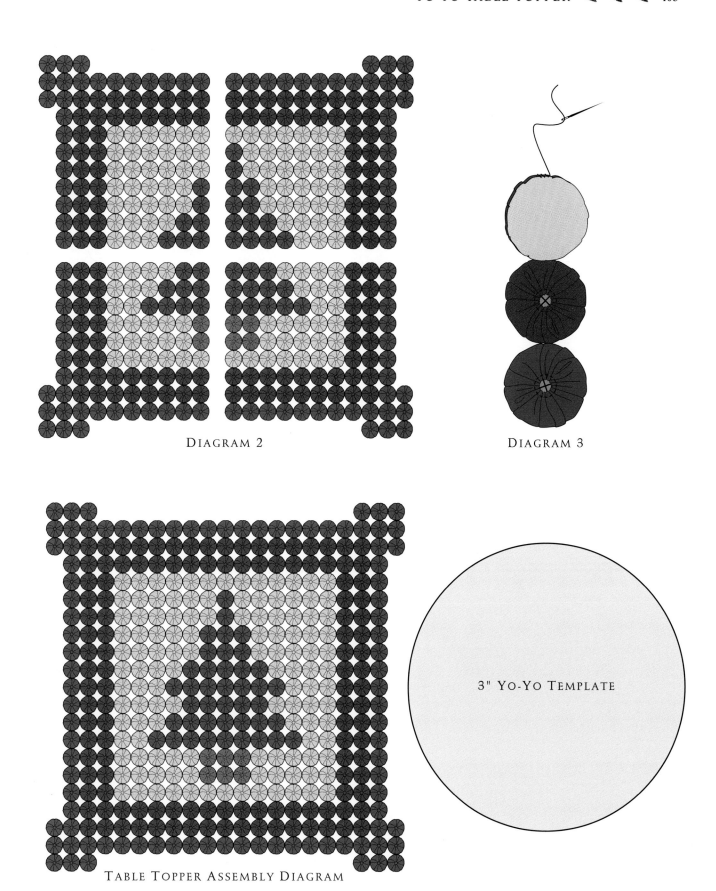

DIAGRAM 2

DIAGRAM 3

3" YO-YO TEMPLATE

TABLE TOPPER ASSEMBLY DIAGRAM

TRIM THE TREE STOCKING

This Christmas stocking, with colorful buttons scattered over a deep green Christmas tree, combines all my favorite things—homespun plaids, ticking, big, bold, chunky shapes, and deep traditional colors. I like to hang several along the stairway for decoration, unfilled, so they're not too heavy. I tuck in extra bits of batting or scrunched scraps of fabric to fill them out a bit. Twining artificial pine garland gets dressed up with twigs, red berries, and white frosted foliage for a simple finishing touch.

Size

Stocking: 12 × 18 inches (unquilted)

Fabrics and Supplies

Yardage is based on 44-inch-wide fabric.

½ yard cream/black plaid fabric for stocking front and back

¼ yard green print fabric for tree appliqué

⅛ yard red print fabric for heart appliqués and ruffle

¼ yard gold print fabric for star appliqués, ruffle, and binding

3 × 5-inch piece dark brown print fabric for tree base

½ yard muslin for lining

Variety of red, black, and gold print fabric scraps for covered button ornaments

Lightweight quilt batting, at least 14 × 19 inches

¼ yard 16-inch-wide fusible webbing

1 skein black embroidery floss

Thirteen 7/16-inch buttons to be covered

Template material

Rotary cutter, mat, and see-through ruler with ⅛-inch markings

Getting Ready

- READ instructions thoroughly before you begin.

- PREWASH and press fabric.

- USE ¼-inch seam allowances throughout unless directions specify otherwise.

- SEAM ALLOWANCES are included in the cutting sizes given.

- PRESS each seam allowance in the direction that will create the least bulk, and whenever possible, press toward the darker fabric.

- TRACE the tree, heart, star, and tree base templates on pages 112–114 onto template material and cut out the shapes.

- CUTTING DIRECTIONS for each section of the quilt are given individually. If you like to cut as you go, simply follow the directions as you get to them. If you'd rather cut all your pieces at the same time, skip ahead to find each of the cutting sections and do all the cutting before you begin to sew. ✔

Fabric Key

▦	Cream/black plaid
■	Green
■	Red
■	Gold
■	Dark brown

Stocking Front

C U T T I N G

From the cream/black plaid fabric:
- Cut one template A for the stocking front

From the green print fabric:
- Cut one 9 × 12-inch piece for the tree

From the red print fabric:
- Cut one 2 × 9-inch piece for the hearts

From the gold print fabric:
- Cut one 3 × 7-inch piece for the stars

From the dark brown print fabric:
- Cut one 3 × 5-inch piece for the tree base

From the muslin:
- Cut one 14 × 19-inch piece for the lining

From the batting:
- Cut one 14 × 19-inch piece

Appliquéing the Stocking Front

1 Position the fusible web (paper side facing up) over the shapes on pages 112–114. Trace one tree base, one large star, two small stars, and four hearts onto the fusible web. Roughly cut around the shapes.

2 Place fusible web shapes, coated side down, on the wrong side of the fabrics chosen for each shape. Press with a hot dry iron, following the manufacturer's directions for your brand of fusible web. Let the fabrics and fusible web cool, cut out the shapes on the tracing lines, and remove the paper backing.

3 Position the appliqué shapes on the stocking front. Refer to DIAGRAM 1 for placement. Press the shapes in place.

DIAGRAM 1

ANCHORING YOUR
BUTTONHOLE STITCHES

🖋 WITH THE PASSAGE OF TIME, I have found that buttonhole stitching can "roll off" the edges of appliqué shapes. If this happens to your buttonhole stitches, you can carefully tack them back in place with matching sewing thread.

🖋 TO PREVENT THIS from happening, take an extra tacking stitch in the same place as you make the buttonhole stitch, as shown. I suggest taking an

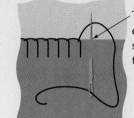

Take a small extra tacking stitch right at this point

extra tacking stitch on each buttonhole stitch going around outer curves, corners, and points. For straight edges, I find that taking a tacking stitch every inch is enough.

---

4 Using three strands of black embroidery floss, appliqué the shapes onto the stocking front with the buttonhole stitch. For more information on the buttonhole stitch, see page 210.

Assembling
the Stocking Front

1 Layer the muslin lining, batting, and stocking front facing up, as shown in DIAGRAM 2. Baste the three layers together and quilt.

2 Machine baste around the quilted stocking front, ¼ inch from the edges.

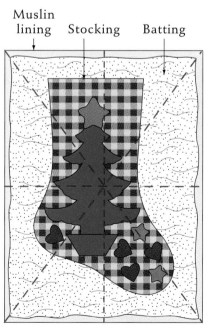

Muslin lining Stocking Batting

DIAGRAM 2

3 Trim the muslin lining and batting even with the raw edges of the stocking front.

4 Cover thirteen ⁷⁄₁₆-inch buttons with the red, black, and gold print fabric scraps. Sew the covered buttons to the tree, referring to the photo on page 107 for placement. The thread should go through to the lining side of the stocking front.

Stocking Back

NOTE: Do not cut the stocking shape from the fabrics designated for the stocking back. The technique that follows treats the stocking back as a rectangular unit of layered fabric and batting. This technique is much easier and more accurate than trying to align so many layers and cut edges. Read through the directions carefully before proceeding.

CUTTING

From the cream/black plaid fabric:
• Cut one 14 × 19-inch rectangle for the stocking back

From the muslin:
• Cut one 14 × 19-inch rectangle for the lining

From the batting:
• Cut one 14 × 19-inch rectangle

Assembling
the Stocking Back

1 Layer the muslin lining, batting, and plaid stocking back, right side up.

2 Lay the stocking front unit, lining side up, on top of the stocking back unit. Pin the stocking front unit in place with right sides facing each other, as shown in DIAGRAM 3.

DIAGRAM 3

3 Referring to DIAGRAM 3, stitch the front and back units together, starting at the dot and ending at the opposite upper edge. Leave the top edge open.

4 Trim the backing, batting, and lining even with the raw edges of the stocking front.

5 Turn the stocking right side out.

DON'T PULL your quilting thread tight by tugging on the needle. This will eventually fray the thread where it passes through the eye of the needle. Instead, grasp the thread between your thumb and forefinger a few inches behind the needle, and pull the thread.

Top Ruffle

C U T T I N G

From the red print fabric:
• Cut one 2 × 32-inch strip for the inner ruffle

From the gold print fabric:
• Cut one 3 × 32-inch strip for the outer ruffle

Assembling the Top Ruffle

1 Sew the red and gold strips together along one long edge, right sides together. Press seam allowances toward the red fabric, as shown in DIAGRAM 4.

DIAGRAM 4

2 Fold the strip in half lengthwise, wrong sides together. Run a gathering stitch ¼ inch from the raw edges, as shown in DIAGRAM 5. Gently pull up the gathering stitches until the ruffle fits the top edge of the stocking.

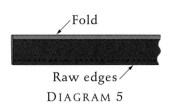

DIAGRAM 5

3 Pin the ruffle to the stocking top with right sides together and raw edges even. The red side of the ruffle should lie next to the stocking. Baste a scant ¼ inch from the raw edges.

Binding and Hanger

C U T T I N G

From the gold print fabric:
• Cut one 2 × 17-inch strip for inner binding
• Cut one 1¼ × 10-inch strip for hanger

Attaching the Binding

1 Fold the 2 × 17-inch strip in half lengthwise, with wrong sides together.

2 Pin the binding to the top edge of the stocking, with raw edges even. Stitch through all layers, with a ¼-inch seam allowance, as shown in DIAGRAM 6.

Stitch ¼" from raw edges

DIAGRAM 6

3 Fold the binding to the inside of the stocking and hand stitch the binding in place. The ruffle will be standing straight up.

4 Stitch the the remainder of the back seam of the stocking closed. Be sure to include the binding and the raw edges of the ruffle in this seam as you stitch it.

Attaching the Hanger

1 Fold the edges of the 1¼ × 10-inch gold strip in toward each other so that they will meet at the center, as shown in DIAGRAM 7.

Fold edges

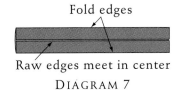

Raw edges meet in center
DIAGRAM 7

2 Fold the strip in half lengthwise once more, and stitch ⅛ inch away from the folded edges, as shown in DIAGRAM 8.

DIAGRAM 8

3 Fold the hanger strip in half crosswise into a loop and sew the hanger strip to the seam allowance of the ruffle and stocking with a medium zigzag stitch. Approximately 2½ inches of the hanger should extend above the ruffle, as shown in DIAGRAM 9.

DIAGRAM 9

Quilting
DESIGNS

🍃 *Very little quilting is necessary on this stocking because so much of its surface is covered by the large appliqué shapes. Simply quilt around the shapes for emphasis.*

🍃 *The buttons will anchor the tree, giving it the kind of texture you can otherwise accomplish by adding more quilting stitches.*

Align with blue line of Template C

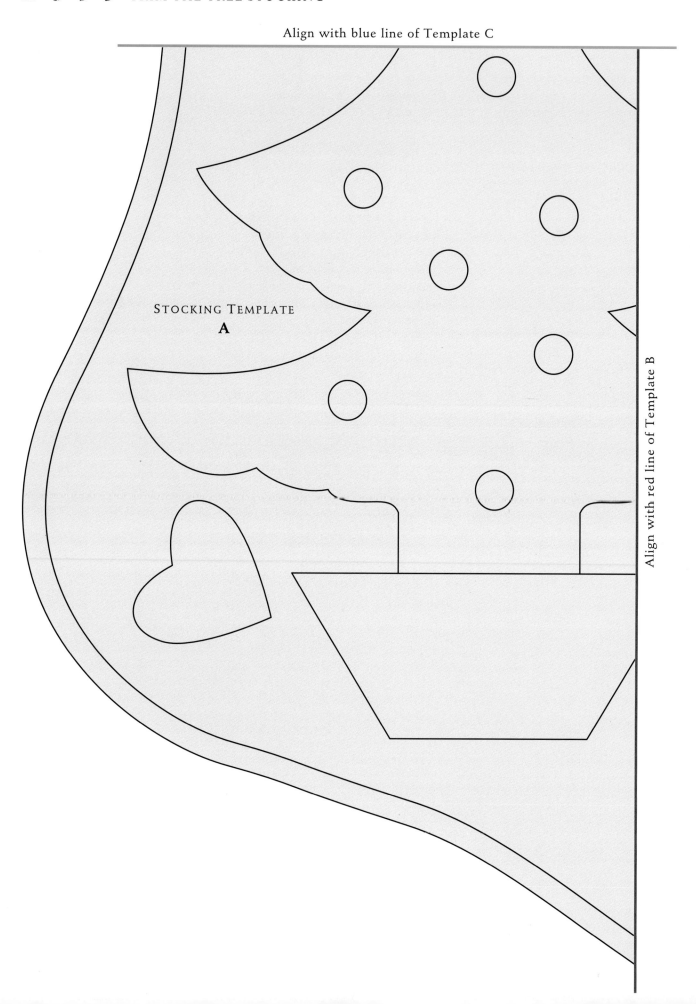

STOCKING TEMPLATE
A

Align with red line of Template B

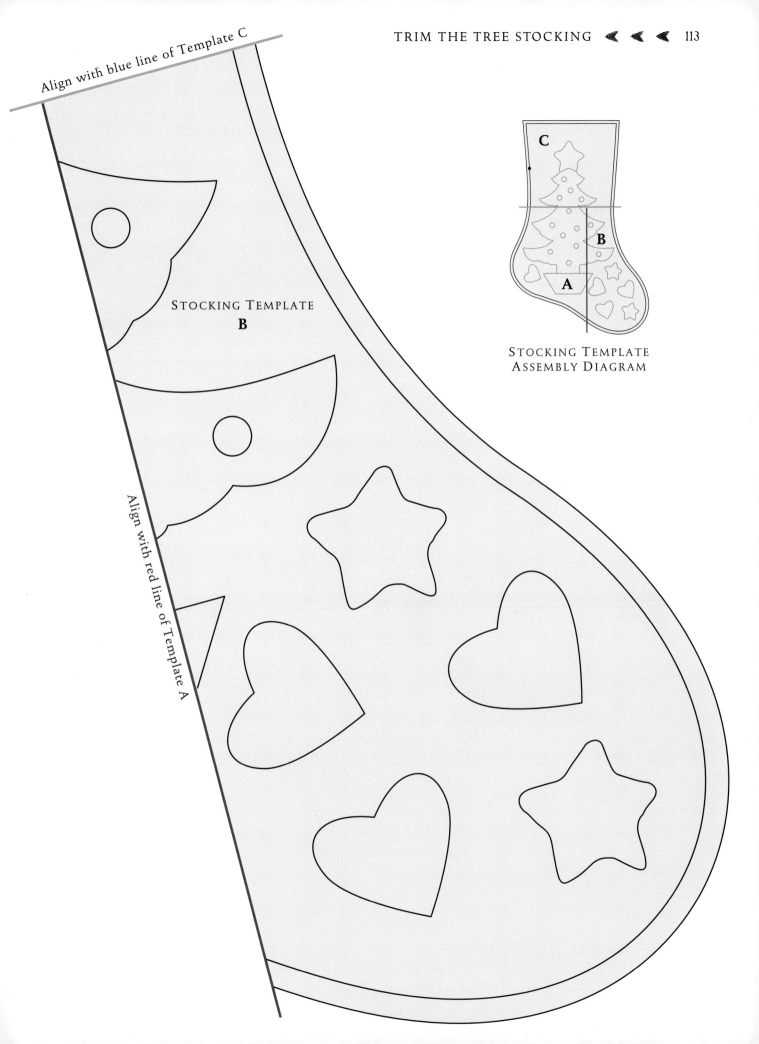

Align with blue line of Template C

STOCKING TEMPLATE
B

Align with red line of Template A

STOCKING TEMPLATE
ASSEMBLY DIAGRAM

STOCKING TEMPLATE
C

Align with blue lines of Templates A and B

CHRISTMAS CANDY

This little wall quilt is as bright and crisp as a jar of peppermints. The two red fabrics are very close in color. I used the darker red print in the border to frame the center of the quilt and the lighter one for highlighting the lattice squares, candy canes, and border pinwheels. A printed tone-on-tone muslin adds a touch of "sugar" to the candy canes, and a soft medium green background print stands out against the darker green lattice and red border strips. The darker green print contains a tiny touch of red and white, which ties the whole top together visually.

Size

Wall Quilt: 15 inches square (unquilted)

Fabrics and Supplies

Yardage is based on 44-inch-wide fabric.

¼ yard light green print fabric for background

¼ yard dark green print fabric for lattice strips and binding

¼ yard red print #1 fabric for candy cane stripes, lattice posts, and pinwheels

⅛ yard beige print fabric for candy canes and pinwheels

¼ yard red print #2 fabric for border

⅝ yard fabric for quilt backing

Lightweight quilt batting, at least 19 inches square

⅜ yard 16-inch-wide fusible web

1 skein black embroidery floss

Rotary cutter, mat, and see-through ruler with ⅛-inch markings

CHRISTMAS CANDY
Getting Ready

- READ instructions thoroughly before you begin.

- PREWASH and press fabric.

- USE ¼-inch seam allowances throughout unless directions specify otherwise.

- SEAM ALLOWANCES are included in the cutting sizes given.

- PRESS seam allowances in the direction that will create the least bulk, and whenever possible, press toward the darker fabric.

- CUTTING DIRECTIONS for each section of the quilt are given individually. If you like to cut as you go, simply follow the directions as you get to them. If you'd rather cut all your pieces at once, skip ahead to find each of the cutting sections and do all the cutting before you begin to sew.

Fabric Key

▦	Light green
■	Dark green
□	Beige
■	Red #1
■	Red #2

Candy Cane Blocks
(MAKE 4)

CUTTING

From the light green print fabric:
- Cut four 4½-inch squares

1 Position the fusible web (paper side facing up) over the candy cane shapes on page 119. Trace four candy canes onto the fusible web. Then trace the stripes and roughly cut around the shapes.

2 Place fusible web shapes, coated side down, on the wrong side of the fabrics chosen for the candy canes and their stripes. Press with a hot dry iron, following the manufacturer's directions for your brand of fusible

WHEN PLANNING color schemes for your quilts, remember that light, bright, and hot colors come forward visually, while dark, dull, and cool colors recede into the background.

TIPS AND TRICKS

web. Let the fabrics cool, cut out the candy canes on the tracing lines, and remove the paper backing. NOTE: It is better to cut the stripes a tiny bit wider than the candy canes so the stripes will be sure to cover the entire width of the candy canes. Cut out stripes along the *outside* edge of the tracing lines and trim the stripes to fit the candy canes, if necessary. Peel off the paper backing.

Appliquéing
the Candy Cane Blocks

1 Center the appliqué pieces on the 4½-inch light green squares and position the stripes on top of the candy canes, as shown in the PLACEMENT DIAGRAM. Press in place with a hot dry iron.

This is how the candy canes should appear when ironed on the background squares

PLACEMENT DIAGRAM

2 Appliqué the shapes in place. Shapes may be ironed on and left as they are, machine appliquéd, or primitive stitched using two strands of black embroidery floss. For more information on the primitive stitch, see page 210.

Quilt Center

C U T T I N G

From the dark green print fabric:
• Cut twelve 1½ × 4½ inch lattice strips

From the red print #1 fabric:
• Cut nine 1½ inch squares

Assembling the Quilt Center

1 Sew a Candy Cane block to each side of a dark green lattice strip, and sew a lattice strip to the other sides of the blocks, as shown in DIAGRAM 1. Repeat for the two remaining Candy Cane blocks.

DIAGRAM 1

2 Sew a dark green lattice strip to both sides of a 1½-inch red #1 square. Add a red lattice post to the ends, as shown in DIAGRAM 2. Make two more of these lattice strips.

DIAGRAM 2

3 Join the Candy Cane blocks with a lattice strip between them. Sew the remaining lattice strips to the top and bottom of the quilt, as shown in DIAGRAM 3.

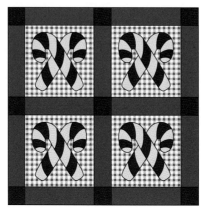

DIAGRAM 3

Border and Pinwheel Corner Blocks

C U T T I N G

NOTE: The yardage given allows for the border pieces to be cut cross-grain.

From the red print #1 fabric:
• Cut one 1⅞ × 44-inch strip

From the beige print fabric:
• Cut one 1⅞ × 44-inch strip

From the red print #2 fabric:
• Cut four 2½ × 11½-inch strips

Piecing the Pinwheels

1 With right sides together, layer the red #1 and beige 1⅞ × 44-inch strips. Press them together, but do not sew. Cut the layered strips into eight 1⅞-inch layered squares. Cut the squares

in half diagonally, as shown in DIAGRAM 4, and stitch a seam ¼ inch from the diagonal edge of each pair of triangles. Press seams toward the red fabric. Make 16 of these triangle-pieced squares.

DIAGRAM 4

2 Sew the triangle-pieced squares together in pairs. Sew the pairs together to form four pinwheels, as shown in DIAGRAM 5.

DIAGRAM 5

Attaching the Border

1 Measure the quilt from left to right through the middle, to determine the length to cut the top and bottom border strips. Cut two 2½-inch-wide red #2 strips this length. Sew these strips to the top and bottom of the quilt.

2 For the side border strips, cut two 2½-inch-wide red #2 strips to the measurement taken in Step 1.

3 Sew the pinwheel blocks to each end of the red #2 side border strips, as shown in DIAGRAM 6.

DIAGRAM 6

4 Sew the border strips to the sides of the quilt, completing the quilt top, as shown in the QUILT ASSEMBLY DIAGRAM.

Putting It All Together

1 Trim the backing and batting so they are 4 inches larger than the quilt top dimensions.

2 Layer the backing, batting, and quilt top. Baste the layers together and quilt.

3 When quilting is complete, remove the basting stitches and trim the excess backing and batting even with the quilt top.

Binding

NOTE: The 2¼-inch-wide strips will make a ¼-inch-wide binding. If you want a wider or narrower binding, adjust the width of the strips you cut. (See page 216 for pointers on how to experiment with binding width.) See "Making and Attaching the Binding" on page 215 to complete your quilt.

CUTTING

From the dark green print fabric:
• Cut two 2¼ × 44-inch strips for cross-grain binding

FOR HAND QUILTING:

❧ *This small quilt actually needs very little quilting. Simply stitch in the ditch around the candy cane shapes, the lattice strips, and the pinwheels in the corners of the border.*

❧ *A purchased quilting stencil with a simple chain or rope design will be effective in the border areas.*

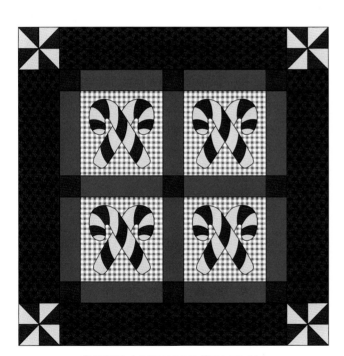

QUILT ASSEMBLY DIAGRAM

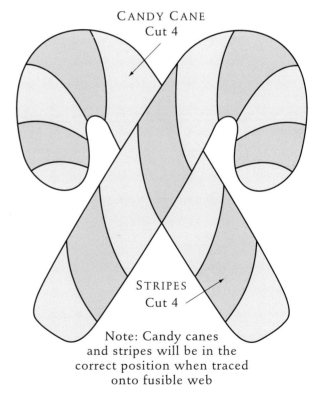

CANDY CANE
Cut 4

STRIPES
Cut 4

Note: Candy canes and stripes will be in the correct position when traced onto fusible web

APPLIQUÉ PATTERNS

CINNAMON HEARTS

Large Quilt and Small Quilt

I wanted these Cinnamon Hearts quilts to look as warm and inviting as their name sounds. I chose warm red fabrics for the hearts and a spicy brown print for the triangles and squares. The two reds contain deeper shades and beige tones that relate to each other, to the background fabric, and to the pieced shapes. Medium green overall prints add visual interest to the unpieced outer borders and draw the eye toward the centers of the quilts. The red bias plaid binding repeats the red colors in the hearts.

Size

Large Quilt: 33 inches square (unquilted)

Fabrics and Supplies

Yardage is based on 44-inch-wide fabric.

¼ yard beige print #1 fabric for heart background

¼ yard red plaid fabric for large heart

⅛ yard small red check fabric for small heart

¼ yard brown print fabric for sawtooth borders

⅛ yard small red check fabric for corner blocks

½ yard beige print #2 fabric for sawtooth borders

¾ yard green print fabric for outer borders

¾ yard red plaid fabric for bias binding

1 yard fabric for quilt backing

Quilt batting, at least 37 inches square

½ yard 16-inch-wide fusible web

1 skein black embroidery floss

Rotary cutter, mat, and see-through ruler with ⅛-inch markings

Getting Ready

- READ instructions thoroughly before you begin.
- PREWASH and press fabric.
- USE ¼-inch seam allowances throughout unless directions specify otherwise.
- SEAM ALLOWANCES are included in the cutting sizes given.
- PRESS seam allowances in the direction that will create the least bulk, and whenever possible, press toward the darker fabric.
- CUTTING DIRECTIONS for each section of the quilt are given individually. If you like to cut as you go, simply follow the directions as you get to them. If you'd rather cut all your pieces at the same time, skip ahead to find each of the cutting sections and do all the cutting before you begin to sew. ✎

Large Quilt Fabric Key

■	Red check
■	Red plaid
□	Beige #1
□	Beige #2
■	Brown
■	Green

Heart Blocks
(MAKE 4)

CUTTING

From the beige print #1 fabric:
- Cut four 6½-inch squares

Appliquéing the Heart Blocks

1 Position the fusible web (paper side facing up) over the heart shapes on page 127. Trace four small and four large hearts. Roughly cut around the shapes.

2 Place fusible web shapes, coated side down, on the wrong side of the fabrics chosen for the hearts. Press with a hot

dry iron, following the manufacturer's instructions for your brand of fusible web. Let the fabric and fusible web cool, cut out on tracing lines, and remove the paper backing.

3 Center the large heart shapes on the four 6½-inch beige squares, as shown in DIAGRAM 1, and press in place with a hot dry iron. Center the small hearts on the large hearts, and press.

DIAGRAM 1

4 Referring to DIAGRAM 1, and working with three

strands of black embroidery floss, appliqué the hearts onto the blocks, using the buttonhole stitch. For more information on the buttonhole stitch, see page 210.

Sawtooth Borders

CUTTING

From the brown print fabric:
- Cut three 2⅜ × 44-inch strips

From the beige print #2 fabric:
- Cut three 2⅜ × 44-inch strips

Piecing the Sawtooth Borders

1 With right sides together, layer the brown and beige

2⅜ × 44-inch strips and press them together. Cut the layered strips into forty-eight 2⅜-inch squares.

2 Cut the squares in half diagonally, as shown in DIAGRAM 2. Stitch ¼ inch from the diagonal edges. Press seam allowances toward the brown fabric. Repeat to make a total of 96 triangle-pieced squares.

DIAGRAM 2

TRIM OFF points of patches to within ¼ inch of seam lines to reduce bulk. Press seams before crossing another seam.

3 Sew 4 triangle-pieced squares together in a row, as shown in DIAGRAM 3. Repeat to make a total of 12 of these units. Make another row with the triangle-pieced squares in the opposite positions, as shown on the right. Make 12 of these units.

DIAGRAM 3

4 Refer to DIAGRAM 4 for placement to assemble the sawtooth borders. Sew the sawtooth border strips together in pairs. Make six of Section A and six of Section B, as shown.

Section A   Section B

DIAGRAM 4

Corner Blocks
(MAKE 9)

C U T T I N G

From the small red check fabric:
• Cut one 2 × 44-inch strip

From the beige print #2 fabric:
• Cut one 2 × 44-inch strip

Piecing the Corner Blocks

1 Sew the red and beige strips together. Press seam allowances toward the red fabric.

2 Cut this strip set into eighteen 2-inch-wide segments, as shown in DIAGRAM 5.

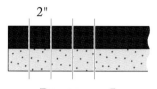

2"

DIAGRAM 5

3 Sew two segments together, alternating colors, as shown in DIAGRAM 6. Repeat to make nine of these Four Patch corner blocks.

DIAGRAM 6

Quilt Center

1 Sew the Section A segments and heart blocks together in two vertical rows, as shown in DIAGRAM 7. Press seam allowances toward the heart blocks.

DIAGRAM 7

2 Sew the Section B segments and corner blocks together in three vertical rows, as shown in DIAGRAM 7 on page 123. Press the seam allowances toward the corner blocks.

3 Referring to DIAGRAM 7, sew the vertical rows together. Press the seam allowances toward the heart blocks.

Outer Border

C U T T I N G

NOTE: The yardage given allows for cutting the border pieces cross-grain.

From the green print fabric:
• Cut four 6½ × 44-inch strips

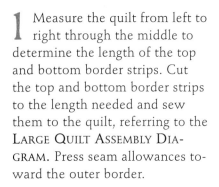

1 Measure the quilt from left to right through the middle to determine the length of the top and bottom border strips. Cut the top and bottom border strips to the length needed and sew them to the quilt, referring to the LARGE QUILT ASSEMBLY DIAGRAM. Press seam allowances toward the outer border.

2 Measure the quilt from top to bottom through the middle, including the border strips just added, to determine the length of the side border strips. Cut the side border strips to the length needed and sew them to the quilt, as shown. Press seam allowances toward the outer border.

LARGE QUILT ASSEMBLY DIAGRAM

Putting It All Together

1 Trim the backing and batting so they are 4 inches larger than the quilt top dimensions.

2 Mark quilting designs on the quilt top.

3 Layer the backing, batting, and quilt top. Baste the layers together and quilt.

4 When quilting is complete, remove basting and trim the excess backing and batting even with the quilt top.

Binding

NOTE: The 2¾-inch strips will make a ⅜- to ½-inch-wide finished binding. If you want a wider or narrower binding, adjust the width of the strips you cut. (See page 216 for pointers on how to experiment with binding width.) See "Making and Attaching the Binding" on page 215 to complete your quilt.

C U T T I N G

From the red plaid fabric:
• Cut enough 2¾-inch bias strips to make a 147-inch strip

CINNAMON HEARTS

Small Quilt

Size

Small Quilt: 18 inches square (unquilted)

Fabrics and Supplies

Yardage is based on 44-inch-wide fabric.

7-inch square of beige print #1 fabric for heart background

5-inch square of red print fabric for small heart

7-inch square of red plaid fabric for large heart

¼ yard chestnut print fabric for sawtooth borders

¼ yard beige print #2 fabric for sawtooth borders

⅛ yard red stripe fabric for corner blocks

½ yard green print fabric for border

⅜ yard red print fabric for binding

⅝ yard fabric for quilt backing

Quilt batting, at least 22 inches square

¼ yard fusible webbing

1 skein black embroidery floss

Rotary cutter, mat, and see-through ruler with ⅛-inch markings

Heart Block

(MAKE 1)

C U T T I N G

From the beige print #1 fabric:
• Cut one 6½-inch square

Appliquéing the Heart Block

Refer to "Appliquéing the Heart Blocks," Steps 1 through 4, in the Cinnamon Hearts large quilt, and appliqué the heart block for the small quilt in the same manner.

Sawtooth Borders

C U T T I N G

From the chestnut print fabric:
• Cut one 2⅜ × 44-inch strip

From the beige print #2 fabric:
• Cut one 2⅜ × 44-inch strip

Piecing the Sawtooth Borders

Refer to "Piecing the Sawtooth Borders," Steps 1 through 4, in the Cinnamon Hearts large quilt, and piece the sawtooth borders for the small quilt in the same manner. Make two of Section A and two of Section B.

Small Quilt Fabric Key

☐	Beige #1
⊡	Beige #2
■	Chestnut
▦	Red plaid
■	Red
■	Green

Corner Blocks

(MAKE 4)

C U T T I N G

From the red stripe fabric:
• Cut one 2 × 18-inch strip

From the beige print #2 fabric:
• Cut one 2 × 18-inch strip

Referring to "Corner Blocks," Steps 1 through 3, in the Cinnamon Hearts large quilt, and "Cutting" above, make a strip set for the corner blocks for the small quilt. Cut this strip set into eight 2-inch segments. Make a total of four corner blocks.

Quilt Center

1 Sew the Section A strips to the top and bottom of the heart block, as shown in DIAGRAM 8.

DIAGRAM 8

2 Sew the corner blocks to the ends of the Section B strips, and sew these rows to the sides of the heart block, as shown in DIAGRAM 8.

Outer Border

C U T T I N G

NOTE: The yardage given allows for the border pieces to be cut cross-grain.

From the green fabric:
• Cut two 3½ × 44-inch strips

Attaching the Outer Border

1 Measure the quilt from left to right through the middle to determine the length of the top and bottom border strips. Cut the

SMALL QUILT ASSEMBLY DIAGRAM

top and bottom border strips to the length needed, and sew them to the quilt, referring to the SMALL QUILT ASSEMBLY DIAGRAM.

2 Measure the quilt from top to bottom through the middle, including the border strips just added, to determine the length of the side border strips. Cut the side border strips to the length needed and sew them to the quilt, referring to the SMALL QUILT ASSEMBLY DIAGRAM.

Putting It All Together

1 Trim the backing and batting so they are 4 inches larger than the quilt top dimensions.

2 Mark quilting designs on the quilt top.

3 Layer the backing, batting, and quilt top. Baste the layers together and quilt.

4 When quilting is complete, remove the basting stitches, and trim the excess backing and batting even with the quilt top.

Binding

NOTE: The 2¾-inch strips will make a ⅜- to ½-inch-wide binding. If you want a wider or narrower binding, adjust the width of the strips you cut. (See page 216 for pointers on how to experiment with binding width.) See "Making and Attaching the Binding" on page 215 to complete your quilt.

C U T T I N G

From the red print fabric:
• Cut two 2¾ × 44-inch strips for cross-grain binding

Quilting DESIGNS

FOR HAND QUILTING:

🌀 *Quilt around the pieced shapes and appliqué hearts in both the large and small quilts to make them stand out from the background fabrics and appear to be slightly stuffed.*

🌀 *Choose a feathered cable design, as shown in* QUILTING DIAGRAM 1, *for quilting the wide, solid borders in the small quilt.*

🌀 *I find it a real joy to hand quilt where there are no seam allowances. There are also fewer restrictions in the types of designs you can choose for solid borders, so select any design that will fit the quilt borders. For the large quilt, you can choose a feather and swag design, as shown in* QUILTING DIAGRAM 2.

QUILTING DIAGRAM 1

QUILTING DIAGRAM 2

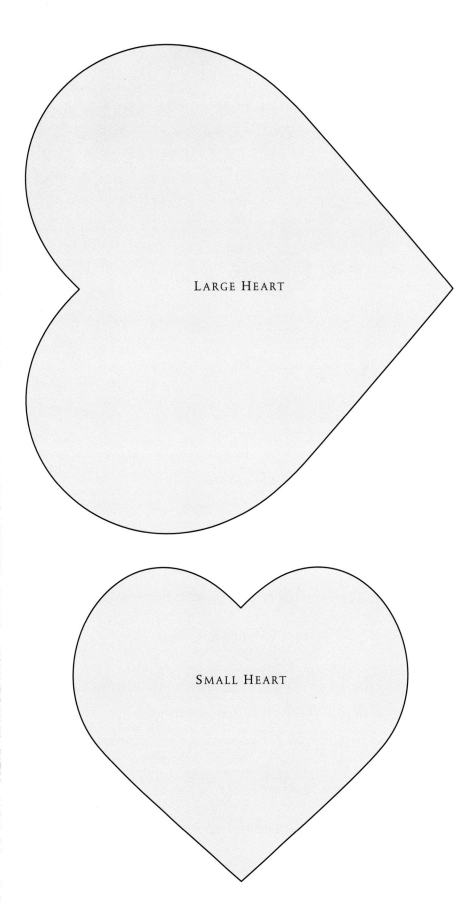

LARGE HEART

SMALL HEART

CHRISTMAS APPLE

The graphic pieced checkerboard pattern in Christmas Apple is a striking place for a floral centerpiece, decorative candles, or a bowl of fresh apples. The pine trees in small-scale, tone-on-tone green prints re-create the depth of color in real trees. The small-scale red fabric in the apples harmonizes well with the size of the blocks; I think that large-scale prints often lose effectiveness in small shapes like these. For the centers of the star blocks in the borders, I chose a plaid that combines three colors from the other prints. I also used the same fabric in the inner red border and the binding.

Size

Table Runner: 24 × 42 inches (unquilted)

Fabrics and Supplies

Yardage is based on 44-inch-wide fabric.

¼ yard blue print fabric for center squares

¼ yard brown plaid fabric for center squares

¼ yard dark red print fabric for inner border

¼ yard red check fabric for apples

⅛ yard dark green print fabric for leaves

¾ yard beige print fabric for background

⅛ yard *each* of four coordinating green print fabrics for trees

⅛ yard brown check fabric for tree trunks

⅛ yard gold plaid fabric for star center

⅛ yard gold print fabric for star

1¼ yards fabric for quilt backing

⅜ yard red print fabric for binding

Quilt batting, at least 28 × 46 inches

Rotary cutter, mat, and wide see-through ruler with ⅛-inch markings

Getting Ready

- READ instructions thoroughly before you begin.

- PREWASH and press fabric.

- USE ¼-inch seam allowances throughout unless directions specify otherwise.

- SEAM ALLOWANCES are included in the cutting sizes given.

- PRESS seam allowances in the direction that will create the least bulk, and whenever possible, press toward the darker fabric.

- CUTTING DIRECTIONS for each section of the quilt are given individually. If you like to cut as you go, simply follow the directions as you get to them. If you'd rather cut all your pieces at the same time, skip ahead to find each of the cutting sections and do all the cutting before you begin to sew. 🍃

Patchwork Center

CUTTING

From the blue print fabric:
- Cut two 3½ × 20-inch strips
- Cut one 3½ × 17-inch strip

From the brown plaid fabric:
- Cut two 3½ × 17-inch strips
- Cut one 3½ × 20-inch strip

Piecing the Patchwork Center

1 To make Strip Set I, sew a 3½ × 20-inch blue strip to each side of a 3½ × 20-inch brown plaid strip, as shown in DIAGRAM 1. Press the seam

allowances toward the brown fabric. Crosscut the strip set into five 3½-inch segments.

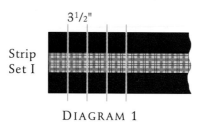

3½"

Strip
Set I

DIAGRAM 1

2 To make Strip Set II, sew a 3½ × 17-inch brown plaid strip to each side of a 3½ × 17-inch blue strip, as shown in DIAGRAM 2. Press seam allowances toward the brown fabric. Crosscut the strip set into four 3½-inch segments.

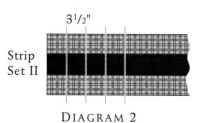

3½"

Strip
Set II

DIAGRAM 2

3 Sew the Strip Set I and Strip Set II segments together, alternating colors, as shown in DIAGRAM 3. Begin and end with a Strip Set I segment. At this time, the piece should measure 9½ × 27½ inches.

DIAGRAM 3

Fabric Key

- ■ Blue
- ▦ Brown plaid
- ■ Dark red
- ■ Red check
- ■ Dark green
- ▢ Beige
- ■ Green #1
- ■ Green #2
- ■ Green #3
- ■ Green #4
- ■ Brown check
- ▦ Gold plaid
- ■ Gold

Inner Border

From the dark red print fabric:
• Cut two 2 × 9½-inch strips
• Cut two 2 × 30½-inch strips

Attaching the Inner Border

1 Sew the 9½-inch-long dark red print border strips to the short edges of the runner center, as shown in DIAGRAM 4. Press seam allowances toward the border.

2 Sew the 30½-inch-long border strips to the long edges of the runner center, as shown in DIAGRAM 4. Press seam allowances toward the border.

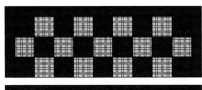

DIAGRAM 4

Apple Blocks
(MAKE 12)

From the red check fabric:
• Cut one 3½ × 44-inch strip; from this strip, cut twelve 3½-inch squares

From the dark green print fabric:
• Cut two 2 × 44-inch strips;

from these strips, cut twenty-four 2-inch squares

From the beige print fabric:
• Cut two 2 × 44-inch strips; from these strips, cut twenty-four 2 × 3½-inch pieces
• Cut two 1¼ × 44-inch strips; from these strips, cut forty-eight 1¼-inch squares

Piecing the Apple Blocks

1 With right sides together, position a 2-inch dark green square on the corner of a 2 × 3½-inch beige piece. Stitch diagonally from corner to corner on the green square, as shown in DIAGRAM 5. Trim away excess fabric, leaving a ¼-inch seam allowance. Press seam allowances toward the dark green fabric. Repeat for the opposite corner, as shown. Repeat to make a total of 12 leaf units.

—Trim to ¼"

DIAGRAM 5

2 With right sides together, position four 1¼-inch beige squares at each corner of a 3½-inch red check square, as shown in DIAGRAM 6.

DIAGRAM 6

3 Stitch diagonally from corner to corner, as shown in DIAGRAM 7. Trim away the excess fabric from each corner, leaving ¼-inch seam allowances.

Press seam allowances toward the red fabric. Repeat Steps 2 and 3 for each of the 12 apple units.

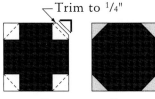

—Trim to ¼"

DIAGRAM 7

4 Sew a leaf unit to the top of each apple unit, as shown in DIAGRAM 8. Sew a 2 × 3½-inch beige piece to the bottom of each apple unit, as shown. Press seam allowances toward the apples. At this point, the Apple block should each measure 3½ × 6½ inches.

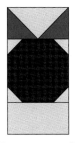

DIAGRAM 8

Tree Blocks
(MAKE 8)

From each of the four green print fabrics:
• Cut one 2⅜ × 44-inch strip. Cut a total of sixty-six 2⅜-inch squares from these four strips. Cut the squares in half diagonally to form 132 triangles. This will allow you extra triangles so you can mix them if you wish.

From the brown check fabric:
• Cut one 1½ × 18-inch strip.

From the beige print fabric:
• Cut two 3 × 18-inch strips.
• Cut two 2⅜ × 44-inch strips; from these strips, cut twenty-four 2⅜-inch squares. Cut the squares in half diagonally to form forty-eight triangles.
• Cut sixteen 2-inch squares.

Piecing the Tree Blocks

NOTE: Mix colors and patterns to give the trees depth; to make all trees identical, see DIAGRAM 9.

1 Sew the green and beige triangles and squares in three horizontal rows, referring to DIAGRAM 9 for color placement. Press seam allowances in each row in one direction, alternating the direction with each row. Join the rows, as shown. Repeat for each tree unit.

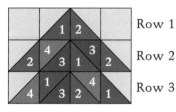

Row 1
Row 2
Row 3

DIAGRAM 9

2 To make Strip Set III for the trunk unit, sew a 3 × 18-inch beige strip to each side of the 1½ × 18-inch brown strip, as shown in DIAGRAM 10. Press seam allowances toward the brown fabric. Crosscut this strip set into eight 2-inch segments, as shown.

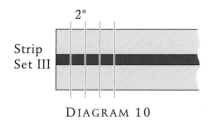

2"

Strip Set III

DIAGRAM 10

3 Sew the trunk units to the trees. At this point, the Tree block should measure 6½ inches square.

Star Blocks
(MAKE 4)

CUTTING

From the gold plaid fabric:
• Cut four 3½-inch squares

From the gold print fabric:
• Cut two 2 × 44-inch strips; from these strips, cut thirty-two 2-inch squares

From the beige print fabric:
• Cut two 2 × 44-inch strips; from these strips, cut sixteen 2 × 3½-inch pieces
• Cut sixteen 2-inch squares

Piecing the Star Blocks

1 With right sides together, position a 2-inch gold print square on a 2 × 3½-inch beige piece, as shown in DIAGRAM 11. Stitch diagonally from corner to corner on the gold square, as shown. Trim away excess fabric, leaving a ¼-inch seam allowance. Press seam allowances toward the gold fabric. Repeat for the opposite corner. Make a total of sixteen star point units.

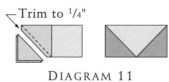

Trim to ¼"

DIAGRAM 11

2 Sew a star point unit to the top and bottom edge of each 3½-inch gold plaid square, as shown in DIAGRAM 12.

DIAGRAM 12

3 Sew a 2-inch beige square to each end of the remaining star point units, as shown in DIAGRAM 13.

DIAGRAM 13

4 Sew one of these units to each side of the Star blocks, as shown in DIAGRAM 14. At this point, the Star block should measure 6½ inches square.

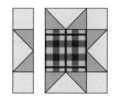

DIAGRAM 14

WHEN JOINING two pieced sections together, here's an easy way to match seams. Before you sew, place a pin directly through both seam lines, making sure that the seam allowance of the top section faces away from you and the seam allowance of the underlying section faces toward you. This will eliminate bulk and produce perfectly aligned seams.

TIPS AND TRICKS

Pieced Border

1 For each of the two short border strips, sew an Apple block to each side of a Tree block, as shown in DIAGRAM 15.

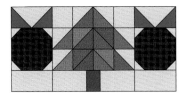

DIAGRAM 15

2 For each of the two long border strips, sew three Tree blocks and four Apple blocks together, alternating blocks, as shown in DIAGRAM 16. Sew a Star block to each end of the border strips, as shown.

Assembling the Table Runner

1 Sew the short pieced border strips to the short edges of the runner top, as shown in the TABLE RUNNER ASSEMBLY DIAGRAM.

2 Sew the long pieced border strips to the long edges of the runner top, as shown.

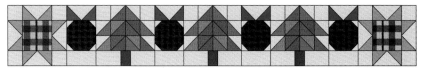

DIAGRAM 16

Putting It All Together

1 Trim the backing and batting so they measure approximately 4 inches larger than the table runner top.

2 Mark quilting designs on the quilt top.

3 Layer the backing, batting, and quilt top. Baste or pin these layers together and quilt.

4 When quilting is complete, remove the basting stitches, and trim the excess backing and batting even with the quilt top.

Binding

NOTE: The 2¼-inch binding strips will produce a ¼-inch-wide binding. If you want a wider or narrower binding, adjust the width of the strips you cut. (See page 216 for pointers on

how to experiment with binding width.) See "Making and Attaching the Binding" on page 215 to complete your quilt.

CUTTING

From the red print binding fabric:
• Cut four 2¼ × 44-inch strips for cross-grain binding

Quilting DESIGNS

FOR HAND OR MACHINE QUILTING:

❧ *Quilt in the ditch of each seam. Also quilt diagonally from corner to corner in the squares at the center of the quilt to create a secondary geometric pattern.*

❧ *Quilt the squares in the corner Star blocks in the same manner as the center squares. Repeating the same type of quilting design in more than one area of a quilt helps to create visual unity throughout the quilt.*

❧ *Quilt in the ditch around the apples, stars, and trees to add texture and highlight the pieced triangles.*

TABLE RUNNER ASSEMBLY DIAGRAM

CHRISTMAS HOUSE

Christmas House is filled with many of my favorite country motifs—stars, pine trees, hearts, and a house with a picket fence. When I choose fabrics for a quilt like this, I like to look for prints, plaids, and checks that feature many of the same colors, in order to unify a variety of different design elements. Here, I decided to use a neutral background that would visually tie the individual blocks together, and I selected small-scale, simple prints and plaids to stay in keeping with the whimsical country style of the quilt.

Size

Wall Quilt: 31 × 34 inches (unquilted)

Fabrics and Supplies

Yardage is based on 44-inch-wide fabric.

⅛ yard red dot fabric for house

⅛ yard black check fabric for windows, chimney, and door

⅛ yard black plaid fabric for roof

¾ yard beige print fabric for background

⅓ yard red check fabric for Nine Patch and hearts

⅛ yard dark green print fabric for trees

⅛ yard brown check fabric for trunks

¼ yard gold print fabric for stars

¼ yard cream print fabric for fence

¼ yard green print fabric for fence background

⅛ yard red plaid fabric for pieced border

⅛ yard tan print for fabric pieced border

⅓ yard black print fabric for narrow inner border and corner squares

½ yard gold/black plaid fabric for outer border

½ yard red dot fabric for binding

1⅓ yards fabric for quilt backing

Quilt batting, at least 35 × 38 inches

Rotary cutter, mat, and see-through ruler with ⅛-inch markings

Getting Ready

- READ instructions thoroughly before you begin.
- PREWASH and press fabric.
- USE ¼-inch seam allowances throughout unless directions specify otherwise.
- SEAM ALLOWANCES are included in the cutting sizes given.
- PRESS seam allowances in the direction that will create the least bulk, and whenever possible, press toward the darker fabric.
- CUTTING DIRECTIONS for each section of the quilt are given individually. If you like to cut as you go, simply follow the directions as you get to them. If you'd rather cut all your pieces at the same time, skip ahead to find each of the cutting sections and do all the cutting before you begin to sew.

House Block
(MAKE 1)

CUTTING

From the red dot fabric:
- Cut three 1½ × 6½-inch pieces for the house
- Cut five 1½ × 2½-inch pieces for the house

From the black check fabric:
- Cut one 2½ × 3½-inch piece for the door
- Cut two 1½ × 2½-inch pieces for the small windows
- Cut one 2½-inch square for the large window
- Cut two 1½-inch squares for the chimneys

From the black plaid fabric:
- Cut one 2½ × 9½-inch strip for the roof

From the beige print fabric:
- Cut two 1½ × 6½-inch pieces for the house background
- Cut one 1½ × 3½-inch piece for the chimney background
- Cut two 1½ × 2½-inch pieces for the chimney background
- Cut two 2½-inch squares for the roof background

Fabric Key

- ■ Red dot
- ■ Black check
- ▦ Black plaid
- ■ Beige
- ■ Red check
- ■ Green
- ■ Brown
- ■ Gold
- ▨ Cream
- ■ Dark green
- ■ Red plaid
- ▨ Tan
- ▨ Black print
- ▦ Gold/black plaid

Piecing the House Blocks

1 To make the roof unit, position the 2½-inch beige squares on the corners of the 2½ × 9½-inch black plaid piece. Stitch diagonally on the beige squares, as shown in DIAGRAM 1. Trim away excess fabric, leaving a ¼-inch seam allowance, as shown. Press seam allowances toward the plaid fabric.

Trim to ¼"

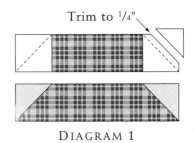

DIAGRAM 1

2 Sew a 1½-inch black check square to each side of the 1½ × 3½-inch beige piece, as shown in DIAGRAM 2. Sew a 1½ × 2½-inch beige piece to each side, creating the chimney unit, as shown.

DIAGRAM 2

3 To make Unit A, sew a 1½ × 2½-inch red dot piece to each side of a 1½ × 2½-inch black check piece, as shown in DIAGRAM 3. Sew the 2½ × 3½-inch black check piece to the bottom of this unit, as shown.

Unit A

DIAGRAM 3

4 To make Unit B, sew a 1½ × 2½-inch red dot piece to each side of a 1½ × 2½-inch black check piece, as shown in DIAGRAM 4. Sew a 2½-inch black check square to the bottom of this unit, and add a 1½ × 2½-inch red dot piece below the black check square, as shown.

Unit B

DIAGRAM 4

5 Sew two each of the 1½ × 6½-inch beige and red dot strips together, as shown in DIAGRAM 5. Sew one of these units to the left side of Unit A and one to the right side of Unit B. Sew Units A and B to each side of the remaining 1½ × 6½-inch red dot strip to make the house unit, as shown.

Unit A   Unit B

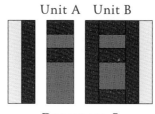

DIAGRAM 5

6 Sew together the chimney, roof, and house base units from Steps 1 through 5, as shown in DIAGRAM 6. At this point, the House block should measure 9½ inches square.

DIAGRAM 6

Nine Patch Blocks
(MAKE 8)

C U T T I N G

From the red check fabric:
• Cut two 1½ × 26-inch strips
• Cut one 1½ × 15-inch strip

From the beige print fabric:
• Cut one 1½ × 26-inch strip
• Cut two 1½ × 15-inch strip

Piecing the Nine Patch Blocks

1 To make Strip Set I, sew a 1½ × 26-inch red check strip to both sides of a 1½ × 26-inch beige strip, as shown in DIAGRAM 7. Press seam allowances toward the red fabric. Crosscut the strip set into sixteen 1½-inch segments, as shown.

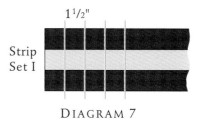

1½"

Strip Set I

DIAGRAM 7

2 To make Strip Set II, sew a 1½ × 15-inch beige strip to both sides of a 1½ × 15-inch red check strip, as shown in DIAGRAM 8. Press seam allowances toward the red fabric. Crosscut the strip set into eight 1½-inch segments, as shown.

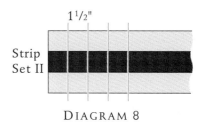

1½"

Strip Set II

DIAGRAM 8

3 Sew a Strip Set I segment to each side of a Strip Set II segment to make each of the Nine Patch blocks, as shown in DIAGRAM 9 on page 138. At this point, the Nine Patch Blocks should measure 3½ inches square.

DIAGRAM 9

Tree Blocks

(MAKE 8)

CUTTING

From the dark green print fabric:
• Cut eight Template A triangles for trees; mark notches on each piece

From the beige print fabric:
• Cut eight Template B triangles; mark a notch on each piece
• Cut eight Template B reversed triangles; mark a notch on each piece
• Cut two 1½ × 12-inch strips for trunk background

From the brown check fabric:
• Cut one 1½ × 12-inch strip for trunks

Piecing the Tree Blocks

1 Referring to DIAGRAM 10, sew a beige B and B reverse piece to the sides of each dark green A triangle, matching notches. Press seam allowances toward the green fabric.

DIAGRAM 10

2 To make tree trunks, sew a 1½ × 12-inch beige strip to either side of the 1½ × 12-inch brown check strip. Press seam allowances toward the brown fabric. Crosscut this strip set into eight 1¼-inch segments, as shown in DIAGRAM 11.

1¼"

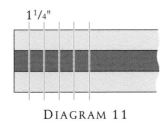

DIAGRAM 11

3 Sew a tree trunk unit to the bottom of each tree unit, as shown in DIAGRAM 12. At this point, the Tree blocks should measure 3½ inches square.

DIAGRAM 12

Quilt Center

1 Referring to DIAGRAM 13, sew a horizontal row consisting of two Tree blocks and one Nine Patch block. Make two of these rows and sew them to the top and bottom of the house block, as shown.

2 Referring to DIAGRAM 13, sew a vertical row consisting of three Nine Patch blocks and two Tree blocks. Make two of these rows and sew them to the sides of the house block, as shown.

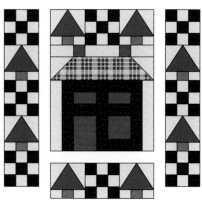

DIAGRAM 13

Star Blocks

(MAKE 5)

CUTTING

From the gold print fabric:
• Cut five 1½-inch squares
• Cut one 1⅞ × 22-inch strip

From the beige print fabric:
• Cut twenty 1½-inch squares
• Cut one 1⅞ × 22-inch strip

Piecing the Star Blocks

1 With right sides together, layer a 1⅞ × 22-inch gold strip and a 1⅞ × 22-inch beige strip. Press the strips together. Cut the layered strips into ten 1⅞-inch squares. Cut the squares in half diagonally, and stitch ¼ inch from the diagonal edges, as shown in DIAGRAM 14. Press seam allowances toward the gold fabric to make twenty 1½-inch triangle-pieced squares.

DIAGRAM 14

2 To make Unit A, sew a 1½-inch beige square to each side of ten of the 1½-inch triangle-pieced squares, as shown in DIAGRAM 15.

Unit A

DIAGRAM 15

3 To make Unit B, sew a 1½-inch triangle-pieced square to each side of the five 1½-inch gold squares, as shown in DIAGRAM 16.

Unit B

DIAGRAM 16

4 Sew a Unit A to each side of a Unit B to make each Star block, as shown in DIAGRAM 17. At this point, the Star blocks should measure 3½ inches square.

 Unit A
Unit B
Unit A

DIAGRAM 17

5 Stitch the five Star blocks together in a row and add this row to the top of the quilt center, referring to the QUILT ASSEMBLY DIAGRAM.

Pieced Border

C U T T I N G

From the tan print fabric:
• Cut nine 3½ × 4½-inch pieces

From the red plaid fabric:
• Cut eight 3½ × 4½-inch pieces

Assembling the Pieced Borders

1 To make side border strips, sew together three red plaid pieces and three tan pieces, as shown in DIAGRAM 18. Sew

these border strips to the sides of the quilt center, referring to the QUILT ASSEMBLY DIAGRAM.

DIAGRAM 18

QUILT ASSEMBLY DIAGRAM

2 To make the top border strip, sew together two red plaid pieces and three tan pieces, as shown in **DIAGRAM 19**. Do *not* sew the top border strip to the quilt center at this time.

DIAGRAM 19

Heart Blocks
(MAKE 2)

From the red check fabric:
• Cut four 1½ × 2½-inch pieces
• Cut two 3½ × 4½-inch pieces

From the beige print fabric:
• Cut eight 1½-inch squares
• Cut four 2½-inch squares

Piecing the Heart Blocks

1 With right sides together, position a 1½-inch beige square on one corner of a 1½ × 2½-inch red check piece, as shown in **DIAGRAM 20**. Stitch diagonally on the beige square and trim away excess fabric, leaving a ¼-inch seam allowance, as shown. Repeat at the other corner. Press seam allowances toward the red fabric. Make two of these units.

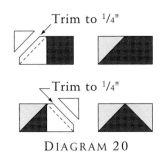

Trim to ¼"

Trim to ¼"

DIAGRAM 20

2 Sew two of the Step 1 units together, creating a heart top unit, as shown in **DIAGRAM 21**. Make two of these heart top units.

DIAGRAM 21

3 With right sides together, position a 2½-inch beige square on the corner of a 3½ × 4½-inch red check piece, as shown in **DIAGRAM 22**. Stitch diagonally on the beige square. Trim away excess fabric, leaving a ¼-inch seam allowance, as shown. Press seam allowances toward the red fabric. Repeat for the opposite corner, as shown. Make two of these heart base units.

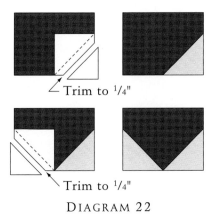

Trim to ¼"

Trim to ¼"

DIAGRAM 22

4 Sew each heart top unit to a heart base unit, as shown in **DIAGRAM 23**.

DIAGRAM 23

5 Sew the Heart blocks to the sides of the top pieced border, referring to the **QUILT ASSEMBLY DIAGRAM** on page 139. Sew this pieced border to the top of the quilt center.

Fence Border

From the cream print fabric:
• Cut one 1½ × 20-inch strip
• Cut twelve 1½ × 4½-inch pieces

From the green print fabric:
• Cut one 1½ × 20-inch strip
• Cut twelve 1½-inch squares
• Cut one 2½ × 20-inch strip

Piecing the Fence Border

1 To make the fence background units, sew the 1½ × 20-inch green and cream print strips together, as shown in **DIAGRAM 24** on the opposite page. Sew the 2½ × 20-inch green strip to the other side of the beige strip, and crosscut the strip set into eleven 1½-inch segments, as shown.

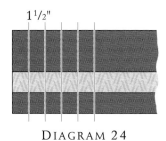

1½"

DIAGRAM 24

2 To make the 12 fence post units, position a 1½-inch green square on the corner of a 1½ × 4½-inch cream piece, as shown in DIAGRAM 25. Stitch diagonally on the green square. Trim away excess fabric, leaving a ¼-inch seam allowance, as shown. Press seam allowances toward the beige fabric.

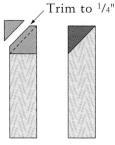

Trim to ¼"

DIAGRAM 25

3 Sew the fence post units and the fence background units together, as shown in DIAGRAM 26. Sew this border strip to the bottom of the quilt center, referring to the QUILT ASSEMBLY DIAGRAM on page 139.

Outer Borders

C U T T I N G

NOTE: The yardage given allows for the border pieces to be cut cross-grain.

From the black print fabric:
• Cut four 1½ × 44-inch strips for the inner border
• Cut four 3½-inch corner squares

From the gold/black plaid fabric:
• Cut four 3½ × 44-inch strips for the outer border

Attaching the Outer Borders

1 Measure the quilt from left to right through the middle to determine the length of the top and bottom narrow border strips. Cut two black print inner border strips to the necessary length and sew them to the top and bottom of the quilt, referring to the QUILT ASSEMBLY DIAGRAM on page 139.

2 Measure the quilt from top to bottom through the middle, including the border strips you just added, to determine the length of the inner side border strips. Cut two black print inner border strips to the

necessary length and sew them to the sides of the quilt, as shown. Press.

3 For the top and bottom outer border strips, measure as in Step 1 for the inner border. Cut the gold/black plaid fabric to the necessary length, and sew the border strips to the top and bottom of the quilt, as shown. Press.

4 For the wide side outer border strips, use the measurement taken in Step 2. Cut the gold/black plaid fabric to the necessary length. Sew the 3½-inch black print squares to the ends of these border strips and sew the wide border strips to the sides of the quilt, as shown in the QUILT ASSEMBLY DIAGRAM on page 139. Press.

Putting It All Together

1 Trim the backing and batting so they are about 4 inches larger than the quilt top.

2 Mark quilting designs on the quilt top.

3 Layer the backing, batting, and quilt top. Baste the layers together and quilt.

4 When quilting is complete, remove the basting stitches, and trim the excess backing and batting even with the quilt top.

DIAGRAM 26

Binding

NOTE: The 2¾-inch binding strips will produce a ⅜-inch-wide binding. If you want a wider or narrower binding, adjust the width of the strips you cut. (See page 216 for pointers on how to experiment with binding width.) See "Making and Attaching the Binding" on page 215 to complete your quilt.

C U T T I N G

From the red dot fabric:
• Cut four 2¾ × 44-inch strips for cross-grain binding

FOR HAND QUILTING:

🌩 *Outline quilt around each of the patchwork motifs in the quilt to make them stand out from the background.*

🌩 *In the 3 × 4-inch blocks at both the top and sides of the house, quilt vertical lines, spacing them at 1-inch intervals.*

🌩 *Choose a purchased quilting stencil with a rope design, as shown in the* QUILTING DIAGRAM, *for the outer border. The soft diagonal lines of the rope make a nice contrast to the plaid fabric in the border.*

QUILTING DIAGRAM

FOR AN UNUSUAL, *fun binding, piece together approximately 18- to 24-inch lengths of a variety of the fabrics in your quilt. If your quilt is a small one, simply cut your strips a shorter length.*

TIPS AND TRICKS

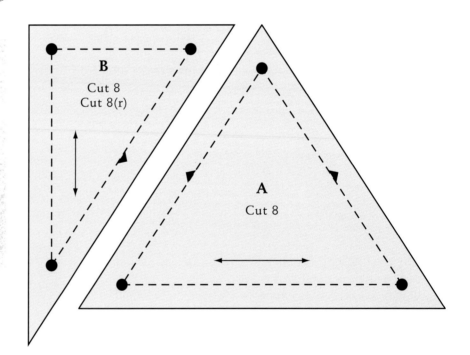

B
Cut 8
Cut 8(r)

A
Cut 8

PINE RIDGE

My fascination with antique woven wool coverlets led me to design this bold, simple, yet striking Pine Ridge quilt. I started with squares and surrounded them with repeating motifs and large Star blocks at the corners to stay in keeping with the tradition of woven coverlets. To create a rich dark center for the quilt, I used deep shades of red and green and subtle prints. The weight of the towering giant pines helps to balance the dark center blocks, and selecting dark greens for the trees adds even more visual strength to the quilt design. This quilt will shield you from chilly temperatures and add a warm glow to any room.

Size

Twin Quilt: 76 × 84 inches (unquilted)

Fabrics and Supplies

Yardage is based on 44-inch-wide fabric.

1¼ yards green print #1 fabric for trees

¾ yard green print #2 fabric for trees

¾ yard green print #3 fabric for trees

¼ yard brown print fabric for trunks

1½ yards gold print fabric for stars and quilt center points

2⅜ yards beige print fabric for background

¾ yard red print #1 fabric for patchwork center and pieced corner sections

1½ yards red print #2 fabric for patchwork center and outer border

1 yard dark green print fabric for patchwork center and inner border

⅞ yard green plaid fabric for patchwork center and pieced corner sections

1 yard gold print fabric for binding

5⅓ yards fabric for quilt backing

Quilt batting, at least 80 × 88 inches

Rotary cutter, mat, and see-through ruler with ⅛-inch markings

PINE RIDGE
Getting Ready

- READ instructions thoroughly before you begin.

- PREWASH and press fabric.

- USE ¼-inch seam allowances throughout unless directions specify otherwise.

- SEAM ALLOWANCES are included in the cutting sizes given.

- PRESS seam allowances in the direction that will create the least bulk, and whenever possible, press toward the darker fabric.

- CUTTING DIRECTIONS for each section of the quilt are given individually. If you like to cut as you go, simply follow the directions as you get to them. If you'd rather cut all your pieces at the same time, skip ahead to find the cutting sections and do all the cutting before you begin to sew. 🍃

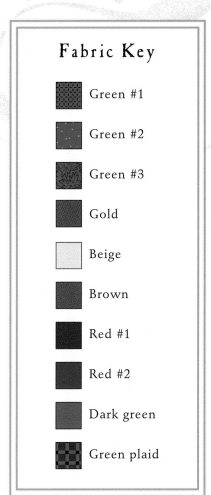

Fabric Key

- Green #1
- Green #2
- Green #3
- Gold
- Beige
- Brown
- Red #1
- Red #2
- Dark green
- Green plaid

Tree Blocks
(MAKE 14)

CUTTING

From the green print #1 fabric:
- Cut six 4½ × 8½-inch pieces
- Cut thirty-six 2½ × 8½-inch pieces

From the green print #2 fabric:
- Cut four 4½ × 8½-inch pieces
- Cut twenty-four 2½ × 8½-inch pieces

From the green print #3 fabric:
- Cut four 4½ × 8½-inch pieces
- Cut twenty-four 2½ × 8½-inch pieces

From the gold print fabric:
- Cut twenty-eight 4½-inch squares for center points

From the beige print fabric:
- Cut one hundred sixty-eight 2½-inch squares for background
- Cut four 3½ × 44-inch strips for background

From the brown print fabric:
- Cut two 2½ × 44-inch strips for trunks

Piecing the Tree Blocks

1 With right sides together, position a 4½-inch gold square on the corner of a 4½ × 8½-inch green piece, as shown in the top portion of DIAGRAM 1. Stitch diagonally on the gold square. Trim away excess fabric, leaving a ¼-inch seam allowance, as shown. Press seam allowances toward the green fabric. Repeat for the opposite corner, creating a tree top unit, as shown. Repeat for the remaining 4½ × 8½-inch green #1, green #2, and green #3 pieces.

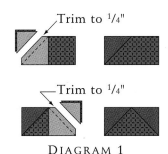

Trim to ¼"

Trim to ¼"

DIAGRAM 1

2 With right sides together, position a 2½-inch beige print square on each corner of a 2½ × 8½-inch green piece to make a tree branch unit, as shown in DIAGRAM 2 on page 146. Stitch diagonally on the beige square. Trim away excess fabric, leaving a ¼-inch seam allowance, as shown. Press seam allowances toward the green fabric. Repeat for the remaining 2½ × 8½-inch green #1, green #2, and green #3 pieces.

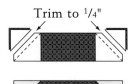

Trim to ¼"

DIAGRAM 2

3 Sew a 3½ × 44-inch beige strip to each side of a 2½ × 44-inch brown strip, as shown in DIAGRAM 3. Repeat to make two strip sets. Crosscut the strip sets into fourteen 4½-inch trunk units, as shown.

4½"

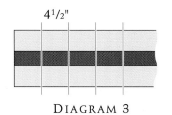

DIAGRAM 3

4 For each tree block, sew six tree branch units together. Add a matching tree top and a trunk unit, as shown in DIAGRAM 4. Press seam allowances toward the tree fabrics. At this point, the tree blocks should measure 8½ × 20½ inches.

NOTE: Make six green #1 tree blocks. Make four green #2 tree blocks. Make four green #3 tree blocks.

DIAGRAM 4

5 Sew four tree blocks together in a row, referring to DIAGRAM 5 for color placement. Repeat.

6 Sew three tree blocks together in a row, referring to DIAGRAM 5 for color placement. Repeat.

Star Blocks
(MAKE 4)

C U T T I N G

From the gold print fabric:
• Cut four 8½-inch squares for Star blocks
• Cut thirty-two 4½-inch squares for Star blocks

From the beige print fabric:
• Cut sixteen 4½-inch squares for background
• Cut sixteen 4½ × 8½-inch pieces for background

From the red print #1 fabric:
• Cut two 4½ × 44-inch strips for corner sections

From the green plaid fabric:
• Cut two 4½ × 44-inch strips for corner sections
• Cut four 4½-inch squares for corner sections

Piecing the Star Blocks

1 With right sides together, position a 4½-inch gold square on the corner of a 4½ × 8½-inch

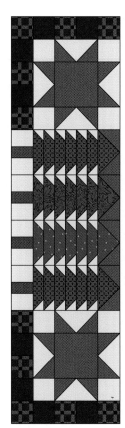

DIAGRAM 5

beige piece, as shown in DIA-GRAM 6. Stitch diagonally from corner to corner on the gold square. Trim away excess fabric, leaving a ¼-inch seam allowance, as shown. Press seam allowances toward the gold fabric. Repeat for the opposite corner. Repeat for each of the 4½-inch gold squares and 4½ × 8½-inch beige pieces.

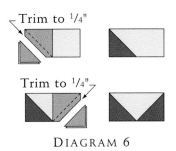

Trim to ¼"

Trim to ¼"

DIAGRAM 6

2 Sew one of these star point units to the top and one to the bottom of each 8½-inch gold square, as shown in DIAGRAM 7.

DIAGRAM 7

3 Sew a 4½-inch beige square to each end of the remaining star point units, as shown in DIAGRAM 8.

DIAGRAM 8

4 Sew a star point to each side of the Star blocks, as shown in DIAGRAM 9. At this time, the

AN ACCURATE ¼-inch seam allowance is critical for making sure that all the parts of a quilt will fit together as they should. Here's an easy way to test for accuracy. Stitch two pieces of scrap fabric together using a ¼-inch seam, as you normally would. Then measure from the stitched line to the raw edge of the fabric. If your machine does not have ¼-inch seam markings, put the needle in the down position. Using a tape measure, measure exactly ¼ inch to the right of the needle and place a piece of masking tape at that point. And when you stitch patches together, press seams and check seam allowances frequently to make sure the units you sew are the correct size. If not, make adjustments if necessary.

Star blocks should measure 16½ inches square.

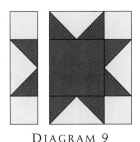

DIAGRAM 9

5 Sew the 4½ × 44-inch red #1 and green plaid strips together, alternating colors, as shown below in DIAGRAM 10. Crosscut this strip set into eight 4½-inch segments, as shown in DIAGRAM 10.

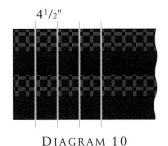

4½"

DIAGRAM 10

6 Sew one of these segments to each Star block, as shown in DIAGRAM 11. Add a 4½-inch

green square to the remaining units, and sew these units to the Star blocks.

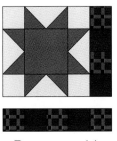

DIAGRAM 11

Patchwork Center

C U T T I N G

From the red print #1 fabric:
• Cut three 8½-inch squares

From the red print #2 fabric:
• Cut three 8½-inch squares

From the green plaid fabric:
• Cut three 8½-inch squares

From the dark green print fabric:
• Cut three 8½-inch squares

Piecing the Patchwork Center

1 Sew the 8½-inch squares together in horizontal rows, as shown in DIAGRAM 12. Sew the rows together to form the patchwork center, and press.

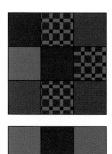

DIAGRAM 12

2 Sew the three tree-block rows to the top and bottom of the quilt center, as shown in DIAGRAM 5 on page 146. Sew a Star block to both sides of the remaining tree units, as shown, and sew these units to the sides of the quilt center.

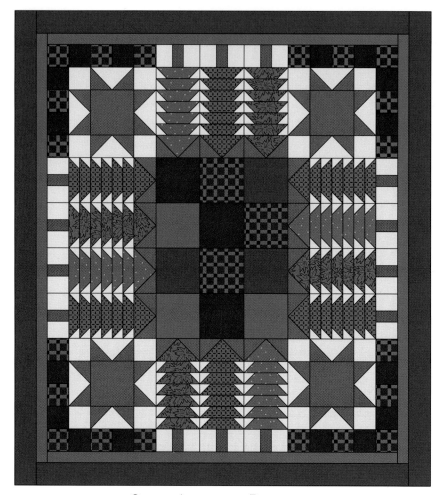

QUILT ASSEMBLY DIAGRAM

Borders

Note: The yardage given allows for the border pieces to be cut cross-grain.

From the dark green print fabric:
• Cut seven 2½ × 44-inch strips for the inner border

From the red print #2 fabric:
• Cut eight 4½ × 44-inch strips for the outer border

Attaching the Borders

1 Measure the quilt from left to right through the middle to determine the length of the top and bottom border strips. Diagonally piece and cut the dark green inner border strips to this length. Sew to the top and bottom of the quilt, as shown in the QUILT ASSEMBLY DIAGRAM, and press.

2 Measure the quilt from top to bottom through the middle to determine the length of the side border strips. Diagonally piece and cut the dark green inner

border strips to this length. Sew them to the sides of the quilt, as shown, and press.

3 For the top and bottom outer border, measure as for the inner border in Step 1. Diagonally piece and trim the red #2 fabric to the necessary lengths and sew to the top and bottom of the quilt, and press.

4 For the side outer border strips, measure as you did for the inner border in Step 2. Sew the border strips to the sides of the quilt, and press.

Putting It All Together

1 Cut the 5⅓-yard length of backing fabric in half crosswise. Remove the selvages and sew the long edges of the two lengths together. Press this seam open. Trim the backing and batting so they are about 4 inches larger than the quilt top.

2 Mark quilting designs on the quilt top.

3 Layer the backing, batting, and quilt top. Baste these layers together and quilt.

4 When quilting is complete, remove the basting stitches and trim the excess backing and batting even with the quilt top.

Binding

NOTE: The 2¾-inch bias strips will produce a ⅜-inch-wide binding. If you want a wider or narrower binding, adjust the width of the strips you cut. (See page 216 for pointers on how to experiment with binding width.) See "Making and Attaching the Binding" on page 215 to complete your quilt.

C U T T I N G

From the gold print fabric:
• Cut nine 2¾ × 44-inch strips for cross-grain binding

Quilting DESIGNS

FOR HAND QUILTING:

❧ The center blocks and outer borders are crosshatched at 2-inch intervals, which creates an old-fashioned overall design.

❧ Quilt the triangles in the tops of the trees, as shown in QUILTING DIAGRAM 1.

❧ Quilt in the ditch around the edges of the trees to make them prominent, and stitch diagonal lines 1 inch inside the edges of each piece, referring to QUILTING DIAGRAM 1.

❧ Quilt two vertical lines inside each tree trunk, as shown in QUILTING DIAGRAM 1, and quilt curved arcs to create the illusion of snow mounds beside the trunks.

❧ Quilt the stars from point to point, as shown in QUILTING DIAGRAM 2, and quilt the background squares and triangles behind the stars with two lines spaced at 1-inch intervals, following each shape.

❧ Choose a commercial stencil with a small rope design, as shown in QUILTING DIAGRAM 3, for the 2-inch dark green borders, because the soft curves are a pleasing contrast to the other straight-line designs.

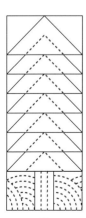

QUILTING DIAGRAM 1

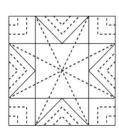

QUILTING DIAGRAM 2

QUILTING DIAGRAM 3

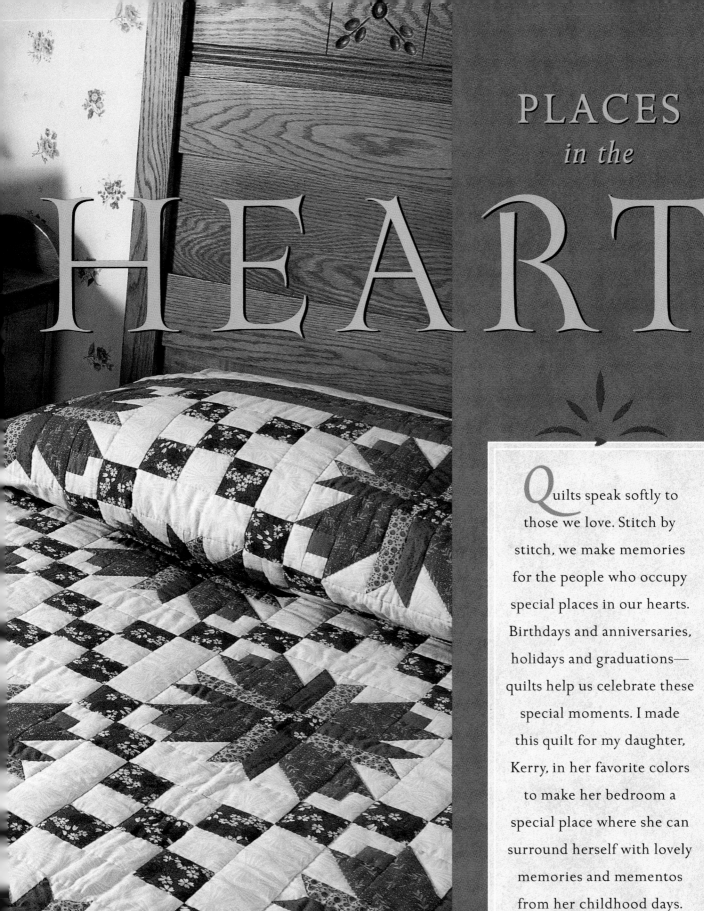

PLACES
in the
HEART

Quilts speak softly to those we love. Stitch by stitch, we make memories for the people who occupy special places in our hearts. Birthdays and anniversaries, holidays and graduations—quilts help us celebrate these special moments. I made this quilt for my daughter, Kerry, in her favorite colors to make her bedroom a special place where she can surround herself with lovely memories and mementos from her childhood days.

DAISY DAYS

The striking potted flower motifs in *Daisy Days* gain visual strength from repetition. The rectangular shape of this charming quilt makes it a perfect choice to display over a mantelpiece or above the headboard of a bed or a jelly cupboard. A beige background print effectively camouflages the seams of the flower pots and the leaves, making them almost seem to float on top of the fabric. Oversize double circles at the center of each flower lend a bold look, and the triangles in the sawtooth borders repeat the shapes of the flower petals, creating a dramatic frame for the quilt center.

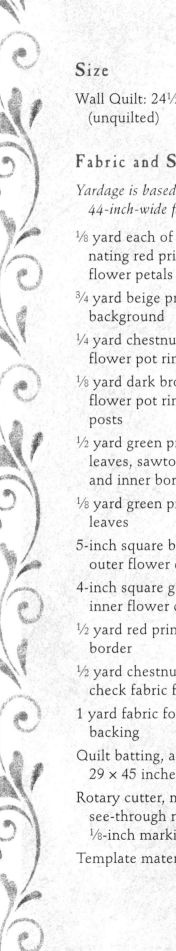

Size

Wall Quilt: 24½ × 41 inches (unquilted)

Fabric and Supplies

Yardage is based on 44-inch-wide fabric.

⅛ yard each of eight coordinating red prints for flower petals

¾ yard beige print for background

¼ yard chestnut print for flower pot rim and base

⅛ yard dark brown print for flower pot rim and corner posts

½ yard green print #1 for leaves, sawtooth border, and inner border

⅛ yard green print #2 for leaves

5-inch square black print for outer flower centers

4-inch square gold print for inner flower centers

½ yard red print for outer border

½ yard chestnut and black check fabric for binding

1 yard fabric for quilt backing

Quilt batting, at least 29 × 45 inches

Rotary cutter, mat, and see-through ruler with ⅛-inch markings

Template material

Getting Ready

- READ instructions thoroughly before you begin.

- PREWASH and press fabric.

- USE ¼-inch seam allowances throughout unless directions specify otherwise.

- SEAM ALLOWANCES are included in the cutting sizes given.

- PRESS seam allowances in the direction that will create the least bulk, and whenever possible, toward the darker fabric.

- TRACE templates A, B, and C from page 159 onto template material and cut them out.

- CUTTING DIRECTIONS for each section of the quilt are given individually. If you like to cut as you go, simply follow the directions as you get to them. If you'd rather cut all your pieces at the same time, skip ahead to find each of the cutting sections and do all the cutting before you begin to sew. ✎

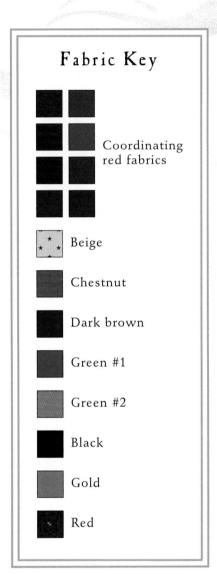

Fabric Key

Coordinating red fabrics

Beige

Chestnut

Dark brown

Green #1

Green #2

Black

Gold

Red

Flower Pot
(MAKE 3)

CUTTING

From the chestnut print fabric:
- Cut three 3½ × 8-inch rectangles
- Cut six 2-inch squares

From the dark brown print fabric:
- Cut nine 2-inch squares

From the beige print fabric:
- Cut six 3½-inch squares

Piecing
the Flower Pot

1 With right sides together, position a 3½-inch beige square at each end of a 3½ × 8-inch chestnut rectangle, as shown in DIAGRAM 1. Draw a diagonal line on the beige squares, and stitch on these lines. Trim seam allowances to ¼ inch, as shown. Press seam allowances toward the darker fabric. Make three of these units, as shown.

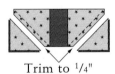

Trim to ¼"

DIAGRAM 1

2 Sew three 2-inch dark brown squares and two 2-inch chestnut squares together, alternating colors, as shown in DIAGRAM 2. Press. Make three of these units.

DIAGRAM 2

3 Sew a unit from Step 1 and a unit from Step 2 together to form each flower pot, as shown

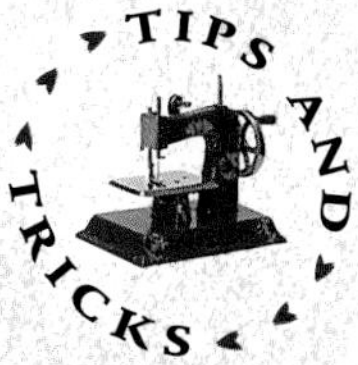

EVEN AFTER prewashing, very dark fabrics may still bleed color. To test for this, sew a piece of the fabric in question to a piece of light fabric and place them in a bowl of cool water. Soak, squeeze out the water, dry, and press the fabrics. If there is no trace of color on the lighter fabric, you should be safe. The peace of mind you'll gain from this process is worth spending the extra time to do this test.

in DIAGRAM 3. At this point, each flower pot should measure 5 × 8 inches.

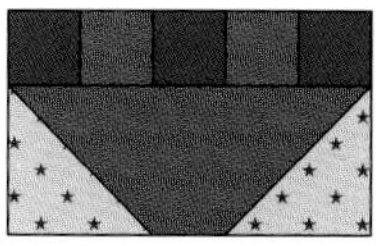

DIAGRAM 3

Leaves

CUTTING

From the green print #1 fabric:
- Cut one 2⅜ × 10-inch strip
- Cut one 2⅜ × 18-inch strip
- Cut three 2 × 3½-inch rectangles

From the green print #2 fabric:
- Cut two 2⅜ × 10-inch strips

From the beige print fabric:
- Cut one 2⅜ × 18-inch strip
- Cut one 2⅜ × 10-inch strip

Piecing the Leaves

1 With right sides together, layer the 2⅜ × 18-inch green #1 strip with the 2⅜ × 18-inch beige strip. Press, but do not sew. Cut the layered strips into six 2⅜-inch squares, as shown in DIAGRAM 4.

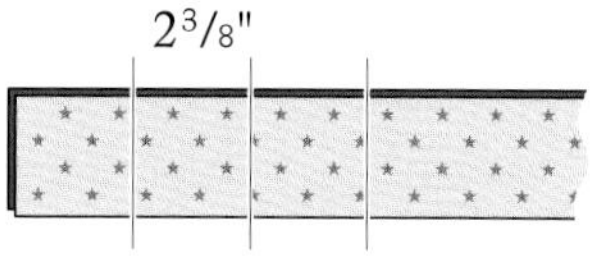

DIAGRAM 4

2 Cut the squares in half diagonally and stitch ¼ inch from the diagonal edges, as shown in DIAGRAM 5. Press seam allowances toward the green #1 fabric to form twelve 2-inch triangle-pieced squares, as shown.

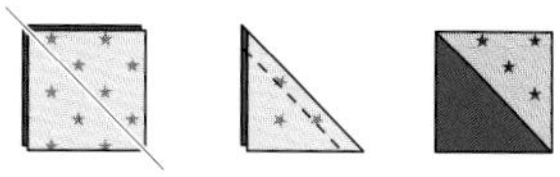

DIAGRAM 5

3 In the same manner, layer the 2⅜ × 10-inch green #2 strip with the 2⅜ × 10-inch beige strip. Cut these layered strips into three 2⅜-inch squares. Cut the squares in half diagonally and stitch ¼ inch from each diagonal edge, as shown in DIAGRAM 6. Press to form six 2-inch triangle-pieced squares.

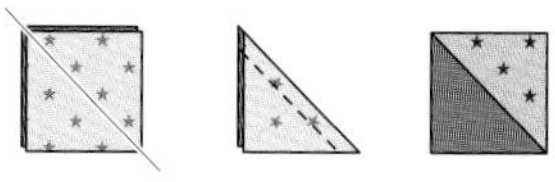

DIAGRAM 6

4 In the same manner, layer the 2⅜ × 10-inch green #1 and green #2 strips. Cut the layered strips into three 2⅜-inch squares. Cut the squares in half diagonally and stitch ¼ inch from each diagonal edge. Press to form six 2-inch triangle-pieced squares, as shown in DIAGRAM 7.

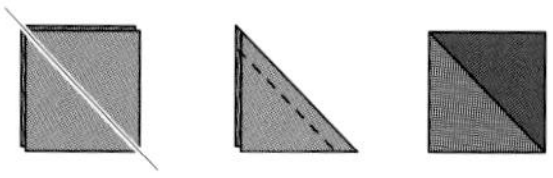

DIAGRAM 7

5 To make a left leaf unit, sew together two triangle-pieced squares from Step 2, one from Step 3, and one from Step 4, as shown in DIAGRAM 8. To make a right leaf unit, reverse the order of the triangle squares, as shown in the diagram. Make three left and three right leaf units.

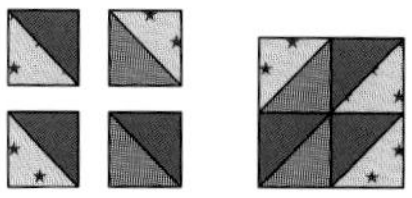

DIAGRAM 8

6 Sew these units to both sides of each 2 × 3½-inch green #1 rectangle, as shown in DIAGRAM 9. Press. Make three of these leaf sections. At this point, each leaf section should measure 3½ × 8 inches.

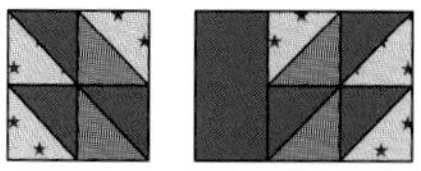

DIAGRAM 9

Quilt Center

CUTTING

From the beige print fabric:
• Cut four 2 × 8-inch rectangles
• Cut one 5 × 29-inch strip

Assembling the Quilt Center

1 Sew each of the leaf and flower pot sections together, as shown in DIAGRAM 10.

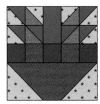

DIAGRAM 10

2 Sew the four 2 × 8-inch beige rectangles and the leaf/pot sections together, as shown in DIAGRAM 11. Press. Add the 5 × 29-inch beige strip to the top of this unit, as shown. At this point, the quilt center should measure 12½ × 29 inches.

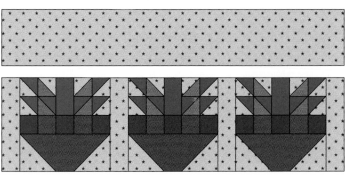

DIAGRAM 11

Flowers
(MAKE 3)

CUTTING

From the eight coordinating red print fabrics for flower petals:
• Cut a total of 24 of template A.

From the black print fabric:
• Cut three of template B, positioning the template on the wrong side of the black print fabric. Trace around template B, leaving ½ inch between each circle. Cut out the fabric circles, adding ¼-inch seam allowances.

From the gold print fabric:
• Cut three of template C in the same manner as for template B.

Piecing the Flowers

1 Fold the red print A pieces in half lengthwise, right sides together, as shown in DIAGRAM 12. Sew a ¼-inch seam along the top edge, and trim away the excess seam allowance at the point, as shown.

Trim

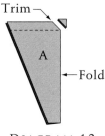

Fold

DIAGRAM 12

2 Turn each A petal right side out, and push the tips out with a blunt pencil. Press, making sure the seam lines are centered on the wrong side and both sides are symmetrical, as shown in DIAGRAM 13.

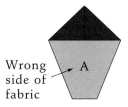

Wrong side of fabric — A

DIAGRAM 13

3 Sew eight petals together for each flower, as shown in DIAGRAM 14. Press all seam allowances in the same direction.

DIAGRAM 14

4 Referring to the QUILT ASSEMBLY DIAGRAM, position the flowers on the quilt center so that the flower petals overlap the stems and just touch the leaf units. Using matching thread, slip stitch the flowers in place.

QUILT ASSEMBLY DIAGRAM

5 To create smooth, well-rounded center circles for the flowers, run a line of basting stitches around each of the black B and gold C circles, placing these stitches halfway between the drawn line and the cut edge of each circle, as shown in DIA-GRAM **15**. After basting each circle, keep the needle and thread attached for Step 6.

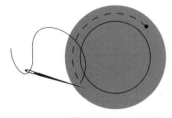

DIAGRAM 15

6 Place the template on the wrong side of each fabric circle and pull on your basting stitches, gathering the fabric over

the template, as shown in DIA-GRAM **16**. When the fabric is tight, space the gathers evenly, and make a backstitch or knot to secure the thread, as shown. Clip the thread, press the circle, and remove the paper template.

DIAGRAM 16

7 Appliqué the gold print C circles to the center of each black print B circle, referring to the QUILT ASSEMBLY DIAGRAM.

8 Appliqué the layered flower centers to the flowers, referring to the QUILT ASSEMBLY DIAGRAM.

Borders

C U T T I N G

NOTE: The yardage given allows for border pieces to be cut cross-grain.

From the green print #1 fabric:
• Cut two 2 × 29-inch strips for the inner border
• Cut two 2 × 12½-inch strips for the inner border
• Cut two 2⅜ × 44-inch strips for the sawtooth border

From the dark brown print fabric:
• Cut four 2-inch squares for the corner posts

From the beige print fabric:
• Cut two 2⅜ × 44-inch strips for the sawtooth border
• Cut four 2-inch squares for the sawtooth border

From the red print fabric:
• Cut two 3½ × 35-inch strips
for the outer border
• Cut two 3½ × 24½-inch strips
for the outer border

Attaching
the Inner Border

1 Sew the 2 × 29-inch green #1
border strips to the top and
bottom of the quilt, referring to
the QUILT ASSEMBLY DIAGRAM
on page 157. Press seam allowances toward the border.

2 Sew a 2-inch brown square
to each end of the 2 × 12½-
inch green border strips, referring
to the QUILT ASSEMBLY DIAGRAM
on page 157. Press. Sew these
border strips to the sides of the
quilt. Press seam allowances toward the border.

Piecing
the Sawtooth Border

1 Layer a 2⅜ × 44-inch green #1
strip and a 2⅜ × 44-inch beige
strip, right sides together, as you
did for the leaf sections. Press,
do not sew. Repeat with the remaining green #1 and beige strips.
Cut the layered strips into thirty-
one 2⅜-inch squares.

2 Cut the squares in half diagonally, and stitch ¼-inch
from the diagonal edges, in the
same manner as for the leaf sections. Press seam allowances toward the green fabric. Make 62
of these triangle-pieced squares.

DIAGRAM 17

3 Referring to DIAGRAM 17,
sew 21 of the triangle-pieced
squares together for each of the
top and bottom sawtooth border
strips. Sew these border strips to
the top and bottom of the quilt,
referring to the QUILT ASSEMBLY
DIAGRAM on page 157. Press
seam allowances toward the
inner border.

4 Sew ten of the triangle-
pieced squares together for
each of the side border strips, as
shown in DIAGRAM 18. Sew a
2-inch beige square to each end
of the side sawtooth border
strips, as shown. Press. Sew
these border strips to the sides of
the quilt, referring to the QUILT
ASSEMBLY DIAGRAM on page 157.
Press seam allowances toward
the inner border.

DIAGRAM 18

Attaching
the Outer Border

1 Sew the 3½ × 35-inch red
print strips to the top and
bottom of the quilt, referring to
the QUILT ASSEMBLY DIAGRAM
on page 157. Press the seam
allowances toward the outer
border.

2 Sew the 3½ × 24½-inch red
print strips to the sides of
the quilt, as shown in the QUILT

ASSEMBLY DIAGRAM on page 157.
Press seam allowances toward
the outer border.

Putting It All
Together

1 Trim the backing and batting
so they are 4 inches larger
than the quilt top dimensions.

2 Mark quilting designs on the
quilt top.

3 Layer the backing, batting,
and quilt top. Baste the layers
together and quilt.

Binding

NOTE: The 2¾-inch binding
strips will produce a ⅜-inch-
wide binding. If you want a
wider or narrower binding, adjust the width of the strips you
cut. (See page 216 for pointers on
how to experiment with binding
width.) See "Making and Attaching the Binding" on page 215
to complete your quilt.

C U T T I N G

From the chestnut and black
check binding fabric:
• Cut enough 2¾-inch bias strips
to make 150 inches of bias
binding

Quilting
DESIGNS

FOR HAND QUILTING:

Quilting in the ditch around the shapes in this quilt will help to accentuate the flower pots and make them almost "pop" off the background fabric.

Quilt the entire background in a grid of horizontal and vertical lines that are spaced 1½ inches apart. Notice that these grid lines are spaced at the same intervals as the triangle-pieced squares in the leaves and the squares in the flower pot rims. This grid will make the flower pots appear almost to float on top of the background fabric.

Quilting in the ditch in the sawtooth border will emphasize the strong design.

Quilt the outer border in a pattern of straight lines that continue outward from the seam lines in the sawtooth border.

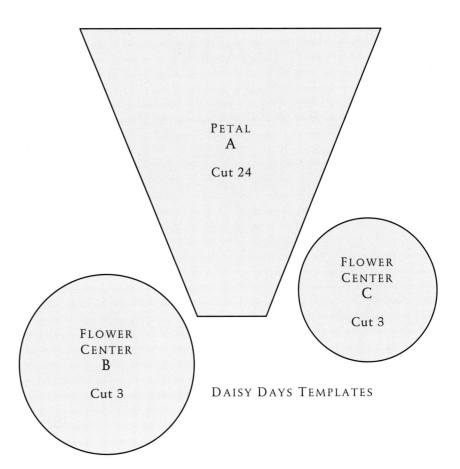

PETAL
A

Cut 24

FLOWER
CENTER
C

Cut 3

FLOWER
CENTER
B

Cut 3

DAISY DAYS TEMPLATES

MEADOW LILY

Meadow Lily has a simple block arrangement that looks more complicated than it is. I chose a creamy beige tone-on-tone print for the background and the borders to enhance the effect of the flower blocks and the single Irish Chains. The flower blocks in the borders echo the colors in the quilt center. When choosing fabrics for your own Meadow Lily quilt, you can create a pleasing color mix by selecting fabrics that share common colors and varying the scale of the prints. Bind your quilt with the border fabric to keep the focus on the colors in the center of your quilt.

Size

Bed Quilt: 72 × 92 inches (unquilted)

Finished Block: 10 inches square

Fabrics and Supplies

Yardage is based on 44-inch-wide fabric.

2 yards purple print fabric for Meadow Lily blocks and middle border

¾ yard maple print fabric for Meadow Lily block centers and inner border

4½ yards beige print fabric for background and outer borders

¾ yard light green print fabric for leaves

¾ yard dark green print fabric for leaves

1 yard purple floral print fabric for Meadow Lily block centers and Nine Patch blocks

1 yard beige print fabric for binding

5½ yards fabric for quilt backing

Quilt batting, at least 76 × 96 inches

Rotary cutter, mat, and see-through ruler with ⅛-inch markings

Getting Ready

- READ instructions thoroughly before you begin.
- PREWASH and press fabric.
- USE ¼-inch seam allowances throughout unless directions specify otherwise.
- SEAM ALLOWANCES are included in the cutting sizes given.
- PRESS seam allowances in the direction that will create the least bulk, and whenever possible, press toward the darker fabric.
- CUTTING DIRECTIONS for each section of the quilt are given individually. If you like to cut as you go, simply follow the directions as you get to them. If you'd rather cut all your pieces at the same time, skip ahead to find each of the cutting sections and do all the cutting before you begin to sew. ✎

Fabric Key

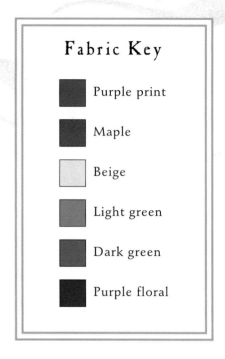

- Purple print
- Maple
- Beige
- Light green
- Dark green
- Purple floral

Meadow Lily Blocks

(MAKE 18 FULL,
4 HALF, AND
4 QUARTER BLOCKS)

CUTTING

From the purple print fabric:
- Cut six 2½ × 44-inch strips; from these strips, cut eighty-four 2½-inch squares
- Cut seven 2⅞ × 44-inch strips

From the maple print fabric:
- Cut four 1½ × 44-inch strips

From the beige print fabric:
- Cut seven 2⅞ × 44-inch strips
- Cut four 1½ × 44-inch strips
- Cut six 1½ × 44-inch strips; from these strips, cut eighty-four 1½ × 2½-inch rectangles

Piecing the Lily Units

1 With right sides together, layer a 2⅞ × 44-inch purple print strip and a 2⅞ × 44-inch beige strip. Layer the remaining purple and beige 2⅞-inch strips in the same manner. Press the strips together, but do not sew.

2 Cut the layered strips into eighty-four 2⅞-inch squares, as shown in DIAGRAM 1.

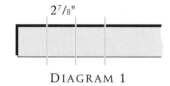

2⅞"

DIAGRAM 1

3 Cut the squares in half, as shown in DIAGRAM 2. Stitch ¼ inch from the diagonal edges, as shown. Press seam allowances toward the darker fabric to make a 2½-inch triangle-pieced square, as shown. Repeat for the remaining squares.

DIAGRAM 2

4 Sew each 1½ × 44-inch maple strip to a 1½ × 44-inch beige strip, as shown in DIAGRAM 3. Press seam allowances toward the maple fabric. Cut these strip sets into eighty-four 1½-inch segments, as shown.

1½"

DIAGRAM 3

5 Sew a 1½ × 2½-inch beige rectangle to each of the segments from Step 4, as shown in DIAGRAM 4.

DIAGRAM 4

6 For each lily unit, sew together two triangle-pieced squares, one unit from Step 5, and one 2½-inch purple print square, as shown in DIAGRAM 5. Make 84 lily units.

DIAGRAM 5

Leaf Units

CUTTING

From the light green print fabric:
• Cut ten 1½ × 44-inch strips; from these strips, cut eighty-four 1½ × 4½-inch rectangles

From the dark green print fabric:
• Cut ten 1½ × 44-inch strips; from these strips, cut eighty-four 1½ × 4½-inch rectangles

From the beige print fabric:
• Cut seven 1½ × 44-inch strips; from these strips, cut one hundred sixty-eight 1½-inch squares

From the purple floral print fabric:
• Cut two 2½ × 44-inch strips; from these strips, cut eighteen 2½-inch squares
• Cut four 1½ × 2½-inch rectangles
• Cut four 1½-inch squares

Piecing the Leaf Units

1 With right sides together, layer a 1½-inch beige square on one end of a light green 1½ × 4½-inch rectangle, as shown in DIAGRAM 6. Draw a diagonal line from corner to corner on the beige square. Stitch on this line, and trim the seam allowance to ¼ inch, as shown. Press the seam allowance toward the darker fabric. Make 84 light green leaf units, as shown.

Trim to ¼"

DIAGRAM 6

2 Repeat Step 1, using the 1½ × 4½-inch dark green rectangles and the 1½-inch beige squares, as shown in DIAGRAM 7. Make sure that the diagonal line is drawn in the *opposite* direction from the lines drawn in Step 1. Make 84 dark green leaf units, as shown.

Trim to ¼"

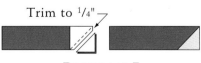

DIAGRAM 7

3 Sew the light green and dark green leaf units together to make 76 pairs, as shown in DIAGRAM 8.

DIAGRAM 8

4 Sew a leaf unit from Step 3 to both sides of a 2½-inch purple print square, as shown in DIAGRAM 9. Make 18 of these units to be used in the full Meadow Lily blocks.

DIAGRAM 9

5 Sew a light green and a dark green leaf unit to both sides of a 1½ × 2½-inch purple print rectangle, as shown in DIAGRAM 10. Make four of these units to be used in the half–Meadow Lily blocks.

DIAGRAM 10

Assembling the Meadow Lily Blocks

1 Sew together four lily units, two leaf units, and one unit from Step 4, as shown in DIA-GRAM 11. Make 18 Meadow Lily blocks, as shown. At this point, the Meadow Lily blocks should measure 10½ inches square.

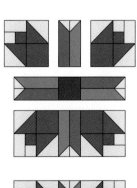

DIAGRAM 11

2 Sew together two lily units, one leaf unit, and one unit from Step 5, as shown in DIAGRAM 12. Make four half–Meadow Lily blocks, as shown. Set these blocks aside to be used for the pieced border.

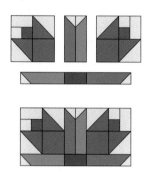

DIAGRAM 12

3 Sew together one lily unit and two leaf units, as shown in DIAGRAM 13. Make four quarter–Meadow Lily blocks, as shown. Set these blocks aside to be used for the pieced border.

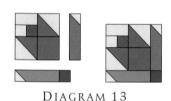

DIAGRAM 13

Nine Patch Blocks

(MAKE 17)

CUTTING

From the purple floral print fabric:
• Cut nine 2½ × 44-inch strips

From the beige print fabric:
• Cut four 2½ × 44-inch strips
• Cut four 6½ × 44-inch strips; from two of these strips, cut thirty-four 2½ × 6½-inch rectangles

Piecing the Nine Patch Blocks

1 To make Strip Set I, sew a 2½ × 44-inch purple floral strip to each side of a 2½ × 44-inch beige strip, as shown in DIAGRAM 14. Make another Strip Set I. Press seam allowances toward the darker fabric. Cut these strip sets into a total of thirty-four 2½-inch segments. NOTE: You may need to make an extra Strip Set I if your fabric is not wide enough.

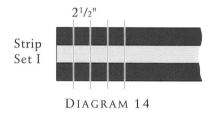

2½"

Strip Set I

DIAGRAM 14

2 To make Strip Set II, sew a 2½ × 44-inch beige strip to each side of a 2½ × 44-inch purple floral strip, as shown in DIAGRAM 15. Press seam allowances toward the darker fabric. Cut this strip set into seventeen 2½-inch segments, as shown. NOTE: You may need to make an extra Strip Set II if your fabric is not wide enough.

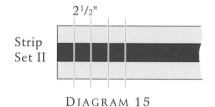

2½"

Strip Set II

DIAGRAM 15

3 Sew two Strip Set I segments and one Strip Set II segment together, matching block intersections, as shown in DIAGRAM 16. Make 17 of these nine-patch units, as shown.

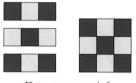

DIAGRAM 16

4 Sew a 2½ × 6½-inch beige rectangle to both sides of each nine-patch unit, as shown in DIAGRAM 17.

DIAGRAM 17

5 To make Strip Set III, sew a 2½ × 44-inch purple floral strip to both sides of a 6½ × 44-inch beige strip, as shown in DIAGRAM 18. Press seam allowances toward the darker fabric. Make two of these strip sets and cut them into thirty-four 2½-inch-wide segments, as shown.

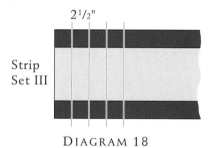

2½"

Strip Set III

DIAGRAM 18

6 Sew one segment from Step 5 to the top and one to the bottom of each nine-patch unit, as shown in DIAGRAM 19.

DIAGRAM 19

Quilt Center

1 Sew the blocks into rows, alternating Meadow Lily blocks and Nine Patch blocks, referring to the QUILT ASSEMBLY DIAGRAM. Press seam allowances toward the Nine Patch blocks.

2 Join the seven horizontal rows to make the quilt center, as shown. The quilt top should measure 50½ × 70½ inches at this time. Adjust seam allowances if necessary.

Borders

NOTE: The yardage given allows for the borders to be cut cross-grain. Press seam allowances toward the borders.

From the maple print fabric:
• Cut seven 1½ × 44-inch strips for the inner border

From the purple print fabric:
• Cut eight 2½ × 44-inch strips for the middle border

From the beige print fabric:
• Cut seven 5½ × 44-inch strips for the outer border
• Cut nine 3½ × 44-inch strips for the outer border

1 Measure the quilt from left to right through the middle to determine the length for the top and bottom inner border strips. Sew the maple inner border strips together with diagonal seams, as shown in DIAGRAM 20. Trim

QUILT ASSEMBLY DIAGRAM

seam allowances to ¼ inch, as shown. Cut two strips to the necessary length.

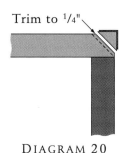

Trim to ¹⁄₄"

DIAGRAM 20

2 Sew a maple inner border strip to the top and bottom edges of the quilt, referring to the QUILT ASSEMBLY DIAGRAM.

3 Measure the quilt from top to bottom through the middle, including the border strips just added, to determine the length for the side inner border strips. Cut two maple inner border strips to the necessary length, and sew them to the sides of the quilt.

Middle Border

1 Measure the quilt from left to right through the middle to determine the length of the top and bottom middle border strips. Sew the purple middle border strips together with diagonal seams in the same manner as for the maple inner borders. Trim seam allowances to ¼ inch and cut two strips to the necessary length.

2 Sew the top and bottom purple print middle border strips to the quilt.

3 Measure the quilt from top to bottom through the middle, including the border strips just added, to determine the length for the side middle border strips. Cut two purple middle border strips to the necessary length and sew them to the sides of the quilt.

Pieced Border

1 Measure the quilt from left to right through the middle. Subtract 10 inches from this measurement to allow for a quarter–Meadow Lily block at each end. Sew the 5½-inch beige border strips together with

diagonal seams, trim seam allowances to ¼ inch, and press. Cut two strips to the necessary length.

2 Sew a quarter–Meadow Lily block to each end of these two beige border strips, as shown in DIAGRAM 21.

3 Sew the beige pieced border strips to the top and bottom edges of the quilt, referring to the QUILT ASSEMBLY DIAGRAM on page 165.

4 Measure the quilt from top to bottom through the middle, including the borders just added. Subtract 20 inches from this measurement to allow for a half–Meadow Lily block at each end. Cut two 5½-inch border strips to the necessary length.

5 Sew a half–Meadow Lily block to each end of these border strips, as shown in DIAGRAM 22.

6 Sew the beige pieced side borders to the quilt.

Outer Border

1 Measure the quilt from left to right through the middle to determine the length for the top

and bottom outer borders. Sew the 3½-inch beige outer border strips together with diagonal seams, as before, and trim the seam allowances to ¼ inch, and press. Cut two strips to the necessary length.

2 Sew the top and bottom beige outer borders to the quilt, referring to the QUILT ASSEMBLY DIAGRAM on page 165.

3 Measure the quilt from top to bottom through the middle, including the borders just added, to determine the length for the side outer borders. Cut two strips to the necessary length, and sew the beige side outer borders to the quilt.

Putting It All Together

1 Prepare the backing for the quilt by cutting the 5½-yard length of backing fabric in half crosswise to make two 2¾-yard lengths. Remove the selvages.

2 Sew the long edges of the two lengths together with one center seam. Press the seam open. Trim the backing and batting so they are about 4 inches larger than the quilt top.

DIAGRAM 21

DIAGRAM 22

3 Mark quilting designs on the quilt top.

4 Layer the backing, batting, and quilt top. Baste the layers together and quilt.

5 When quilting is complete, remove the basting stitches, and trim the excess backing and batting even with the quilt top.

Binding

NOTE: The 2¾-inch binding strips will produce a ⅜-inch binding. If you want a wider or narrower binding, adjust the width of the strips you cut. (See page 216 for pointers on how to experiment with binding width.) Refer to "Making and Attaching the Binding" on page 215 to complete your quilt.

CUTTING

From the beige print fabric:
• Cut nine 2¾ × 44-inch strips for cross-grain binding

Quilting
DESIGNS

FOR HAND QUILTING:

✿ *To decide on quilting designs that I want to use, I like to think about what should be most visually prominent in the finished quilt. For this project, I wanted the squares and clusters of flowers to advance, so I decided to emphasize each element by stitching along the seams of these pieces. Another benefit of this kind of quilting is that no marking is required.*

✿ *Quilt the purple border and the maple border as one unit, using a commercial stencil that features a 2½-inch floral motif, as shown in the* QUILTING DIAGRAM *at right.*

✿ *Cross-hatching at 2-inch intervals finishes off the border and works nicely behind the clusters of lilies at the corners.*

QUILTING DIAGRAM

In Bloom

The magic of In Bloom lies in the simplicity of its design and the repeat of the motif as it changes direction in alternating rows. Using fabrics in similar colors will impart a feeling of uniformity throughout the quilt, and a variety of two-color and tone-on-tone prints will hold the viewer's interest. Muslin for the background and borders allows the flowers and the grid lattice-work to remain the focal features. Because the pieces of this quilt are large and the construction is uncomplicated, you can piece the blocks very quickly and soon have a bed-size quilt ready for the quilt frame.

Size

Bed quilt: 90 × 102 inches (unquilted)

Finished Block: 9 inches square

Fabrics and Supplies

Yardage is based on 44-inch-wide fabric.

¾ yard *each* of assorted gold print, purple print, and pink print fabrics for flowers

1⅝ yards dark green print fabric for leaves

7 yards muslin for background

2 yards medium green print fabric for lattice

1 yard fabric for binding

8 yards fabric for quilt backing

Quilt batting, at least 94 × 106 inches

Rotary cutter, mat, and see-through ruler with ⅛-inch markings

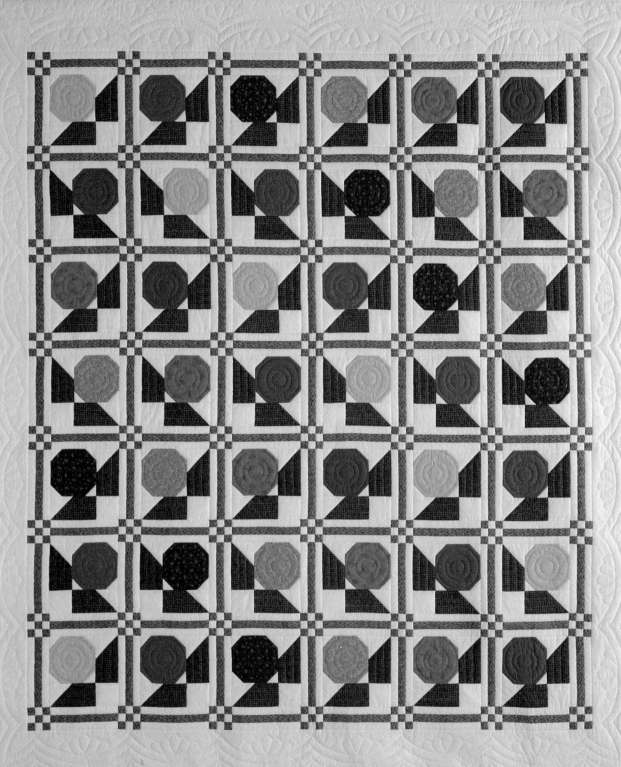

Getting Ready

- READ instructions thoroughly before you begin.
- PREWASH and press fabric.
- USE ¼-inch seam allowances throughout unless directions specify otherwise.
- SEAM ALLOWANCES are included in the cutting sizes given.
- PRESS seam allowances in the direction that will create the least bulk, and whenever possible, press toward the darker fabric.
- CUTTING DIRECTIONS for each section of the quilt are given individually. If you like to cut as you go, simply follow the directions as you get to them. If you'd rather cut all your pieces at the same time, skip ahead to find each of the cutting sections and do all the cutting before you begin to sew. 🍃

Fabric Key

Flower prints

Dark green

Medium green

Muslin

Flower Blocks

(MAKE 42 TOTAL—14 FROM EACH COLOR OF FABRIC)

C U T T I N G

From the pink print fabrics:
- Cut a total of three 6½ × 44-inch strips; from these strips, cut fourteen 6½-inch squares

From the purple print fabrics:
- Cut a total of three 6½ × 44-inch strips; from these strips, cut fourteen 6½-inch squares

From the gold print fabrics:
- Cut a total of three 6½ × 44-inch strips; from these strips, cut fourteen 6½-inch squares

From the dark green print fabric:
- Cut fourteen 3½ × 44-inch strips; from these strips, cut eighty-four 3½ × 6½-inch rectangles

From the muslin:
- Cut nine 2 × 44-inch strips; from these strips, cut one hundred sixty-eight 2-inch squares
- Cut eleven 3½ × 44-inch strips; from these strips, cut one hundred twenty-six 3½-inch squares

Piecing the Flower Blocks

1 With right sides together, position a 2-inch muslin square at each corner of a 6½-inch pink square, as shown in DIAGRAM 1. Draw a diagonal line from corner to corner on each muslin square, and stitch on these lines. Trim seam allowances to ¼-inch, as shown, and press seam allowances toward the pink fabric. Referring to DIAGRAM 1, make 14 of these units using gold squares, 14 using purple squares, and 14 using pink squares.

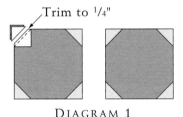

Trim to ¼"

DIAGRAM 1

2 With right sides together, position a 3½-inch muslin square on the corner of a 3½ × 6½-inch dark green rectangle, as shown in DIAGRAM 2. Draw a diagonal line from corner to corner on the muslin square, as shown, and stitch on this line. Trim seam allowances to ¼-inch, as shown, and press toward the dark green fabric. Repeat to make 42 of these left leaf units.

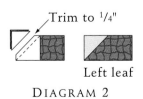

Trim to ¼"

Left leaf

DIAGRAM 2

3 Repeat Step 2, this time re-
versing the direction of the
seam, as shown in DIAGRAM 3.
Make 42 of these right leaf units.

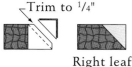

Right leaf
DIAGRAM 3

4 Sew a left leaf unit to a
flower unit, as shown in DI-
AGRAM 4. Press seam allowances
toward the leaf unit. Repeat for
all 42 flower units.

DIAGRAM 4

5 Sew a 3½-inch muslin
square to each of the right
leaf units, as shown in DIAGRAM
5. Press seam allowances toward
the leaf units.

DIAGRAM 5

6 Sew a right leaf unit created
in Step 5 to each of the 42
flower units, as shown in DIA-
GRAM 6. At this point, the
Flower blocks should measure
9½ inches square.

DIAGRAM 6

Lattice Strips

CUTTING

From the medium green print
fabric:
• Cut twenty-five 1½ × 44-inch
strips

From the muslin:
• Cut fifty 1½ × 44-inch strips

Piecing
the Lattice Strips

Sew a 1½ × 44-inch muslin strip
to both sides of a 1½ × 44-inch
medium green strip, as shown in
DIAGRAM 7. Press seam allowances toward the green strip. Sew
the remaining medium green and
muslin strips together in the same
manner to make 25 strip sets.
Crosscut the strip sets into a total
of 97 segments, each 9½ inches
wide, as shown.

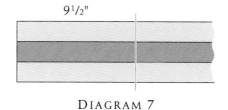

DIAGRAM 7

Nine-Patch
Lattice Posts

CUTTING

From the medium green print
fabric:
• Cut ten 1½ × 44-inch strips

From the muslin:
• Cut eight 1½ × 44-inch strips

Piecing
the Nine-Patch
Lattice Posts

1 To make Strip Set I, sew a
1½ × 44-inch medium green
strip to both sides of a 1½ × 44-
inch muslin strip, as shown in
DIAGRAM 8. Press seam allowances toward the green strip.
Make a total of four of Strip Set
I, and crosscut them into a total
of 112 segments, each 1½ inches
wide, as shown.

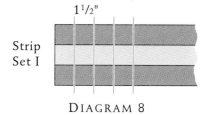

DIAGRAM 8

2 To make Strip Set II, sew a
1½ × 44-inch muslin strip to
both sides of a 1½ × 44-inch
medium green print strip, as
shown in DIAGRAM 9. Press
seam allowances toward the
green strip. Make two of Strip
Set II, and crosscut them into 56
segments, each 1½ inches wide,
as shown.

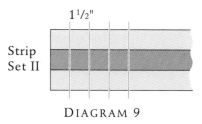

DIAGRAM 9

3 Sew a Strip Set I segment to both sides of a Strip Set II segment, as shown in DIAGRAM 10. Press. Make 56 nine-patch lattice posts, as shown.

DIAGRAM 10

Quilt Center

1 Referring to the QUILT ASSEMBLY DIAGRAM for color placement, sew together a horizontal row of six Flower blocks alternating with seven lattice strip segments. Refer to the QUILT ASSEMBLY DIAGRAM to determine which direction the Flower blocks should face within each row. Make seven of these horizontal rows. Press seam allowances toward the Flower blocks.

2 To make the lattice strips between the rows of Flower blocks, sew together a horizontal row of seven nine-patch lattice posts and six lattice segments, referring to the QUILT ASSEMBLY DIAGRAM. Make eight of these horizontal lattice strips. Press seam allowances toward the nine-patch lattice posts.

3 Referring to the QUILT ASSEMBLY DIAGRAM, sew the horizontal flower rows and horizontal lattice strips together to form the quilt center. Press.

Border

CUTTING

NOTE: The yardage given allows for the border pieces to be cut cross-grain.

From the muslin:
• Cut twelve 8 × 44-inch strips

Attaching the Border

1 Measure the quilt from left to right through the middle to determine the length of the top and bottom border strips. For

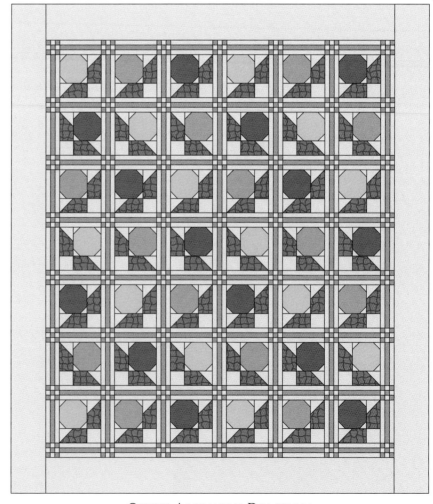

QUILT ASSEMBLY DIAGRAM

each of the top and bottom border strips, piece together three muslin border strips with diagonal seams, and cut them to the necessary length. For more information on diagonal seams, see page "Border Basics" on page 211. Sew these border strips to the top and bottom of the quilt. Press seam allowances toward the border.

2 Measure the quilt from top to bottom through the middle, including the borders you just added, to determine the length of the side border strips. For each of the side border strips, piece together three muslin strips with diagonal seams, and cut them to the necessary length. Sew these border strips to the sides of the quilt. Press seam allowances toward the border.

Putting It All Together

1 Cut the 8-yard length of backing fabric in thirds crosswise to make three 2⅔-yard pieces. Remove the selvages and sew the long edges of the lengths together. Press these seams open. Trim the backing and batting so

they are about 4 inches larger than the quilt top dimensions.

2 Mark quilting designs on the quilt top.

3 Layer the backing, batting, and quilt top. Baste the layers together and quilt.

4 When quilting is complete, remove the basting stitches, and trim the excess backing and batting even with the quilt top.

Binding

NOTE: The 2¾-inch binding strips will produce a ⅜-inch-wide binding. If you want a wider or narrower binding, adjust the width of the strips you cut. (See page 216 for pointers on how to experiment with binding width.) See "Making and Attaching the Binding" on page 215 to complete your quilt.

C U T T I N G

From the binding fabric:
• Cut ten 2¾ × 44-inch strips for cross-grain binding

Quilting DESIGNS

FOR HAND QUILTING:

🌸 *Choose quilting designs that will enhance the shapes of the flowers in this quilt. Notice how the concentric circles make the snowball blocks appear rounder than they are.*

🌸 *Channel quilting in the leaves accentuates the straight lines and acts as a welcome contrast to the circular motion of the blooms in the Flower blocks.*

🌸 *Quilting in the ditch beside the green pieces in the lattice gridwork makes those green pieces seem more visually prominent.*

🌸 *Cross-hatching in the borders expresses the same feeling of simplicity as in the design of this quilt.*

STICKS AND STONES

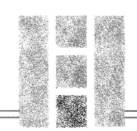

Sticks and Stones has a cheerful, warm childlike quality, and it makes a great "get it done in a hurry" project. All it takes are six coordinating fabrics; one of these should be much lighter than the other five, to be used for the background of the Stones blocks. Notice that the stones fabric in the center of these blocks is echoed in the border. This repetition helps to guide the eye outward from the center to the edges of the quilt. The diagonally striped border travels around the quilt, adding visual movement without the need for complicated piecing.

Size

Bed Quilt: 78 × 90 inches (unquilted)

Finished Block: 6 inches square

Fabrics and Supplies

Yardage is based on 44-inch-wide fabric.

1 yard *each* of three coordinating print fabrics for Sticks blocks

2¾ yards gold print fabric for Stones blocks and corner squares

1½ yards blue print fabric for Stones block centers and outer border

1¼ yards red print fabric for outer border

⅞ yard red print fabric for binding

5½ yards fabric for quilt backing

Quilt batting, at least 82 × 94 inches

Rotary cutter, mat, and see-through ruler with ⅛-inch markings

Getting Ready

- READ instructions thoroughly before you begin.
- PREWASH and press fabric.
- USE ¼-inch seam allowances throughout unless directions specify otherwise.
- SEAM ALLOWANCES are included in the cutting sizes given.
- PRESS seam allowances in the direction that will create the least bulk, and whenever possible, press toward the darker fabric.
- CUTTING DIRECTIONS for each section of the quilt are given individually. If you like to cut as you go, simply follow the directions as you get to them. If you'd rather cut all your pieces at the same time, skip ahead to find each of the cutting sections and do all the cutting before you begin to sew. 🍃

Fabric Key

- Coordinating fabrics
- Gold
- Blue
- Red

Sticks Blocks
(MAKE 72)

CUTTING

From each of the three coordinating print fabrics:
- Cut twelve 2½ × 44-inch strips

Piecing the Sticks Blocks

Sew three 2½ × 44-inch coordinating print strips together to make a strip set, as shown in DIAGRAM 1. Make 12 of these strip sets. Press all seam allowances in the same direction. Crosscut the strip sets into seventy-two 6-½-inch segments, creating the Sticks blocks. Check

IF YOU are a beginner, avoid being tempted by a project that is too advanced and complicated. Rather, try to select a smaller project or one that has just a few design elements, which will allow you to gain confidence. Sticks and Stones is a perfect project for a beginning quilter.

TIPS AND TRICKS

to make sure that each block is 6½ inches square.

6½"

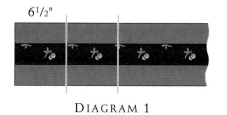

DIAGRAM 1

Stones Blocks
(MAKE 71)

CUTTING

From the gold print fabric:
- Cut thirty-four 2½ × 44 strips; from 24 of these strips, cut 142 rectangles, each 2½ × 6½ inches

From the blue print fabric:
- Cut five 2½ × 44-inch strips

Piecing the Stones Blocks

1 With right sides together, sew a 2½ × 44-inch gold strip to both sides of a 2½ × 44-inch blue print strip, as shown in DIAGRAM 2. Make five of these strip sets. Press seam allowances

toward the blue fabric. Crosscut the strip sets into seventy-one 2½-inch segments, as shown.

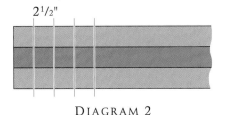

2½"

DIAGRAM 2

2 With right sides together, sew a 2½ × 6½-inch gold rectangle to both sides of the segments made in Step 1, creating the Stones blocks, as shown in DIAGRAM 3. Press seam allowances toward the gold fabric. At this point, the Stones blocks should measure 6½ inches square.

DIAGRAM 3

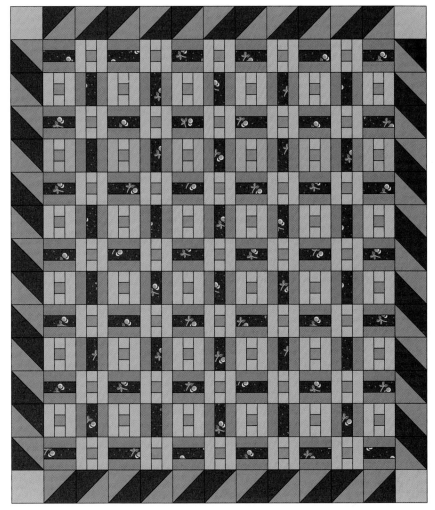

QUILT ASSEMBLY DIAGRAM

Quilt Center

1 Sew the blocks into 13 horizontal rows of 11 blocks each. Alternate the Sticks blocks and Stones blocks in each row, as shown in the QUILT ASSEMBLY DIAGRAM. Press seam allowances toward the Stones blocks.

2 Sew the 13 horizontal rows together. The quilt center should measure 66½ × 78½ inches. If necessary, trim seam allowances so that the pieced border will fit.

Border

C U T T I N G

NOTE: The yardage given allows for border pieces to be cut cross-grain.

From the red print fabric:
• Cut five 6⅞ × 44-inch strips

From the blue print fabric:
• Cut five 6⅞ × 44-inch strips

From the gold print fabric:
• Cut four 6½-inch squares

Piecing the Border

1 With right sides together, layer the 6⅞ × 44-inch red strips and the 6⅞ × 44-inch blue strips. Press together, but do not sew. Layer the remaining strips in the same manner.

2 Cut the layered strips into twenty-four 6⅞-inch squares. Cut the squares in half diagonally, as shown in DIAGRAM 4 on page 178. Sew a ¼-inch seam along the diagonal edge to form 48 triangle-pieced squares, as shown.

DIAGRAM 4

3 Sew 11 triangle-pieced squares together for the top border strip and 11 for the bottom border strip, referring to the QUILT ASSEMBLY DIAGRAM on page 177. Sew the top and bottom border strips to the quilt, and press.

4 Sew 13 triangle-pieced squares together for each side border. Add a 6½-inch gold print corner square to both ends of the side border strips, referring to the QUILT ASSEMBLY DIAGRAM on page 177. Sew the side border strips to the quilt, and press.

Putting It All Together

1 Prepare the backing for the quilt by cutting the 5½-yard length of backing in half crosswise to make two 2¾-yard lengths. Remove the selvages.

2 Sew the long edges of the two lengths together. Press this seam allowance open. Trim backing and batting so they are about 4 inches larger than the quilt top.

3 Mark quilting designs on the quilt top.

4 Layer the backing, batting, and quilt top. Baste the layers together and quilt.

5 When quilting is complete, remove the basting stitches, and trim the excess backing and batting even with the quilt top.

Binding

NOTE: The 2¾-inch binding strips will produce a ⅜-inch-wide binding. If you want a wider or narrower binding, adjust the width of the strips you cut. (See page 216 for pointers on how to experiment with binding width.) See "Making and Attaching the Binding" on page 215 to complete your quilt.

C U T T I N G

From the red print fabric:
• Cut nine 2¾ × 44-inch strips for cross-grain binding

Quilting DESIGNS

FOR MACHINE QUILTING:

❧ *Use a large pattern of meander quilting over the entire surface of this quilt to enhance the simple patchwork blocks and to allow you to finish it quickly.*

FOR HAND QUILTING:

❧ *Another option is to quilt in the ditch of the patchwork blocks to accentuate the individual "sticks" and "stones." If you elect this option, quilting in the ditch of the diagonal border seams will also be very effective.*

❧ *In the corner border blocks, quilt a square shape in the center to echo the "stones" in the pieced blocks, or simply quilt diagonal lines from corner to corner in both directions.*

RAINING CATS AND DOGS

The colors in Raining Cats and Dogs are youthful, happy, and more vivid than pastels, yet with a soft and comforting feel. I often think of them as "Dick and Jane" colors because it's so easy for many of us to visualize the colorful pages of those books. The cats' and dogs' heads are actually adaptations from a pair of pot holders that originally belonged to my grandmother. I decided to set them against a plaid background fabric that contributes to a whimsical country look without competing with the other prints in the quilt.

Size

Crib Quilt: 48 × 58 inches (unquilted)

Fabrics and Supplies

Yardage is based on 44-inch-wide fabric.

1 yard red floral print fabric for inner blocks and corner squares

1 yard blue print fabric for lattice strips

2/3 yard gold print #1 fabric for lattice posts and cat heads

3/4 yard green print fabric for inner border and corner squares

1¼ yards gold check fabric for background squares

3/8 yard red print #1 fabric for cat bows

1/4 yard gold print #2 fabric for dog noses

3/8 yard red print #2 fabric for dog ears/eyes

1/3 yard green floral print fabric for dog bows

1/8 yard black fabric for dog and cat eyes/noses

5/8 yard green print fabric for binding

3 yards fabric for quilt backing

Quilt batting, at least 52 × 62 inches

1 skein black embroidery floss

Freezer paper

Rotary cutter, mat, and see-through ruler with 1/8-inch markings

RAINING CATS AND DOGS

Getting Ready

- READ instructions thoroughly before you begin.

- PREWASH and press fabric.

- USE ¼-inch seam allowances throughout unless directions specify otherwise.

- SEAM ALLOWANCES are included in the cutting sizes given.

- PRESS seam allowances in the direction that will create the least bulk, and whenever possible, press toward the darker fabric.

- TRACE the templates on pages 186–189 onto freezer paper. For more information on the freezer paper appliqué method of hand appliqué, see page 209.

- CUTTING DIRECTIONS for each section of the quilt are given individually. If you like to cut as you go, simply follow the directions as you get to them. If you'd rather cut all your pieces at the same time, skip ahead to find each of the cutting sections and do all the cutting before you begin to sew. ✍

Fabric Key

- Red floral
- Blue
- Gold #1
- Gold #2
- Green print
- Gold check
- Red #1
- Red #2
- Green floral
- Black

Quilt Center

CUTTING

From the red floral print fabric:
- Cut four 6½-inch squares
- Cut two 8½ × 44-inch strips; from these strips, cut two 8½-inch squares and six 6½ × 8½-inch pieces

From the blue print fabric:
- Cut four 2½ × 44-inch strips; from these strips, cut seven 2½ × 8½-inch pieces and ten 2½ × 6½-inch pieces

From the gold print #1 fabric:
- Cut six 2½-inch squares

Assembling the Quilt Center

1 With right sides together, sew a 2½ × 6½-inch blue lattice strip to both sides of a 6½ × 8½-inch red floral piece, as shown in DIAGRAM 1. Sew a 6½-inch red floral square to both sides of the blue lattice strips, as shown. Make two of these units.

DIAGRAM 1

2 With right sides together, sew a 2½ × 8½-inch blue lattice strip to both sides of a 8½-inch red floral square, as shown in DIAGRAM 2. Then sew

a 6½ × 8½ red floral piece to both sides of the blue lattice strips, as shown. Make two of these units.

DIAGRAM 2

3 To construct the horizontal lattices, sew a 2½-inch gold #1 square to each side of a 2½ × 8½-inch blue lattice strip, as shown in DIAGRAM 3 on page 182. Sew a 2½ × 6½-inch blue lattice strip to the outer side of the gold squares, as shown. Make three of these horizontal lattices.

DIAGRAM 3

4 Sew the block strips and horizontal lattices together to form the quilt center, referring to the QUILT ASSEMBLY DIAGRAM. At this point, the quilt top should measure 24½ × 34½ inches.

IF YOU have extra blocks left over from a project or extra fabric cut for additional blocks, save them and add other leftover blocks to them to create your very own sampler.

TIPS AND TRICKS

QUILT ASSEMBLY DIAGRAM

Inner Border

CUTTING

From the green print fabric:
• Cut four 4½ × 44-inch strips

Attaching the Inner Border

1 Measure the quilt from left to right through the center to determine the length of the top and bottom border strips. Cut the green print inner border strips to this length and sew them to the top and bottom of the quilt, referring to the QUILT ASSEMBLY DIAGRAM.

2 Measure the quilt from top to bottom through the middle, including the border strips just added, to determine the length of the side border strips. Cut the two remaining green print inner border strips to this length and sew them to the sides of the quilt, referring to the QUILT ASSEMBLY DIAGRAM.

Outer Border

CUTTING

NOTE: Templates for the cat and dog heads are found on pages 186–189. Read appliqué instructions before cutting the pieces.

From the gold check fabric:
• Cut fourteen 8½-inch squares

From the gold print #1 fabric:
• Cut seven cat heads

From the red print #1 fabric:
• Cut seven cat bows

From the gold print #2 fabric:
• Cut seven dog nose sections

From the red print #2 fabric:
• Cut seven dog ears/eyes sections for the right side of each dog head and seven for the left side of each dog head

From the green floral print fabric:
• Cut seven dog bows

From the blue print fabric:
• Cut eighteen 2½ × 8½-inch strips

From the red floral print fabric:
• Cut one 4½ × 44-inch strip

From the green print fabric:
• Cut one 4½ × 44-inch strip

From the black fabric:
• Cut seven right eyes, seven left eyes, and seven noses for the cats
• Cut seven right eyes, seven left eyes, and seven noses for the dogs

Appliquéing the Cat and Dog Blocks

1 Using the freezer paper method for hand appliqué, prepare the appliqué pattern pieces. For more information on the freezer paper method, see page 209.

2 Transfer the head and bow shapes for the cats and dogs on pages 186–189 onto the 8½-inch gold check background squares by positioning each square over one of the tracing diagrams on pages 186–189. Make sure the cat or dog shape is centered and at least ¼ inch away from the raw edges of the fabric to allow for seam allowances. Lightly trace the cat and dog shapes onto the fabric. If you cannot see the lines of the tracing diagram through your fabric, photocopy the tracing diagram. Then place both the background square and tracing diagram over a light box or tape them on a window, and trace the shapes. Trace seven cat heads and seven dog heads onto the background squares.

3 To appliqué a cat block, position and pin a gold #1 cat head on a background square, aligning it with the traced lines. With matching thread, appliqué the cat head by hand with small slip stitches. If you are using the

freezer paper method, needle turn the seam allowance under the edge of the paper. The only exception to this technique is in any area that will be overlapped by another fabric, such as the lower edge of the cat head. Clip curves as needed and remove the freezer paper. For more information on removing the freezer paper, see "Freezer Paper Method" on page 209.

4 Position and pin the red #1 bow on the background square, aligning it with the traced lines, and appliqué it in place in the same manner. Remove the freezer paper.

5 Repeat Steps 3 and 4 for the remaining six cat blocks.

6 To appliqué a dog block, position and pin a gold #2 dog nose section to a background square, aligning it with the traced lines. Appliqué the top edge only. The remaining edges will be overlapped by the ears/eyes and bow. Remove the freezer paper.

7 Place a green floral bow on the background square, aligning it with the traced lines, and appliqué with small slip stitches. Remove the freezer paper.

8 Place the left and right red #2 ears/eyes sections on the background squares, aligning them with the traced lines, and appliqué. Remove the freezer paper.

9 To trace the cat and dog eyes, nose, and embroidery lines from pages 186–189 onto the faces, turn each block over

and carefully trim away the back layer of fabric to approximately ¼ inch inside your stitching lines. When the background fabric is trimmed away, it will be easy to lightly trace the facial features onto each face.

10 Appliqué the eyes and noses in place on each dog and cat head. With two strands of black embroidery floss, stitch around the cat and dog eyes, noses, bows, and heads by hand with the outline stitch. For more information on the outline stitch, see page 210.

Assembling the Outer Border

1 For the top and bottom outer border strips, sew together three appliqué blocks and four 2½ × 8½-inch blue pieces, alternating the position of the cat and dog heads, as shown in **DIAGRAM 4**. Sew these border strips to the top and bottom of the quilt.

Top border

Bottom border
DIAGRAM 4

2 For the side outer border strips, sew four appliqué blocks and five 2½ × 8½-inch blue pieces together, as shown in **DIAGRAM 5** on page 184.

Side borders
DIAGRAM 5

3 To make the corner squares, sew a 4½ × 44-inch red floral strip and a 4½ × 44-inch green print strip together, and cut into eight 4½-inch segments, as shown in DIAGRAM 6.

4 Sew the segments together in pairs to make four corner squares, as shown in DIAGRAM 7.

5 Sew the corner squares to the ends of the side borders, as shown in DIAGRAM 8, and sew the side border strips to the quilt.

Putting It All Together

1 Cut the 3-yard length of backing fabric in half crosswise. Remove the selvages and

sew the long edges of the two lengths together. Press this seam open. Trim the backing and batting so they are about 4 inches larger than the quilt top.

2 Mark quilting designs on the quilt top.

3 Layer the backing, batting, and quilt top. Baste the layers together and quilt.

4 When quilting is complete, remove the basting stitches and trim the excess backing and batting even with the quilt top.

Binding

NOTE: The 2¾-inch strips will produce a ⅜-inch-wide binding. If you want a wider or narrower

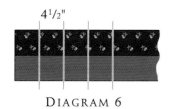

4½"

DIAGRAM 6

DIAGRAM 7

DIAGRAM 8

binding, adjust the width of the strips you cut. (See page 216 for pointers on how to experiment with binding width.) See "Making and Attaching the Binding" on page 215 to complete your quilt.

From the green print fabric:
• Cut six 2¾ × 44-inch strips for cross-grain binding

Quilting DESIGNS

FOR HAND QUILTING:

☁ *The quilting designs selected for Raining Cats and Dogs reflect the design of the quilt top, which helps to maintain a feeling of sweet simplicity in the quilt.*

☁ *Quilt the plain center blocks in a 2-inch straight grid, echoing the overall design of the center squares.*

☁ *Quilt the lattice strips in the ditch of the seams.*

☁ *Choose a very simple 3-inch floral quilting stencil for the green inner border.*

☁ *Outline quilt around the appliqués and inside the stitched details to make the dogs and cats stand out from the background fabric and give them greater visual dimension and personality.*

OPTIONAL MACHINE APPLIQUÉ

✐ MACHINE APPLIQUÉ is a quick and easy way to add the appliqué pieces to this quilt. It also stands up well to repeated washings. You will need a machine that has a buttonhole or zigzag stitch.

STEP 1

1 LAY THE FUSIBLE WEB over the appliqué pattern pieces on pages 186–189 with the paper side up, and trace the shapes. Cut roughly ½ inch outside the traced lines, as shown in Step 1.

Trace second
line here

2 ON EACH SHAPE, draw a line about ⅜ inch inside the first line you traced, as shown in Step 2.

STEP 2

3 WHEN FUSING A LARGE SHAPE, it is a good idea to fuse only the edges so that the large shape will not look stiff in your finished quilt. To make this easier, cut away the fusible web on this second line to leave the center of each shape open, as shown in Step 3.

Cut fusible
web away

STEP 3

4 WITH A HOT DRY IRON, following the manufacturer's directions for your brand of fusible web, press the coated side of each fusible web shape to the wrong side of its fabric, as shown in Step 4, and let the shapes cool.

5 CUT OUT EACH SHAPE along the first line you traced, except at any area where there will be another shape overlapping it. At these areas, leave about ¼ inch of extra fabric outside the turning line, as shown in Step 5, so that the appliqué shape can be layered underneath another shape. Peel off the paper backing from each appliqué shape.

STEP 4

6 POSITION THE APPLIQUÉ shape on the block. Fuse the remaining shapes, then layer, and press.

7 SET YOUR MACHINE to the buttonhole or zigzag/satin stitch. You may need to place a paper towel under the background block to stabilize it before machine appliquéing. It is a good idea to stitch a sample to make sure you're getting the results you want. After you have finished appliquéing, tear away the paper towel.

8 MACHINE APPLIQUÉ the eyes and nose in place.

9 USING TWO STRANDS of black embroidery floss, stitch the cats' and dogs' ears, mouths, whiskers, and bow knot details by hand with the outline stitch.

Overlapping area
STEP 5

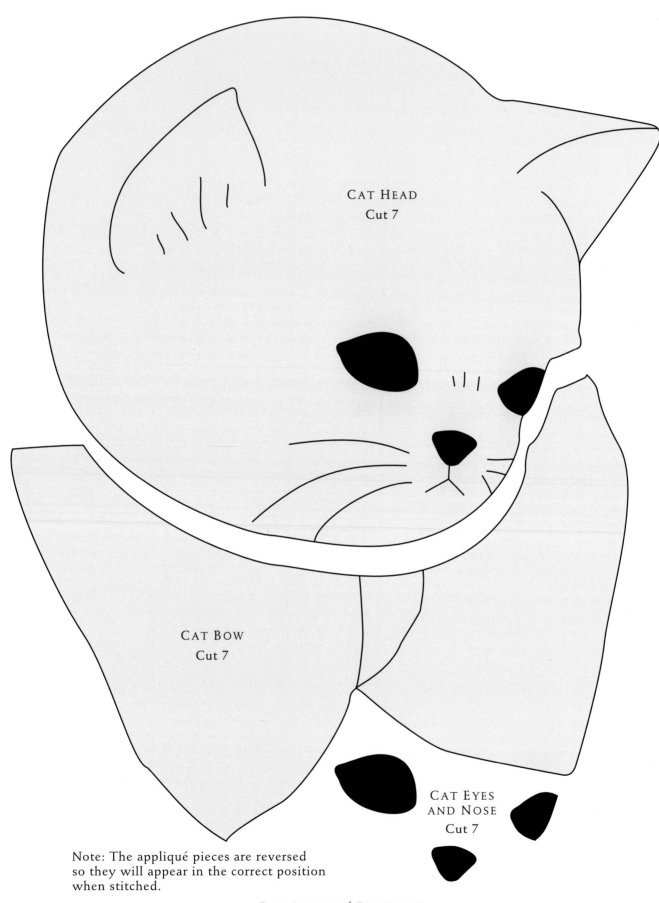

CAT HEAD
Cut 7

CAT BOW
Cut 7

CAT EYES
AND NOSE
Cut 7

Note: The appliqué pieces are reversed
so they will appear in the correct position
when stitched.

CAT APPLIQUÉ PATTERNS

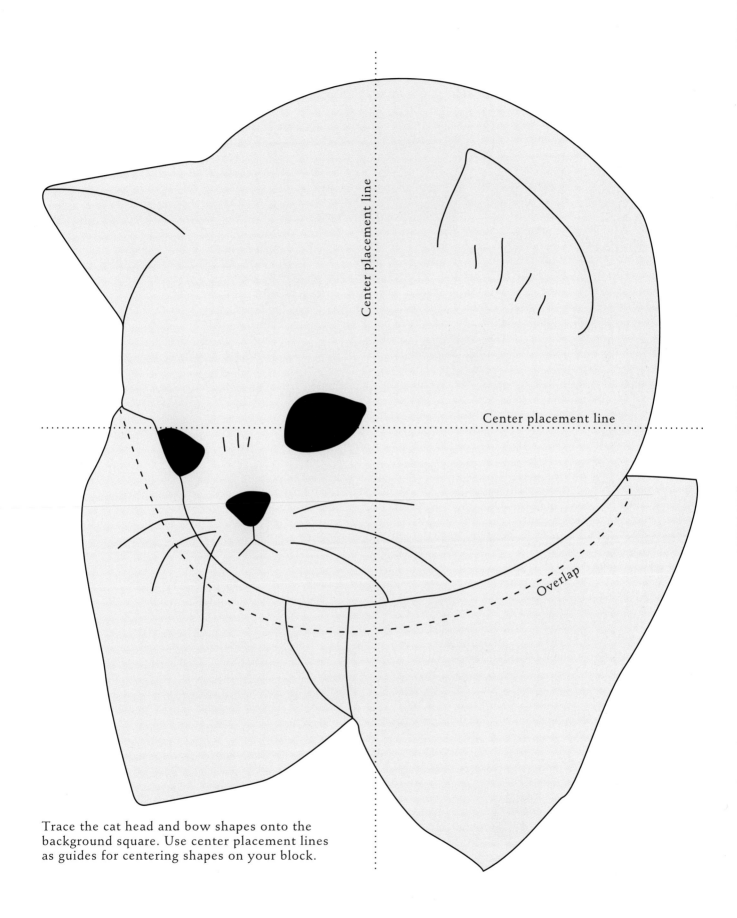

Center placement line

Center placement line

Overlap

Trace the cat head and bow shapes onto the
background square. Use center placement lines
as guides for centering shapes on your block.

CAT TRACING DIAGRAM

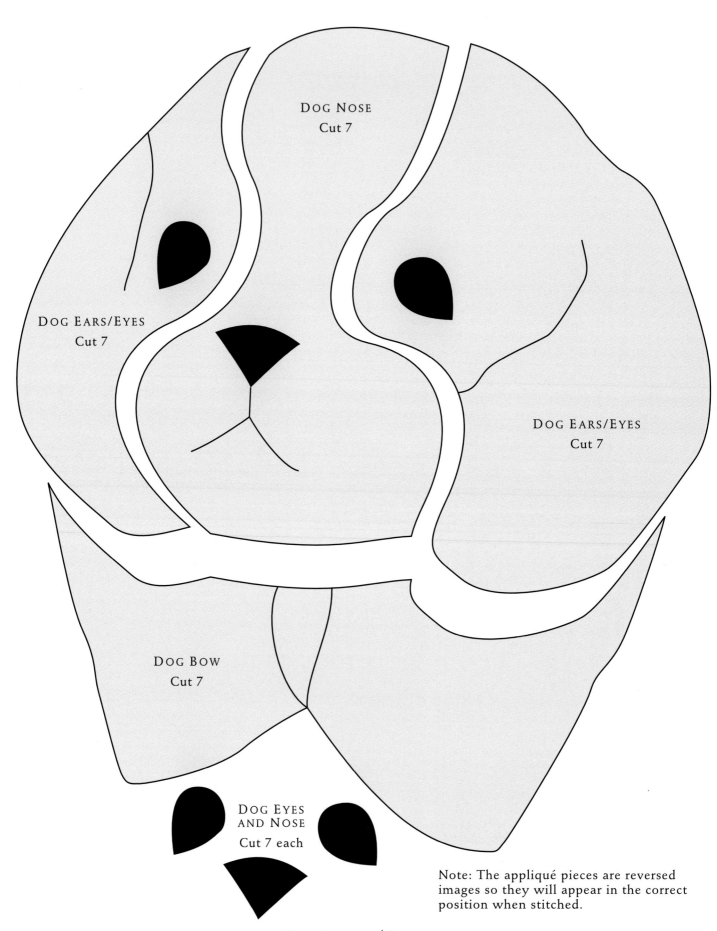

DOG NOSE
Cut 7

DOG EARS/EYES
Cut 7

DOG EARS/EYES
Cut 7

DOG BOW
Cut 7

DOG EYES
AND NOSE
Cut 7 each

Note: The appliqué pieces are reversed images so they will appear in the correct position when stitched.

DOG APPLIQUÉ PATTERNS

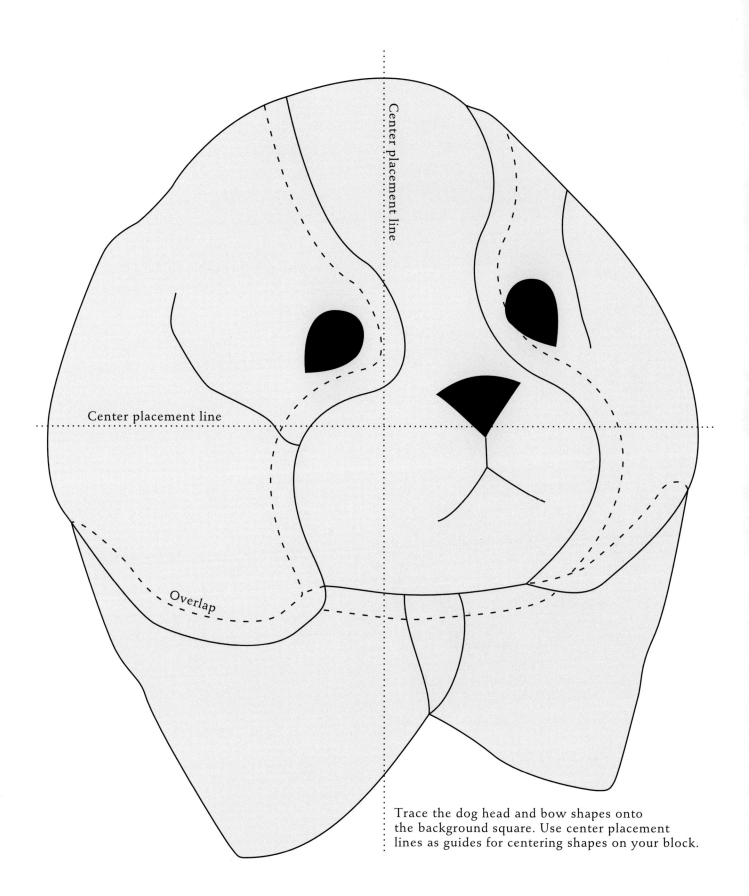

Center placement line

Center placement line

Overlap

Trace the dog head and bow shapes onto the background square. Use center placement lines as guides for centering shapes on your block.

DOG TRACING DIAGRAM

HOME PLACE

There are some quilts that are just right for setting the mood of a country-style bedroom, complete with a warm, inviting atmosphere. Home Place is one of those designs. The quiet, restful greens and overall pattern of the Nine Patch squares and vertical lattice strips create a calm quilt that will add color to a room. This design is also subtle enough to harmonize well with other home decorating elements, such as striped or floral wallpaper, patterned upholstery, or decorative artwork. This quilt is meant to be loved and enjoyed every day.

Size

Bed Quilt: 90 × 108 inches (unquilted)

Finished Nine Patch Block: 4½ inches square

Fabrics and Supplies

Yardage is based on 44-inch-wide fabric.

4¼ yards dark green print fabric for Nine Patch blocks, alternate blocks, and outer border

3⅞ yards beige print fabric for background

2½ yards green floral print fabric for lattice strips

¾ yard chestnut print fabric for inner border

1 yard dark green print fabric for binding

8¼ yards fabric for quilt backing

Quilt batting, at least 94 × 112 inches

Rotay cutter, mat, and see-through ruler with ⅛-inch markings

Getting Ready

- READ instructions thoroughly before you begin.

- PREWASH and press fabric.

- USE ¼-inch seam allowances throughout unless directions specify otherwise.

- SEAM ALLOWANCES are included in the cutting sizes given.

- PRESS seam allowances in the direction that will create the least bulk, and whenever possible, press toward the darker fabric.

- CUTTING DIRECTIONS for each section of the quilt are given individually. If you like to cut as you go, simply follow the directions as you get to them. If you'd rather cut all your pieces at the same time, skip ahead to find each of the cutting sections and do all the cutting before you begin to sew. ✒

Fabric Key

◼ Dark green

◻ Beige

◼ Green floral

◼ Chestnut

Nine Patch Blocks
(MAKE 88)

CUTTING

From the dark green print fabric:
- Cut twenty-three 2 × 44-inch strips

From the beige print fabric:
- Cut nineteen 2 × 44-inch strips

Piecing the Nine Patch Blocks

1 To construct Strip Set I, sew a 2 × 44-inch dark green strip to both sides of a 2 × 44-inch beige strip, as shown in DIAGRAM 1. Press seam allowances toward the darker fabric. Make nine of Strip Set I and crosscut

them into a total of 176 segments, each 2 inches wide, as shown.

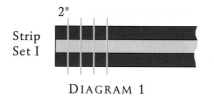

2"

Strip Set I

DIAGRAM 1

2 To construct Strip Set II, sew a 2 × 44-inch beige strip to both sides of a 2 × 44-inch dark green strip, as shown in DIAGRAM 2. Press seam allowances toward the darker fabric. Make five of Strip Set II and crosscut them into a total of 88 segments, each 2 inches wide, as shown.

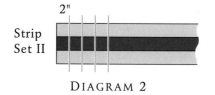

2"

Strip Set II

DIAGRAM 2

3 Sew a Strip Set I segment to both sides of a Strip Set II segment, as shown in DIAGRAM 3, creating a Nine Patch block. Make a total of 88 Nine Patch blocks, as shown. At this point, the Nine Patch blocks should measure 5 inches square.

DIAGRAM 3

Quilt Center

CUTTING

From the beige print fabric:
- Cut six 5 × 44-inch strips; from these strips, cut forty-four 5-inch squares

- Cut twelve 5 × 44-inch strips for Strip Set III

From the dark green print fabric:
- Cut six 5 × 44-inch strips for Strip Set III

From the green floral print fabric:
- Cut fifteen 5 × 44-inch strips for the lattice strips

Assembling the Quilt Center

1 To construct Strip Set III, sew a 5 × 44-inch beige strip to both sides of a 5 × 44-inch dark green strip, as shown in DIAGRAM 4. Press seam allowances toward the lighter fabric. Make six of Strip Set III and crosscut them into a total of 40 segments, each 5 inches wide, as shown.

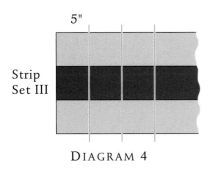

DIAGRAM 4

2 Sew a Nine Patch block to both sides of a 5-inch beige square, as shown in DIAGRAM 5. Press seam allowances toward the lighter fabric. Make 44 of these units, as shown.

DIAGRAM 5

3 Sew together a vertical row of 11 units from Step 2 and 10 Strip Set III segments from

PRESSING FOR STRIP-CUTTING ACCURACY

🖊 WHEN SEWING strips of fabric together for strip sets, it is important to press the seam allowances nice and flat, usually toward the darker fabric. Be very careful not to stretch the fabric while you are pressing. This can cause a curved "rainbow" effect in your strip set and affect the accuracy and shapes of the segments you cut from it.

🖊 I LIKE to press the wrong side of a strip set first, with the strips placed perpendicular to the length of my ironing board. Then I turn the strip set over and press again on the right side. This prevents little pleats from forming at the seams. Avoid laying the strip set lengthwise on the ironing board, which seems to encourage the kind of rainbow effect shown here.

Step 1, as shown in the QUILT ASSEMBLY DIAGRAM on page 194. Make four of these vertical rows, as shown. Press.

4 To make a lattice strip, sew together three 5 × 44-inch green floral strips with diagonal seams. For more information on diagonal seams, see "Border Basics" on page 211. Make five of these lattice strips. Trim each of the five pieced strips to the same length as your vertical rows.

5 Pin and sew the vertical rows and lattice strips together, creating the quilt center, as shown in the QUILT ASSEMBLY DIAGRAM on page 194. Press seam allowances toward the lattice strips.

Borders

CUTTING

NOTE: The yardage given allows for the border pieces to be cut cross-grain.

From the chestnut print fabric:
- Cut ten 2 × 44-inch strips for the inner border

From the dark green print fabric:
- Cut eleven 5½ × 44-inch strips for the outer border

QUILT ASSEMBLY DIAGRAM

4 Measure the quilt from top to bottom through the middle, including the borders you just added, to determine the length for the outer side borders. Trim two 5½-inch dark green border strips to this length, sew them to the sides of the quilt, and press.

Putting It All Together

1 Prepare the backing for the quilt by cutting the 8¼-yard length of backing fabric in thirds crosswise to form three equal lengths that measure about 2¾ yards each. Remove the selvages and sew the long edges of the three lengths together so that the seams run horizontally. Press.

2 Trim the backing and batting so they are 4 inches larger than the quilt top dimensions.

3 Mark quilting designs on the quilt top.

Attaching the Borders

1 Sew the 2 × 44-inch chestnut inner border strips together with diagonal seams. For more information on diagonal seams, see page 211. Measure the quilt from left to right through the middle to determine the length of the top and bottom inner borders. Cut two chestnut strips to this length and sew them to the top and bottom of the quilt. Press seam allowances toward the border.

2 Measure the quilt from top to bottom through the middle, including the borders you just added, to determine the length for the inner side borders. Trim two chestnut strips to this length, sew them to the sides of the quilt, and press.

3 Sew the 5½ × 44-inch dark green strips together with diagonal seams. Measure the quilt from left to right through the middle to determine the length of the top and bottom outer borders. Trim two strips to this length, sew them to the top and bottom of the quilt, and press.

A SLIVER of hard bar soap like Dial is ideal for marking medium to dark fabrics. It rubs off very easily, and it's always simple to create a clean, sharp edge on the soap by breaking off a small piece. Avoid facial soaps with ingredients like oatmeal.

TIPS AND TRICKS

4 Layer the backing, batting, and quilt top. Baste the layers together and quilt.

5 When quilting is complete, remove the basting stitches, and trim the excess backing and batting even with the quilt top.

Binding

NOTE: The 2¾-inch strips will produce a ⅜-inch-wide binding. If you want a wider or narrower binding, adjust the width of the strips you cut. (See page 216 for pointers on how to experiment with binding width.) See "Making and Attaching the Binding" on page 215 to complete your quilt.

CUTTING

From the dark green print binding fabric:
• Cut eleven 2¾ × 44-inch strips for cross-grain binding

Quilting
DESIGNS

FOR HAND OR MACHINE QUILTING:

🌿 *The alternating green unpieced blocks are the perfect place for a small, continous-line floral design like the one in QUILTING DIAGRAM 1.*

🌿 *All of the background areas contain meander quilting, with no quilting in the green sections of the Nine Patches. This makes the Nine Patch blocks stand out more.*

🌿 *A simple trailing vine design like the one shown in QUILTING DIAGRAM 2 accentuates the vertical lines in the quilt and offers a nice contrast to the other quilting motifs.*

🌿 *The feathered quilting design in QUILTING DIAGRAM 3 covers both the narrow brown borders and the green outer borders.*

QUILTING DIAGRAM 2

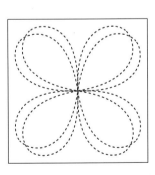

QUILTING DIAGRAM 1

QUILTING DIAGRAM 3

LOOK

*T*he look that is identified with Thimbleberries quilts is a direct reflection of my personal taste and lifestyle. Over the years, I have realized that I want my home, quilts, and quilted accessories to be warm and inviting, and the dark rich colors and "unfussy" designs of my quilts convey that. These projects have a casual, traditional style that you can blend comfortably with antiques and the best of country-style decor. These are quilts you can treasure for years to come.

Thimbleberries
STYLE

My Color Palette

Color has become the most identifiable element of the Thimbleberries style. Many years ago, I discovered that there was no color I did not like as long as I could use darker shades of it. Virtually all colors will work together, and even those usually considered clashing can be compatible if they are dark enough. The colors on these pages show how I like to work with color in designing quilts and also make handy color guides for choosing fabrics for your own quilts.

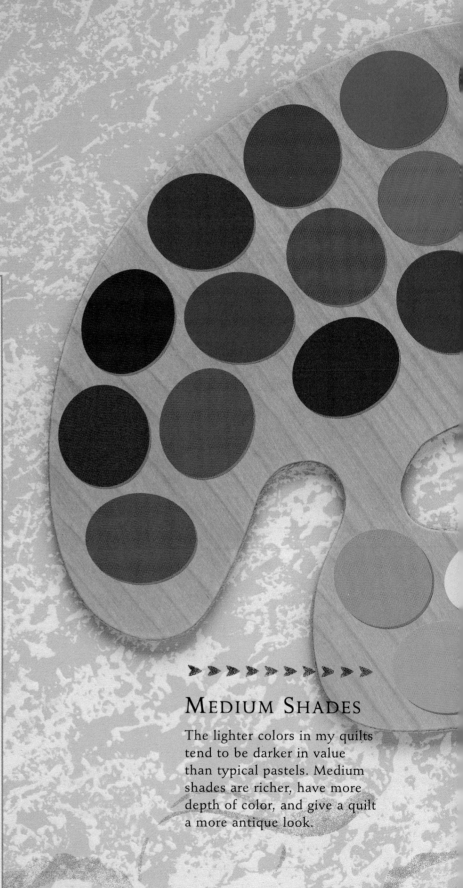

>>>>>>>>>>>>>

MEDIUM SHADES

The lighter colors in my quilts tend to be darker in value than typical pastels. Medium shades are richer, have more depth of color, and give a quilt a more antique look.

DARKER COLORS

Dark values of red, green, blue, and brown, along with a touch of black, feature prominently in my quilts. These colors create bold contrast and contribute to a strong quilt design.

MELLOW TONES

Incorporating a range of deep, mellow gold fabrics helps to impart the same feeling of warmth I see in old quilts. These colors also enhance the other colors in my palette.

NEUTRAL BACKGROUNDS

Beige and cream shades make effective backgrounds for the rich, dark colors I use. These neutral tones soften a quilt without being as sharp or vibrant as "white-whites." This is the same effect that can be seen in antique furniture, textiles, and artwork, where whites have aged to gentle creams over time, and vibrant, clear colors are faded and soft.

Fabric Types

One of the connections all quiltmakers have to each other is their love of fabric. As a young child, my mother would often point out to me the good characteristics of a piece of fabric she was considering buying, so I learned early on to take note of things like quality, scale of print, and how fabrics would be used in a quilt. On these pages, I have gathered some fabrics from my sewing studio to help illustrate important elements to consider when selecting fabrics for any quilt project.

PRINTED PLAINS

"Printed plain" is a term I use to refer to any print that I treat as a solid color in a quilt. These fabrics are usually tone-on-tone color combinations with subtle allover meandering prints. They lend visual texture to a quilt and have a softening effect on the design.

LOW-CONTRAST PLAINS

These fabrics offer color, design, and texture without a lot of differences in color values. They are interesting to look at without being so visually demanding that they take over a quilt design. Low-contrast prints are also great blenders, which help to coordinate colors throughout a quilt.

➤➤➤➤➤➤➤➤➤➤➤➤➤➤➤

LARGE-SCALE PRINTS

I use large-scale prints quite sparingly, usually no more than one per quilt, and in combination with many other prints and plaids. Effective places to use large-scale prints are outside borders and large patches, where the full print is easily visible without being distorted by lots of seams.

PLAIDS AND CHECKS

Both plaids and checks are staples in my fabric repertoire. In some cases, the grainline of a plaid or check is important to me, while other times it is not a concern. For example, when I am cutting plaids or checks into many small pieces that will be placed every which direction in a quilt, I cut them without regard to grainline. If I am cutting out big, bold plaid borders, I take care to use a pair of scissors, so that I can follow lines of the plaid perfectly to make the quilt appear straight and square.

STRONG GRAPHIC PRINTS

It takes just a little bit of a graphic print to add spark to a quilt. These fabrics are prints that stand out because of bold images or strong color definition, so I use them sparingly, because they can sometimes interfere with and distract from a pieced design. It can be fun to use graphic, strong prints in places like narrow borders, lattice strips, or bindings.

Characteristics of Thimbleberries Quilt Designs

Thimbleberries quilts are generally simple, uncomplicated designs, most often making use of color and fabric rather than complicated piecing techniques to enhance the overall designs of the quilts. I lean toward traditional patterns, symmetry, and repetition of pattern. I like to use these elements to create quilts and accessories that will blend comfortably with the best of country-style decor.

PRINTED BACKS ▶▶▶▶

I often use large-scale prints or piece
coordinating fabrics together to
create an interesting quilt back. I
always use really large pieces of
fabric, perhaps three different prints
that are the same length as the quilt,
or a large piece of fabric that is bordered by compatible prints. This will
keep the number of seams to a mini-
mum, which you'll appreciate during
the quilting process.

TRADITIONAL, CASUAL, CLASSIC, CLEAN LINES

My quilt designs are like many of
the antique classics that I refer to as
"prairie patchwork." These quilts
have straight lines, simple bold
shapes, and pattern repeats that all
add up to what I consider everyday
quilts. They are great for adding
color, texture, and warmth to a room
and provide handcrafted goodness.

ADDED EMBELLISHMENTS

A bit of embroidery, a few French
knots, or buttonhole stitching can
do wonders for a quilt. These extra
stitches lend dimension and color,
as well as definition, to any quilt
design. Whether you like working
by hand or machine, try out the
various effects you can create with
embroidery stitches.

MANY PRINTS IN COMBINATION

The combination of a large number
of fabrics is a wonderful treat for the
eye. Even if the pattern of the blocks
is the same throughout a quilt, subtle
changes in color and print can create
lovely visual effects. I think using
lots of fabrics together is reminiscent
of old-fashioned country scrap quilts.

Fabric Shopping Tips

A good piece of fabric is always the beginning of my creativity. To choose fabrics for getting the Thimbleberries look in your quilts, visit your local quilt shop with this book in hand, and use the following tips for finding fabrics you'll love.

🍃 USE THE THIMBLEBERRIES PALETTE: A good way to start is to gather fabrics that match the shades you like on pages 198–199. Remember to look for color first, then for print or pattern.

🍃 LOOK FOR COMPATIBLE FABRIC DESIGNS: You will probably discover that you already have strong personal preferences in fabric design. When I shop, my own preference is for fabrics that have a similar feel. For example, sophisticated prints do not mix well with fabrics that have obvious primitive motifs, nor do country novelties blend well with Victorian florals.

🍃 PLAN FOR VARIETY: Try varying the fabric combinations you put together; for example, group some prints that have geometric figures with some small florals, or mix stripes with small dots and, of course, plaids with checks.

🍃 BRING YOUR OWN FABRIC VIEWER: Cut a 2-inch square out of the center of a piece of typing paper and take it with you when you shop for fabric. Place the paper over any fabric you are considering, and let it show through the hole. This will help put the print into perspective. It can be amazing how different fabric looks when viewed in small pieces. Sometimes a whole bolt can be overwhelming.

🍃 STEP BACK: Always view your fabric selections from a distance of about 15 feet, the same distance at which you will be likely to view a finished quilt across a room. This will tell you a lot about how the scale of each fabric will appear from a distance and help you decide whether you will like the look of the fabrics in the finished quilt.

🍃 TRY OUT DIFFERENT COMBINATIONS: Unfold a bolt length of a fabric you're considering for a background fabric, and then arrange fabrics you're considering for the borders along the sides of the first bolt. Then add several more fabrics you like to these, folding each fabric into smaller pieces and lining them up as they may occur in a finished quilt. This will give you a realistic overview of the color and print combinations you've grouped together. Taking time to play and experiment with fabrics before you purchase them will help you determine which combinations you really like.

🍃 MY BUYING FORMULA: I haven't changed my buying formula for years because it has it has served me well. My own rule of thumb is to buy a 1-yard piece when I like a fabric and think the color and print are good and workable for many of the quilts I make. If I really like a fabric, I always buy 3 yards of it, knowing that I will probably use it in more than one project or feature it prominently in a large quilt. Often, I even go so far as to purchase 6 yards of fabric when I know it will make a great backing or it is a print I know I will want to keep around for a while.

Thimbleberries
GUIDE TO QUILTMAKING

Fabric Facts

For best results, stick with 100 percent cotton broadcloth or dress-weight fabrics. Cotton is easy to press because its "memory" allows it to retain a crease for some time. The soft and lightweight quality of cotton makes it easy to quilt through three layers of a quilt sandwich. Cotton can be manipulated to match tricky points, and it is flexible enough to ease around curves. The quilts in this book are all made of 100 percent cotton fabrics.

Selecting Fabrics

The yardages given for the quilts and projects in this book are based on 44-inch-wide fabric, but to allow for slight variations and possible shrinkage, we use a width of 40 inches as the guideline for calculating required yardage for the projects. These yardages are adequate for each project, allowing up to ¼ yard extra as a margin for error, so you'll always have enough in case there's a cutting error or some other mishap. The extra

fabric is there if you need it, and if you don't, you can add it to your scrap bag for future projects. The yardages have been double-checked for accuracy, but you may want to buy extra fabric, just to be safe. Even the most experienced quilters sometimes make mistakes. Check the fabric widths before you buy— the fabric may be narrower than 44 inches. You may also lose some yardage in the prewashing and preshrinking process.

Pretreating Fabrics

Always prewash, dry, and press your fabrics. Prewashing shrinks fabric slightly and removes any finishes and sizing, making the cloth softer and easier to handle.

Washing will also let the fabrics bleed—something you want to happen *before* you stitch the fabric into your quilt. Wash fabrics in an automatic washer with warm water and a mild detergent or a soap sold specifically for washing quilts. Dry fabrics in the dryer on a medium setting. I usually recommend pretreating fabric the same way you plan to treat it in the completed quilt.

Rotary Cutting

The directions for most of the quilts in this book have been written for rotary cutting, which is faster and more accurate than the traditional method of making templates and using scissors to cut individual pieces. Use the following general guidelines to ensure both safety and accuracy when rotary cutting.

Always:

• Keep rotary cutters out of the reach of children. The blades are extremely sharp!
• Be sure to slide the blade guard into place *whenever* you stop cutting.
• Cut *away* from yourself.
• Square off the left end of your fabric before measuring and cutting pieces, as shown in

A LARGE cutting mat (23 × 35 inches) makes rotary cutting easier and more accurate. Less folding and handling of the fabric is needed when using a larger cutting mat.
WHEN CUTTING multiple fabric layers, try the large-size rotary cutter with 2½-inch blades. Larger blades slice through several layers more easily and efficiently than medium-size blades. And always remember safety precautions.

TIPS AND TRICKS

DIAGRAM 1. Line up the selvages and place a ruled square on the fold. Place a 6 × 24-inch ruler against the side of the square to get a 90 degree angle. Hold the ruler in place, remove the square, and cut along the edge of the ruler. If you are left-handed, work from the other end of the fabric.

6" × 24" ruler

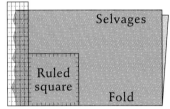

DIAGRAM 1

Cutting Strips, Squares, and Rectangles

Cut strips on the crosswise grain, as shown in DIAGRAM 2, unless instructed otherwise. Strips can then be cut into squares or rectangles, as needed.

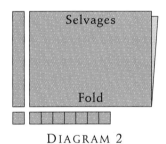

DIAGRAM 2

Check often to make sure that your fabric is square and the strips are straight rather than angled, as shown in DIAGRAM 3. If necessary, refold the fabric, square off the edge, and begin cutting again.

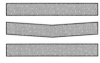

DIAGRAM 3

Cutting Triangles from Squares

The cutting instructions often direct you to cut strips, then squares, and then triangles, as in Brown-Eyed Susan, Harvest Mix, and many others. This method is simple and accurate. The size of the square given in the project will be ⅞ inch larger than the desired finished size of the triangle-pieced square.

For example, for a 2-inch finished triangle-pieced square, each square would be $2\frac{7}{8} \times 2\frac{7}{8}$ inches. Cut a $2\frac{7}{8}$-inch-wide strip of both colors. Layer these strips right sides together and press. Cut the layered strips into $2\frac{7}{8}$-inch squares. You will get two triangle-pieced squares for each pair of squares you cut. Cut the layered squares in half diagonally to make perfect triangles. Sew the triangles together ¼ inch from the diagonal edge, as shown in DIAGRAM 4, and press the seam allowances toward the darker of the two fabrics.

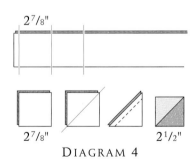

DIAGRAM 4

Cutting Side and Corner Triangles

For projects with side and corner triangles, the instructions will indicate to cut them larger than necessary. This will allow you to truly square up the quilt, and it also eliminates the frustration of

ending up with precut side and corner triangles that do not match your pieced blocks. Refer to "Trimming Side and Corner Triangles" on page 211.

To cut triangles, start by cutting squares. The project directions will tell you what size to make the squares and whether to cut them in half diagonally to make two triangles, as shown in DIAGRAM 5A, or to cut them in quarters diagonally to make four triangles, as shown in DIAGRAM 5B. This cutting method will produce side and corner triangles with the straight of grain running along the outside edges of the quilt.

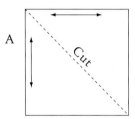

Arrows indicate straight grain

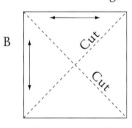

DIAGRAM 5

Making and Using Templates

The template patterns in this book are full-size, so no enlarging or drafting is necessary.

Fine-point or extra-fine-point permanent felt-tip pens are excellent for marking templates. The lines don't smear and the fine points help ensure accuracy. Regular lead pencils also work well, but you may find that the lines are not as easy to see.

At Thimbleberries, we use posterboard or manila folders for making our templates. To do this, place a sheet of tracing paper over the book page and trace the pattern. Glue the tracing paper to the cardboard or manila folder and cut out your templates. Take care to cut off the marking lines as you go. If you cut beyond to the outside edge, you will be adding size to the template when you trace the shape onto fabric. Copy all identification labels, grain lines, and other necessary information onto your templates. Check them against the printed pattern for accuracy.

Thin semitransparent template plastic also makes excellent, durable templates. You can lay the plastic over the book page and carefully trace the patterns directly onto the plastic. Then cut out each shape with scissors. Take care to be as accurate as possible when tracing and cutting templates. Accurate templates are critical for precise piecing.

The patchwork patterns in this book include seam allowances. They are printed with a solid outer line, which is the cutting line, and a dashed inner line, which is the sewing line. We've included dots at the seam intersections, as shown in DIAGRAM 6, to help in matching up and pinning the pieces together for accurate placement. If you wish to mark the seam intersec-

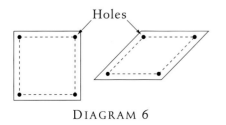

Holes

DIAGRAM 6

tions on your fabric, make holes in your templates at the dots with a heavy needle or a ⅛-inch paper-hole punch.

The holes need to be large enough to accommodate the point of a pencil or marker. Draw around the templates on the wrong side of the fabric, as shown in DIAGRAM 7. This line is the cutting line.

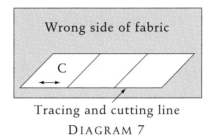

Wrong side of fabric

C

Tracing and cutting line
DIAGRAM 7

Piecing Precisely

An exact ¼-inch seam allowance is extremely important in quiltmaking. A difference of as little as 1/16 inch on several pattern pieces can alter the dimensions of your quilt by as much as an inch or more.

Some sewing machines have a presser foot that measures exactly ¼ inch from the point where the needle goes into the fabric to the edge of the presser foot. Measure to determine whether this is true for your machine. If you cannot use your presser foot as a reliable seam guide, you may wish to mark an exact ¼-inch line on your machine. Lift the presser foot and measure over precisely ¼ inch from the needle. Lay a piece of ¼-inch masking tape at that point to help you guide your fabric.

Before sewing a block, sew a test seam to make sure you are taking accurate ¼-inch seams.

Adjust your machine to sew 10 to 12 stitches per inch. Select a neutral-color thread that blends well with the fabrics you are using. It is a good practice always to cut and piece a sample block before you cut all your fabrics. This will allow you to make certain your color choices work well together and you are cutting the pieces accurately.

Press patchwork seams to one side, toward the darker fabric whenever possible, to prevent them from shadowing through lighter fabrics. Since seams will be stitched down when crossed with another seam, you will need to think about the direction in which you want them to lie.

Chain Piecing

Chain piecing, or assembly-line piecing, can help speed up the process of stitching many of the same-size or -shape pieces together. Referring to DIAGRAM 8, run pairs of pieces or units through the sewing machine one after another without cutting the thread. Once all the units are

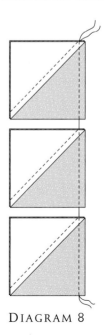

DIAGRAM 8

sewn, snip them apart and press. You can continue to add on more pieces to these units in the same assembly-line fashion until the sections are complete.

Strip Piecing

When squares and rectangles are combined in a repeated pattern, you can simplify assembly by using strip piecing. With strip piecing, you sew together a series of horizontal strips into a strip set. The strip set is then cut into segments. A rotary cutter, used with a see-through ruler with ⅛-inch markings, is ideal for this kind of straight-line cutting. Strips from the strip set are cut ½ inch wider than the finished size of the patch to allow for ¼-inch seam allowances.

When sewing strips of fabric together for strip sets, it is important to press the seam allowances, usually toward the darker fabric. Be very careful not to stretch as you press, causing the "rainbow effect" shown in DIAGRAM 9. This will affect the accuracy and shape of the pieces cut from the strip set. I like to press the wrong side first, with the strips perpendicular to the ironing board. Then I flip the piece over and press on the right side, to prevent little pleats from forming at the seams. Laying the strip set lengthwise on the ironing board seems to encourage the rainbow effect.

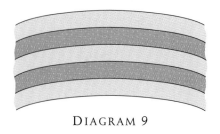

DIAGRAM 9

Pressing Pointers

Pressing is an important step during piecing and assembling a quilt top. Some quilters prefer a dry iron, but I use a steam iron to press pieces. Experiment to see which works best for you. Press by bringing the iron down gently and firmly onto the fabric from above. Ironing your pieces by sliding the iron back and forth across the fabric may stretch them out of shape. Here are some other tips to help you press properly.

• Press a seam before crossing it with another seam.
• Press seam allowances to one side, not open.
• Whenever possible, press seams toward darker fabrics.
• Press seams of adjacent rows of blocks, or rows within blocks, in opposite directions so the pressed seams will abut as the rows are joined (see DIAGRAM 10).
• Press appliqués very gently from the wrong side of the background fabric. They are prettiest when slightly puffed.

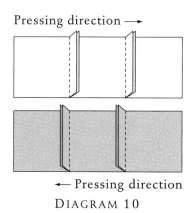

Pressing direction ⟶

⟵ Pressing direction
DIAGRAM 10

Hand Appliqué

Some of the quilts in this book include appliqué, often in combination with patchwork. I use the

needle turn, or freezer paper method, which is especially effective for larger appliqué pieces.

Choose thread to match the appliqué pieces and stitch each appliqué to the background fabric with a blind hem or appliqué stitch, as shown in DIAGRAM 11. The stitches should be a snug ⅛ inch apart, or closer. Use a long thin needle—called a sharp—in size number 11 or 12.

DIAGRAM 11

When making appliqué blocks, always work from the background to the foreground. When one appliqué piece will overlap or cover another, stitch the underneath piece to the background fabric first. Note that on the appliqué pattern pieces, the area to be overlapped by another piece is indicated with a dotted or dashed line.

The patterns for appliqué pieces in this book are finished-size and are printed with only a single line. Draw around these templates on the right side of the fabric, as shown in DIAGRAM 12, leaving ½ inch between the pieces. The lines you draw will be your guides for turning under the edges of the appliqué pieces. Then add a scant ¼-inch seam allowance as you cut out the pieces.

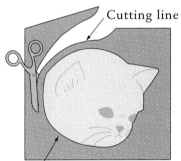

Cutting line

Tracing and fold-under line
DIAGRAM 12

Freezer Paper Method

With the freezer paper method, the freezer paper forms a base around which the fabric is shaped.

TEMPLATES MADE from freezer paper can be reused. This saves a lot of time tracing when you need to stitch multiple appliqués from the same pattern piece.

TIPS AND TRICKS

1 Trace the posterboard templates for the appliqués from the book onto template material and cut them out.

2 Using the posterboard template, trace the appliqué shape onto the noncoated, or dull, side of the freezer paper and cut out the shape.

3 With a dry iron set at wool, press the coated, or shiny, side of the freezer paper template to the wrong side of the fabric. Be sure to allow ½ inch between shapes for seam allowances, as in DIAGRAM 12.

4 Cut out the appliqué shape ⅛ to ¼ inch outside of the paper edge to allow for seam allowance. Clip concave curves, if necessary, to allow you to turn them under more easily, as shown in DIAGRAM 13.

DIAGRAM 13

5 Pin the appliqué shape to the quilt block or top. Appliqué the shape to the quilt with a blind hem stitch as shown in DIAGRAM 11 on the opposite page, turning the seam allowance under against the edge of the paper.

6 Remove the freezer paper by one of two methods. One method is to leave ½ inch of

WHENEVER YOU visit your local quilt shop or other specialty needlework stores, take some time to scout for unusual threads and yarns that can be used for embellishing your quilts. Unique threads, like the new metallic embroidery floss by DMC, or variegated pearl cotton, can add new visual dimension to your hand stitching.

TIPS AND TRICKS

the appliqué shape unstitched. Finger press the fabric over the paper. Then slide your needle into this opening to loosen the freezer paper from the appliqué. Gently pull the freezer paper out, and the fold should still be in the fabric. Finish stitching the appliqué in place. Another way to remove the freezer paper is to slit the fabric from the wrong side and remove the paper.

Primitive Appliqué

Primitive appliqué, in which shapes are fused onto the background fabric and then enhanced by embroidery stitches, is a popular look for whimsical designs, such as Checkerboard Cherries and Christmas Candy.

1 Trace appliqué pattern pieces from the book onto template material.

2 Place the appliqué templates face down on the paper side of the fusible web, and trace.

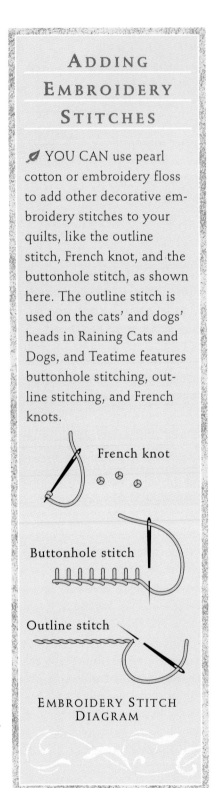

ADDING EMBROIDERY STITCHES

🍃 YOU CAN use pearl cotton or embroidery floss to add other decorative embroidery stitches to your quilts, like the outline stitch, French knot, and the buttonhole stitch, as shown here. The outline stitch is used on the cats' and dogs' heads in Raining Cats and Dogs, and Teatime features buttonhole stitching, outline stitching, and French knots.

French knot

Buttonhole stitch

Outline stitch

EMBROIDERY STITCH DIAGRAM

3 Cut out the shapes loosely and place the rough side of the web against the wrong side of the fabric. Follow the manufacturer's directions and fuse with a dry iron. Let the fabric and the web cool.

4 Cut out the shapes along the drawn lines and peel off the backing.

5 Position the appliqué shapes on the quilt and press in place with a hot dry iron according to the manufacturer's directions.

6 Using three strands of embroidery floss, stitch around the appliqué shape with the primitive stitch, as shown in DI-AGRAM 14. Stitches are about ⅛ inch long and ⅛ inch apart. The primitive stitch is very quick and easy and outlines the shapes nicely.

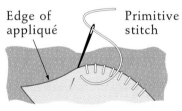

Edge of appliqué   Primitive stitch

DIAGRAM 14

Machine Appliqué

Machine appliqué is a quick and easy way to add appliqué pieces to projects without spending a lot of time doing hand stitching. Machine appliqué also stands up well to repeated washings.

You'll need a sewing machine that has a zigzag stitch setting. Set your machine to a medium-width zigzag stitch and a very short stitch length. Test this satin stitch on a scrap of fabric. Your stitches should form a band of color and they should be ⅛ to ³⁄₁₆ inch wide. If necessary, loosen the top tension slightly so the top thread is just slightly pulled to the wrong side.

The appliqué piece should be either fused, pinned, or basted to the background fabric. See Steps 1 through 4 under "Primitive Appliqué" on page 209 for instructions on using fusible web.

1 Stabilize the background fabric to give more control and eliminate puckering. You can use a sheet of typing paper or a commercial stabilizer such as Tear-Away. Pin it to the wrong side of the background fabric where you will be stitching.

2 Machine satin stitch around the edges of the appliqué pieces, covering the raw edges. Change thread colors as necessary to match the pieces. When stitching is complete, carefully tear away the stabilizer from the wrong side. You can also use a machine buttonhole stitch or other decorative stitch to stitch down the edges after fusing or stabilizing.

Squaring up Blocks

To square up your blocks, first check the seam allowances. This is usually where the problem occurs, and it is always best to alter within the block rather than trim the outer edges. Next, make sure you have pressed accurately. Sometimes a block can become distorted by overly enthusiastic pressing.

To trim up block edges, I like to use one of the many clear plastic squares available on the market. Determine the center of the block; mark it with a pin. Lay the square over the block and align as many perpendicular and horizontal lines as you can to the seams in your block. This will indicate where the block is off. Do not trim off all the excess on one side; this usually results in real distortion of the pieces in the block and the block design. Take a little off all sides until the block is square. When assembling many blocks, make sure all blocks are the same size.

Pin and sew blocks together in horizontal, vertical, or diagonal rows as directed in the instructions. Press seams between blocks in opposite directions from row to row. Join the rows, abutting the pressed seam allowances so the intersections will match perfectly.

If you are assembling a large quilt top, join rows into pairs first and then join the pairs to keep it more manageable.

Press the completed top on the wrong side first, carefully clipping and removing hanging threads. Then press the front, making sure all seams are flat.

Assembling a Quilt Top

To assemble your quilt top, refer to the QUILT ASSEMBLY DIAGRAM, the quilt photograph, and the step-by-step diagrams in each project. Lay out all the blocks, alternate blocks, and corner and side triangles as appropriate for the quilt. Position them right side up as they will be in the completed quilt.

Trimming Side and Corner Triangles

To trim oversize side and corner triangles before adding borders to a quilt, use a wide acrylic ruler, cutting mat, and rotary cutter.

• Begin at a corner first and line up your ruler ¼ inch beyond the points of the corners of the blocks, as shown in DIAGRAM 15. Lightly draw a line along the edge of the ruler. Repeat this along all four sides of the quilt top, lightly marking cutting lines.

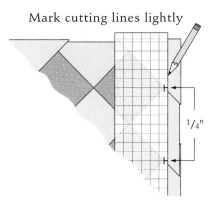

Mark cutting lines lightly

1/4"

DIAGRAM 15

• Check all the corners before you do any cutting. Make sure they are 90 degree angles. Adjust the cutting lines as needed to ensure square corners.
• When you are certain that everything is as parallel and perpendicular as it can be, line up your ruler over the quilt top. Using your marked lines as guides, cut away the excess fabric with your rotary cutter, leaving the ¼-inch seam allowance beyond the block corners (see DIAGRAM 16).

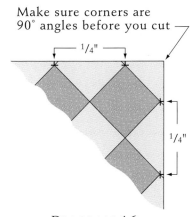

Make sure corners are 90° angles before you cut

1/4"

1/4"

1/4"

DIAGRAM 16

Border Basics

For most of the quilts in this book, the borders are straight rather than mitered. At Thimbleberries, we cut most of our borders cross-grain. The exceptions are when we need a long strip of fabric to match plaids. It is generally more cost-efficient to cut crosswise, but if your quilt is very large, it may not matter. We sometimes cut the top and bottom borders cross-grain and cut the sides lengthwise. I may also cut a floral print border on the lengthwise grain to preserve the repeat of the design. My goal is to make the borders work for each individual quilt. I don't have a rigid rule.

To piece border strips, I like to use diagonal seams, which are less visible in the finished quilt than straight seams. I think diagonal seams work better for quilting, too, because they eliminate the possibility of a seam always appearing in any one spot in a quilting design. The exception to this is when I am trying to match plaids or some other printed or directional fabric which would look better with straight seams.

To sew two border strips together diagonally, place them together at a 90 degree angle with right sides together, as shown in DIAGRAM 17 on page 212. Each strip should extend ¼ inch beyond the other. Sew the strips together, taking care to start and stop your stitching precisely at the V-shaped notch where the two strips meet, as shown. Trim away the excess fabric, leaving a ¼-inch seam allowance.

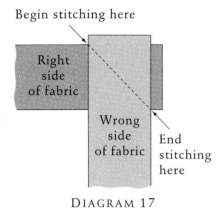

Begin stitching here

Right side of fabric

Wrong side of fabric

End stitching here

DIAGRAM 17

Tips for Plaid Borders

When cutting woven plaids cross-grain, cut along a thread. This will ensure that the plaid stays perpendicular. (When cutting other cross-grain borders, it is not necessary to cut along a thread.) If the border strips need to be longer than the width of the fabric, cut them on the lengthwise grain to avoid piecing. I think it is worth the extra expense to have a continuous plaid design uninterrupted by a seam. Seams are easier to blend when using a fabric with an overall print design.

Cut *all* border strips so they have the same plaid pattern repeat. This usually means using scissors, not a rotary cutter, and actually following the plaid thread line. Also, depending on the plaid, you may have to waste a few inches between border strips to make sure they fall on the same pattern repeat, as shown in DIAGRAM 18.

Next, remember to sew them onto the quilt in the same fashion, paying attention to which part of the plaid should go next to the quilt and which should be on the outside edge. The more complicated the plaid, the more there is to watch, as shown in DIAGRAM 19.

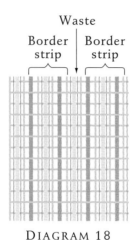

Waste

Border strip | Border strip

DIAGRAM 18

DIAGRAM 20

This part of the plaid must go on the inside on all 4 border strips

DIAGRAM 19

I like to take a different approach when I'm working with a plaid fabric such as the one shown in DIAGRAM 20, which has hearts in it. I would cut this fabric cross-grain with scissors, following a thread line, so I could have the hearts pointing outward and away from the center of the quilt.

All of these are guidelines rather than steadfast rules. Many quilters like the casual, unplanned look they get by cutting borders from plaids without planning the placement. This may actually be more like the antique quilts we love so much.

Quilting Designs

For each quilt in this book, I have made suggestions for quilting designs in the boxes called "Quilting Designs." Some projects lend themselves to very simple quilting patterns, such as outline quilting, while others are beautifully accented by cables, feathers, and floral designs. You can duplicate my designs, create your own, or choose from quilting stencils available at quilt shops or mail-order catalogs.

Marking the Quilting Design

When you're ready to mark the quilt top, choose one of the following markers. They will be visible on the fabric of your quilt and can be brushed out or will wear away after the quilting is completed. Make sure you make your lines very light, no matter what type of pencil you use.

• Quilter's silver pencils
• An artist's white pencil
• Chalk pencils and powdered chalk markers

- Hard lead 0.5 millimeter pencil
- Thin slivers of hand soap

To mark a quilting design, use a commercially made stencil, make your own stencil, or trace the design from a printed source.

If your marks will stay visible for a long time, mark the entire quilt top before layering. If you are using a powdered chalk marker or a chalk pencil, you will need to mark the quilting lines just before quilting them (after you've layered and basted).

Quilt Backings

Many of the quilts in this book are large enough to need pieced backings. There are instructions for the quilt back in each of the projects. I usually don't put the seam down the center of the quilt. I often put the seam off to one side so that I have a larger piece of leftover fabric.

Cut off all selvage edges from the backing fabric before sewing. Sew the pieces together with a ¼-inch seam allowance, and press these seams open. The backing will lie flatter, and it will be easier to quilt through the seam area if the seam is open rather than pressed to one side.

When it is sewn together, the backing should be larger than your completed quilt top so that there is a 2-inch margin of backing and batting on each side of the quilt. This will accommodate the natural tendency of these layers to "shrink," or draw up, during the quilting process.

Quilt Battings

There are many wonderful choices when it comes to the middle layer of your quilt. We use a lightweight batting, such as a polyester light batting, for hand quilting. It resembles soft, old quilts, and I can get nicer quilting stitches with a light polyester batting. For machine quilting, we also use polyester light batting.

Whatever batting you use, make sure to take it out of the plastic bag and let it rest for a day or two before layering, to let it breathe, get the loft up, and get any wrinkles out. Or you can put it in your dryer on the air-only cycle for 10 to 15 minutes.

Layering and Basting

The quilt top, batting, and backing layers must be anchored securely so that the finished quilt will lie flat and smooth. To prepare the quilt sandwich for quilting in a hoop, place the pressed backing right side down, and position the batting on top of it, smoothing out any wrinkled spots. To keep the backing taut, use masking tape at the corners or clamp it to a table with large binder clips.

Place the quilt top over the batting, right side up. Make sure it is centered, and smooth out any wrinkles. Remove any loose or hanging threads. The backing and batting should be at least 2 inches larger than the quilt top on all four sides.

Baste these three layers together with white thread so there won't be any residue of color left in your quilt when the thread is removed. Begin in the middle of the quilt and baste a grid of horizontal and vertical rows that are approximately 4 to 6 inches apart. Use a long darning needle or even a 3-inch dollmaking needle to make the stitching go faster. Thread a few needles in advance with very long lengths of thread.

To use a large floor frame in which the quilt is stretched out to its full dimensions, attach the backing first. Some old frames allow you to use tacks, while some require pinning to a muslin sleeve on the frame. Make sure the batting is nice and taut. Then lay the batting on. Smooth it out and position the quilt top over it. Make sure it is stretched slightly to create some tension for a smooth quilting surface. Tack or pin to the frame.

For machine quilting, use 1-inch-long rustproof, nickel-plated safety pins to baste a quilt sandwich together. Pin from the center outward, approximately every 3 inches, taking care not to place the pins where you intend to quilt.

Quilting

Under "Quilting Designs" in each project, you'll see whether each project is suitable for hand quilting, machine quilting, or both. However you decide to quilt your projects, the tips that follow will be helpful.

Choosing Thread Color for Quilting

Most quilters choose a neutral color thread; white and off-white are the most common, but complementary or contrasting threads are also effective. My preference is to match thread as closely as possible to the general tone of the fabrics in the quilt, because I like to see the texture created by quilting, rather than the color of a contrasting thread. I often change thread colors to match the fabrics in a quilt top so that the thread is not such a stark contrast between one area and another. For machine quilting, I like to use a neutral color in the bobbin and change the top thread to match the fabric of the quilt top. There is a lot of thread laid down in machine quilting, and a contrasting color can affect the overall color of a quilt. The more you match the thread, the less it affects the colors of your quilt. It hides little glitches in your stitching, too.

Hand Quilting

• Use a hoop or frame to keep tension on the quilt as you stitch. To insert the quilt into the hoop, place the quilt over the smaller, inner hoop and then place the larger, outer hoop over the quilt. Adjust the top hoop so that there is even tension on the quilt. Do not keep the tension so tight that it makes stitching difficult.
• Use short quilting needles, called betweens, in size 9 or 10.
• Use 100 percent cotton or cotton-covered polyester quilting thread.
• Start with an 18-inch length of quilting thread. This will be long enough to keep you going for a while but not long enough to tangle easily.
• With knotted thread, insert the needle through the top and batting about ½ inch away from the place where you will begin your quilting. Bring the needle to the surface in position to make the first stitch. Gently tug on the thread to "pop" the knot through the top and bury it in the batting, as shown in DIAGRAM 21.

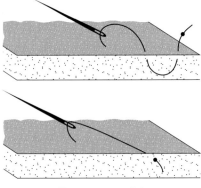

DIAGRAM 21

• Quilt by making running stitches about 1/16 to 1/8 inch long through all the layers. Use a thimble to push the needle down until you feel the tip of the needle with your finger underneath. Then guide the needle back up through the quilt. As you begin to feel comfortable with this "rocking" technique, you may like taking more stitches at one time. Try to keep the stitches straight and even. This is more important than tiny stitches.
• To end a thread, place your needle close to your last stitch, parallel to the quilt, and wind the thread around it two or three times. Insert the tip of the needle through the quilt top and batting only, at the correct stitch length, and bring the needle out approximately ½ inch away from the quilting line. Gently tug the thread to "pop" the knot through the quilt top so that it lodges in the batting layer, and clip it close to the quilt top.

Machine Quilting

We use 100 percent cotton thread for machine quilting, or sometimes cotton-wrapped polyester, but not nylon. We use a stitch length of 12 stitches per inch, which makes the quilting stitches nestle into the quilt sandwich. When cotton batting is used in machine quilted projects, it puckers up after washing, and the stitches seem almost buried.

THREAD SEVERAL needles with quilting thread before you begin. Keep them handy while you work so you won't have to stop to thread a needle every time you finish stitching with a length of thread.

TIPS AND TRICKS

- Use a walking foot or an even feed foot on your sewing machine for quilting straight lines. Use a darning or machine embroidery foot for free-motion or meander quilting.
- Leave long thread ends at the beginning and ending of a design so that later you can go back with a needle to knot and bury them in the batting layer. Pull the bobbin thread up to the top so that it doesn't get bunched up underneath.
- For free-motion quilting, disengage the feed dogs of your machine so you can manipulate the quilt freely. Choose continuous-line quilting designs so you won't have to lift the needle when quilting the design. Guide the quilt under the needle with both hands, working at an even pace so your stitches will be consistent in length.

Binding

Binding finishes the raw edges of the quilt, giving the edges strength and durability. The bindings are cut either cross-grain or on the bias, as specified in the each project. There is some stretch in cross-grain binding and much greater stretch in bias binding. Although bias binding will work for any quilt, it is essential for projects that have curved edges, such as Town Square Tree Skirt. Also, if you're using a plaid fabric, cutting binding strips on the bias will create a diagonal effect in the finished binding. If you cut plaid binding strips on the cross grain, you will end up with relatively boring-looking straight lines of plaid along the quilt edges.

At Thimbleberries, we make French-fold, or double-fold,

binding for all our quilts. This binding can be cut straight-grain or on the bias. Straight-grain binding can be used on all quilts except those with rounded corners or curved or scalloped edges.

We have given yardage and cutting directions for a standard binding width, but you may want to vary the width of your binding to accommodate a thicker or thinner batting. Or if you simply prefer a wider or narrower binding, see "Binding Width" on page 216. Generally, you will need the perimeter of the quilt plus 12 to 20 inches for mitering corners and ending the binding. One yard of fabric is usually enough to make binding for a large quilt. Follow the instructions below for straight-grain or bias binding. Attach the binding to the quilt as described below, mitering it at the corners.

Bias Binding

1 Cut bias strips with a rotary cutter, using the 45 degree angle on your ruler. Straighten the left edge of your fabric, as described on page 206. Align the 45 degree line on your ruler with the bottom edge of the fabric, as shown in DIAGRAM 22A, and cut along the edge of the ruler to trim off the corner. Move the ruler across the fabric, cutting parallel strips in the needed width, as shown in DIAGRAM 22B.

2 Join the strips, right sides together, as shown in DIAGRAM 23, and stitch, using a ¼-inch seam allowance. Start and stop exactly at the V notch of the two strips. Press the seam open. Continue adding strips as needed.

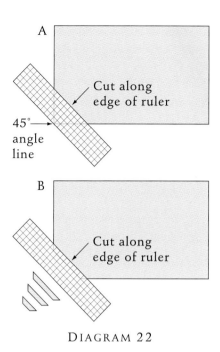

DIAGRAM 22

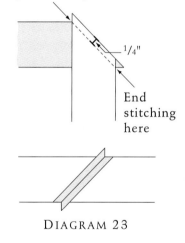

DIAGRAM 23

Straight-Grain Binding

1 Cut the needed number of strips as specified in the project instructions. Cut straight strips across the fabric width.

2 Join the strips using diagonal seams. Place two border strips together at a 90 degree angle with right sides together, as shown in DIAGRAM 24. Each strip should extend ¼ inch

beyond the other. Stitch across diagonally, making sure to start and end your stitching precisely at the V notch of the two strips.

3 Trim off the excess to leave a ¼-inch seam allowance. Press the seam open.

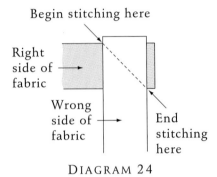

DIAGRAM 24

Binding Width

To figure out how wide to cut your binding, multiply the desired width of the binding by 6. For example, for a ½-inch finished binding, multiply ½ by 6, which means you need to cut a 3-inch-wide strip. If you are using a thicker batting, you may need to add another ¼ to ½ inch. Recalculate yardage requirements if you decide to make a binding wider than the project directions specify. I always cut a sample binding and try it to see if it works—it should cover the edge and fold to the back easily. Sometimes the batting thickness really does affect the width of the binding.

Preparing a Quilt for Binding

1 Use a large see-through ruler or square to square up and trim away the excess batting and backing even with the quilt top.

2 Securely hand baste all three layers together a scant ¼ inch from the raw edges to keep the layers from shifting and prevent puckers from forming.

Attaching the Binding

1 After the binding strips are sewn together, fold them in half lengthwise, wrong sides together, and press.

2 Unfold and cut the beginning end at a 45 degree angle. Press the edge under ¼ inch. Refold the strip.

3 Begin attaching the binding along the bottom lower left side. Do not begin binding at a corner.

4 With raw edges of the binding and quilt top even, start stitching about 2 inches from the diagonal cut end, using a ⅜-inch seam allowance. Stop stitching ⅜ inch from the corner.

5 Clip the thread and remove the quilt from under the presser foot.

6 Fold the binding strip up and away from the corner of the quilt, forming a 45 degree angle, as shown in DIAGRAM 25A. Then refold the binding down even with the raw edge of the quilt, as shown in DIAGRAM 25B. Begin sewing at the upper edge, as shown. Miter all four corners in this manner.

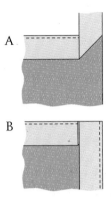

DIAGRAM 25

7 As you approach the point where you started, trim the end of the binding, making sure the end is long enough to tuck inside the beginning of the binding and that the two ends overlap about ⅜ inch. Stitch the remaining binding to the quilt.

8 Turn the folded edge of the binding over to the back side of the quilt, covering the stitching line. Hand sew the binding in place, folding in the mitered corners as you go. Add several stitches to the folds of the miters on both the front and back to hold them in place, as shown in DIAGRAM 26.

DIAGRAM 26

INDEX

METRIC EQUIVALENCY CHART

mm=millimeters

cm=centimeters

Yards to Meters

YARDS	METERS	YARDS	METERS	YARDS	METERS	YARDS	METERS	YARDS	METERS
1/8	0.11	2 1/8	1.94	4 1/8	3.77	6 1/8	5.60	8 1/8	7.43
1/4	0.23	2 1/4	2.06	4 1/4	3.89	6 1/4	5.72	8 1/4	7.54
3/8	0.34	2 3/8	2.17	4 3/8	4.00	6 3/8	5.83	8 3/8	7.66
1/2	0.46	2 1/2	2.29	4 1/2	4.11	6 1/2	5.94	8 1/2	7.77
5/8	0.57	2 5/8	2.40	4 5/8	4.23	6 5/8	6.06	8 5/8	7.89
3/4	0.69	2 3/4	2.51	4 3/4	4.34	6 3/4	6.17	8 3/4	8.00
7/8	0.80	2 7/8	2.63	4 7/8	4.46	6 7/8	6.29	8 7/8	8.12
1	0.91	3	2.74	5	4.57	7	6.40	9	8.23
1 1/8	1.03	3 1/8	2.86	5 1/8	4.69	7 1/8	6.52	9 1/8	8.34
1 1/4	1.14	3 1/4	2.97	5 1/4	4.80	7 1/4	6.63	9 1/4	8.46
1 3/8	1.26	3 3/8	3.09	5 3/8	4.91	7 3/8	6.74	9 3/8	8.57
1 1/2	1.37	3 1/2	3.20	5 1/2	5.03	7 1/2	6.86	9 1/2	8.69
1 5/8	1.49	3 5/8	3.31	5 5/8	5.14	7 5/8	6.97	9 5/8	8.80
1 3/4	1.60	3 3/4	3.43	5 3/4	5.26	7 3/4	7.09	9 3/4	8.92
1 7/8	1.71	3 7/8	3.54	5 7/8	5.37	7 7/8	7.20	9 7/8	9.03
2	1.83	4	3.66	6	5.49	8	7.32	10	9.14

Inches to Millimeters and Centimeters

INCHES	MM	CM	INCHES	CM	INCHES	CM
1/8	3	0.3	9	22.9	30	76.2
1/4	6	0.6	10	25.4	31	78.7
3/8	10	1.0	11	27.9	32	81.3
1/2	13	1.3	12	30.5	33	83.8
5/8	16	1.6	13	33.0	34	86.4
3/4	19	1.9	14	35.6	35	88.9
7/8	22	2.2	15	38.1	36	91.4
1	25	2.5	16	40.6	37	94.0
1 1/4	32	3.2	17	43.2	38	96.5
1 1/2	38	3.8	18	45.7	39	99.1
1 3/4	44	4.4	19	48.3	40	101.6
2	51	5.1	20	50.8	41	104.1
2 1/2	64	6.4	21	53.3	42	106.7
3	76	7.6	22	55.9	43	109.2
3 1/2	89	8.9	23	58.4	44	111.8
4	102	10.2	24	61.0	45	114.3
4 1/2	114	11.4	25	63.5	46	116.8
5	127	12.7	26	66.0	47	119.4
6	152	15.2	27	68.6	48	121.9
7	178	17.8	28	71.1	49	124.5
8	203	20.3	29	73.7	50	127.0